Making the Word of God Fully Known

Australian College of Theology Monograph Series

SERIES EDITOR GRAEME R. CHATFIELD

The ACT Monograph Series, generously supported by the Board of Directors of the Australian College of Theology, provides a forum for publishing quality research theses and studies by its graduates and affiliated college staff in the broad fields of Biblical Studies, Christian Thought and History, and Practical Theology with Wipf and Stock Publishers of Eugene, Oregon. The ACT selects the best of its doctoral and research masters theses as well as monographs that offer the academic community, scholars, church leaders and the wider community uniquely Australian and New Zealand perspectives on significant research topics and topics of current debate. The ACT also provides opportunity for contributors beyond its graduates and affiliated college staff to publish monographs which support the mission and values of the ACT.

Rev Dr Graeme Chatfield
Series Editor and Associate Dean

Making the Word of God Fully Known

Essays on Church, Culture, and Mission
in Honor of Archbishop Philip Freier

Edited by
PAUL A. BARKER and
BRADLY S. BILLINGS

Foreword by
JUSTIN WELBY

WIPF & STOCK · Eugene, Oregon

MAKING THE WORD OF GOD FULLY KNOWN
Essays on Church, Culture, and Mission in Honor of Archbishop Philip Freier

Australian College of Theology Monograph Series

Copyright © 2020 Wipf and Stock Publishers. All rights reserved. Except for brief quotations in critical publications or reviews, no part of this book may be reproduced in any manner without prior written permission from the publisher. Write: Permissions, Wipf and Stock Publishers, 199 W. 8th Ave., Suite 3, Eugene, OR 97401.

Wipf & Stock
An Imprint of Wipf and Stock Publishers
199 W. 8th Ave., Suite 3
Eugene, OR 97401

www.wipfandstock.com

PAPERBACK ISBN: 978-1-7252-5908-9
HARDCOVER ISBN: 978-1-7252-5909-6
EBOOK ISBN: 978-1-7252-5910-2

Manufactured in the U.S.A. JANUARY 7, 2020

Scripture quotations are from the New Revised Standard Version Bible, copyright © 1989 National Council of the Churches of Christ in the United States of America. Used by permission. All rights reserved worldwide.

Contents

Synopsis of Archbishop Philip's Career | ix
Contributors | xi
Foreword by Justin Welby | xvii
Introduction by Paul A. Barker and Bradly S. Billings | xix

1 Making the Word of God Fully Known | 1
  —Paul A. Barker

2 A Diocese in Mission: Coaching and Parish Renewal in the Diocese of Melbourne | 16
  —Richard Trist

3 Cathedrals: Home Churches, Houses of Prayer for all People | 36
  —Andreas Loewe

4 The Changing Context of Ministry Through the Pastoral Offices: New Challenges and Opportunities for Traditional Ministry | 47
  —Colleen O'Reilly

5 Ministry and Mission: Considerations for Parishes Urban and Rural | 64
  —Andrew Curnow

6 Aspects of Multicultural Mission in Melbourne | 83
  —Len Firth

7 Towards an Australian Anglican Ecclesiology | 98
  —Bradly S. Billings

Indigenous Australians

8   Archbishop Philip Freier and Aboriginal Ministry in the Northern Territory | 117
    —Joy Sandefur

9   "Each in Our Own Language": The Translation of the Bible into Australian Indigenous Languages | 133
    —Peter Adam

10 James and Angelina Noble: Pioneer Australian Anglican Missionaries | 159
    —Wei Han Kuan

Women

11 No Longer Male and Female: Women's Leadership and the New Testament in Australian Anglicanism | 181
    —Dorothy A. Lee and Muriel Porter

12 Our Father in Heaven, or Is It Our Mother in Heaven? | 199
    —Kevin Giles

The Church in the World

13 At the Third Altar: The Vocation of the Church in the World | 213
    —Stephen Pickard

14 When Theology Risks Life and Limb: The Role of the Church in Humanitarian Practice | 225
    —Bob Mitchell

15 Te Rongopai, Te Tiriti, Te Pouhere; Gospel, Treaty, Constitution: Church, Culture, and Justice in Aotearoa New Zealand | 247
    —Philip Richardson

Theology and Personhood

16 Identity Angst: Narrative Identity and Anglican Liturgy | 263
    —Brian Rosner

17 "Walking with a Limp": Some Personal and Pastoral Reflections on Trauma | 280
    —John Harrower

Synopsis of Archbishop Philip's Career

Philip Leslie Freier
Born: February 9, 1955, Brisbane, Queensland

Teaching Career

AFTER TRAINING AND OBTAINING his qualification as a teacher, Philip Freier served indigenous communities on Thursday Island, Kowanyama, and Yarrabah, before becoming an advisory teacher in Aboriginal education with the Queensland Education Department. He was converted to Christianity whilst serving indigenous Christians in North Queensland, where he also met his wife, Joy, and decided to seek ordination in the Anglican Church.

Ministry Roles and Positions

Dr. Freier has held a range of roles and positions in the Anglican Church, across three dioceses, as deacon, priest and bishop. Ordained deacon in 1983 and priest in 1984 for the Diocese of Carpentaria, he served parishes in Kowanyama (1983-1988) and Banyo (1988-1993), and was rector of Bundaberg in the Diocese of Brisbane (1993-1999), and an Examining Chaplain to the Archbishop of Brisbane during the same period of time.

Dr. Freier was consecrated bishop on 22 July, 1999 in St John's Cathedral, Brisbane, at the age of 44, and served as Bishop of the Northern Territory from 1999 to 2006. He was installed as the 13th Archbishop of Melbourne on 16 December 2006. He was elected Primate of the Anglican Church of Australia in July 2014.

In addition to his leadership of the Diocese of Melbourne and Standing Committee of the General Synod, Dr. Freier is patron and visitor to numerous schools and organizations and is the present Chair of the Board of the Brotherhood of St Laurence.

Academic Awards and Achievements

Dr. Freier initially trained as a teacher, obtaining qualifications in applied science and education, and the Master of Educational Studies from the University of Newcastle. He studied theology at Morpeth College, Newcastle, being awarded the Bachelor of Divinity in 1984. In 2000 Dr. Freier successfully completed his doctoral thesis for James Cook University on the history of the Anglican mission to Mitchell River—*Living with the Munpitch: the history of Mitchell River Mission, 1905–1967*.

Dr. Freier has also served as Chair, Board of Delegates, the Australian College of Theology, and Chair of the Doctrine Commission of the General Synod. He was admitted as a Fellow of the Australian Institute of Company Directors in 2002.

Contributors

Peter J. H. Adam OAM

Peter Adam was ordained in Melbourne in 1970 and has served in the diocese as Priest in Charge and then Vicar of St. Jude's Carlton, Principal of Ridley College, Canon of St. Paul's Cathedral, Chaplain of Melbourne University, and Archdeacon for Parish Development. He has published a number of commentaries, books, and articles in the areas of Bible, theology, church history, and ministry practice. He has also served on the General Synod Doctrine Commission and the board of the Australian College of Theology. He currently trains preachers in Australia and overseas and supervises research students. He also mentors people in ministry. His current research interests include the theology and practice of preaching, the theology and practice of ministry, and Indigenous issues.

Paul A. Barker

Paul Barker has been an Assistant Bishop in the Diocese of Melbourne since 2016. Formerly, he was Regional Coordinator for Langham Preaching in Asia and lecturer in Old Testament and Preaching in various Bible Colleges in Malaysia, Thailand, Myanmar, India, and Pakistan, among other places, while based for seven years in Malaysia. Paul's doctorate on the Book of Deuteronomy, through the University of Bristol, was published by Paternoster. He has written books aimed for pastors on Deuteronomy, Amos, Psalms, and Kings and edited a book called *Tackling Trauma*.

Bradly S. Billings

Brad Billings is an Assistant Bishop in the Diocese of Melbourne with responsibility for theological education and the ordination process. Prior to his consecration in 2016, he was a parish priest for fifteen years. He has lectured as an adjunct for many years in biblical studies and published in a variety of areas, including the New Testament and early Christianity, historical and pastoral theology, pilgrimage, and church polity and governance. Brad received his doctorate, on textual criticism, from the Australian College of Theology, and his Masters (Classics and Archaeology), on housing in ancient Ephesus, from the University of Melbourne. With a keen interest in church law, governance, and Anglican polity, Brad has been highly involved in the development of diocesan legislation and policy in recent years from the perspective of a practitioner.

Andrew Curnow AM

Bishop Andrew Curnow is Provincial Officer for the Anglican Province of Victoria, a part-time role assisting the Metropolitan of Victoria. He retired as Bishop of Bendigo in February 2018 after serving for fifteen years and before that was an Assistant Bishop in the Diocese of Melbourne for ten years. Bishop Andrew served on the Standing Committee of General Synod for eighteen years and was responsible for writing two major reports on the future of the dioceses in Australia, delivered at General Synods in 2014 and 2017. He has a passion for rural ministry, and he also currently serves on the board of Anglicare Victoria.

Wei-Han Kuan

Wei-Han Kuan is the State Director of the Church Missionary Society – Victoria. His doctoral research in Anglican evangelical history focused on the themes of leadership and long-term continuity. It has been published as *Foundations of Anglican Evangelicalism in Victoria, 1847–1937* (ACT Monograph Series, 2019). With his wife and three children, he is a part of St. Alfred's Anglican Church Blackburn North.

Len Firth

Len Firth teaches students with a refugee background at Ridley College Melbourne. He is also Archdeacon of Essendon in the Anglican Diocese of Melbourne. Len (with Jill) spent twelve years as a CMS Australia missionary in Groote Eylandt as well as Hong Kong, where he taught in the Ming Hua Theological Seminary. He was Principal of St. Andrew's Hall, the CMS Australia Training College (2000–2007). In the Diocese of Melbourne, he has also served as the Archdeacon for Multicultural Ministry and Archdeacon of Sudanese Ministry. His research interests are primarily in Bible and missiology. He recently presented on "Zechariah and the Mission of God" at the Tyndale Fellowship OT Conference 2019. Len is married to Jill, who teaches Biblical Hebrew and Old Testament, also at Ridley College.

Kevin Giles

Kevin Giles (ThD) retired from full-time Anglican parish ministry in 2006. He continues in active ministry and as a theologian and author. His most recent book is *What the Bible Actually Teaches on Women* (Cascade, 2018).

John Harrower OAM

John Harrower is Bishop Assisting the Primate of the Anglican Church of Australia. John worked as a chemical engineer and Director of the Industries Assistance Commission in Melbourne prior to nine years of CMS missionary service as university chaplain, publisher, and church planter during Argentina's "Dirty War." Returning to Melbourne, he engaged in youth and interfaith issues, in particular Islam, while Vicar of the Glen Waverley Anglican Church. In 2000, John was awarded the Medal of the Order of Australia "for service to the community through the Anglican Church and as a missionary." Bishop of Tasmania from 2000 to 2015, he led a pastoral response to survivors of child sexual abuse.

Dorothy A. Lee

Dorothy Lee is the Stewart Research Professor of New Testament at Trinity College Theological School, University of Divinity. She has been involved in theological education for over thirty years and is an Anglican priest and Canon of both St. Paul's Cathedral Melbourne and Holy Trinity Cathedral

Wangaratta. She is widely published in the area of New Testament, with a particular focus on the Gospels. Her most recent published book is *The Gospels Speak: Addressing Life's Questions* (New York: Paulist, 2017). She is about to publish a book on women and leadership in the New Testament.

Andreas Loewe

Andreas Loewe is Dean of Melbourne and responsible for the worship, mission, and life of St. Paul's Cathedral. His research centers on theology as well as ecclesiastical and music history, in particular about ways in which Scripture can be communicated through music. A Fellow and Lecturer at the Melbourne Conservatorium of Music and a Fellow of the Royal Historical Society, he has published widely, including *Johann Sebastian Bach's St. John Passion (BWV 245): A Theological Commentary,* Studies in the History of Christian Traditions (Brill, 2014) and, with Katherine Firth, *Journeying with Bonhoeffer: Six Steps on the Path to Discipleship* (Morning Star, 2019).

Bob Mitchell AM

The Rev. Dr. Bob Mitchell is an Anglican minister and the current CEO of Anglican Overseas Aid. His PhD research focused on the distinctive contribution of Christian faith in implementing international development and humanitarian programs. Dr. Mitchell is the author of *Faith-Based Development* (Orbis, 2017) and he serves on the International Advisory Board of The Christian Journal for Global Health and the Council of the University of Divinity. A lawyer by background, Dr. Mitchell has a strong desire to see enhanced governance of faith-based organizations and is a board member of several Christian organizations and networks.

Colleen O'Reilly

The Rev. Dr. Colleen O'Reilly is the Senior Chaplain to Trinity College, Parkville, and was until 2019 the Vicar of St. George's Malvern. Prior to ordination in Melbourne in 1995, she was a Diocesan Lay Reader in Sydney and taught Pastoral and Liturgical Theology in the Sydney College of Divinity. She is a member of the General Synod Liturgy Commission and the Australian (Ecumenical) Consultation on Liturgy.

Stephen Pickard

Stephen Pickard is Executive Director of the Australian Centre for Christianity and Culture, Director of the Strategic Research Centre in Public and Contextual Theology, and Professor of Theology, Charles Sturt University Canberra. He has been a bishop in the Anglican Church of Australia since 2007 and is currently an Assistant Bishop in the Diocese of Canberra and Goulburn. He has served in a range of ministerial and academic appointments over three and half decades in Australia and the United Kingdom. His teaching and writing is in the area of ecclesiology, ministry, and mission and includes *Liberating Evangelism* (Trinity Press International, 1998), *Theological Foundations for Collaborative Ministry* (Ashgate, 2009), *In-Between God: Theology, Community and Discipleship* (AFT, 2011), *and Seeking the Church: An Introduction to Ecclesiology* (SCM, 2012).

Muriel Porter OAM

Muriel Porter is a Melbourne journalist and author. Formerly a member of the General Synod, she was a leader in the decades-long struggle to see women ordained as priests and bishops in the Anglican Church. She has written numerous books on the contemporary Australian religious scene, the most recent being *The New Scapegoats: The Clergy Victims of the Anglican Church Sexual Abuse Crisis* (Morning Star, 2017). An Honorary Research Fellow of the University of Divinity, she is a member of the adjunct faculty of Trinity College Melbourne.

Philip Richardson

Philip Richardson is Bishop of Waikato and Taranaki, where he has been bishop for twenty years. He has been Archbishop and Primate in the Anglican Church of Aotearoa, New Zealand and Polynesia for the last six years. His primacy is unique within the Anglican Communion in that it is shared between three Archbishops, representing Māori, Pasefika, and Pākehā. Prior to becoming bishop, Philip was head of a University College at the University of Otago with a particular interest in Christian ethics. As a bishop of a predominantly rural diocese, he has been committed to identifying and implementing new forms of ministry where church and community interface in the rural context.

Brian S. Rosner

Brian Rosner (PhD, Cambridge) is the Principal of Ridley College, having formerly taught at Moore Theological College and the University of Aberdeen. In 2012, he was ordained by Archbishop Philip Freier in St. Paul's Cathedral and is actively involved in the life of the diocese. Brian is the author or editor of more than a dozen books, including *The New Dictionary of Biblical Theology* (IVP, 2000), *the Pillar commentary on 1 Corinthians* (co-author Roy E. Ciampa; Eerdmans, 2010), *Greed as Idolatry: The Origin and Meaning of a Pauline Metaphor* (Eerdmans, 2007), *Paul and the Law: Keeping the Commandments of God* (Inter-Varsity, 2013), and most recently, *Known by God: A Biblical Theology of Personal Identity* (Zondervan, 2017).

Joy Sandefur

Joy Sandefur has walked alongside and worked with Aboriginal people over many years. As a member of Wycliffe Bible Translators, Joy was part of the Kriol Bible translation team. Her PhD thesis is a study of the Aboriginal church at Ngukurr in the Northern Territory. She has spent further years in the Northern Territory as a BCA staff worker, on the staff of Nungalinya (a training college for Aboriginal Christians), supporting Anglican Aboriginal churches in Arnhem Land, preparing Aboriginal women for ordination, and facilitating an Aboriginal congregation in Darwin. Joy is a retired Anglican priest.

Richard McL. Trist

Richard Trist is Dean of the Anglican Institute and Senior Lecturer in Pastoral Theology at Ridley College Melbourne. He has been teaching at the college since 2007, and prior to this was in parish ministry in Australia and the United Kingdom. Richard has a DMin from the Australian College of Theology and postgraduate qualifications in professional supervision. He is a Canon of St. Paul's Cathedral Melbourne and a member of the General Synod Commission for Mission and Ministry.

Foreword

Justin Welby

It is a real pleasure to commend this remarkable collection of essays in honor of Archbishop Philip Freier on the occasion of his sixty-fifth birthday and to take the opportunity to add my own words of personal gratitude for his long and fruitful ministry, both in the Anglican Church of Australia and in the global Anglican Communion.

I was delighted to be able to preside at the service in St Paul's Cathedral Melbourne in August 2014, when Archbishop Philip was installed as Primate of the Anglican Church of Australia. On that occasion, I said that there is "no greater hope for the world than a church abounding in holiness and wisdom." Archbishop Philip has, over his years of service, embodied that wisdom and holiness for the good of the global Anglican Church. It is as clear now as it was then that Archbishop Philip is held in the highest regard by the people of his Diocese of Melbourne as well as in the broader community. This holds true across the rich diversity of the Australian church, to which he has made an extraordinarily significant and lasting contribution in a variety of ways over an extended period of time.

I have had the opportunity to witness and experience all this first hand as Archbishop Philip, from the beginning of his primacy, has been a prominent and important contributor across the Anglican Communion. His service has included, but not by any means been limited to, his role on the Anglican Consultative Council, the Anglican-Roman Catholic

International Commission, and the Anglican Centre in Rome. I personally have valued his wisdom and diplomacy in his support for the Church of Ceylon at a critical time. His encouragement to the church there was recognized by the Standing Committee and the wider Anglican Communion and has meant that the Church of Ceylon is taking forward its journey to become an autonomous Province. Archbishop Philip has been of special assistance, both to the Anglican Communion and to me personally, in the Oceania region. He has played an immensely important role in facilitating dialogue with, and encouraging the ministry of, our brothers and sisters in Papua New Guinea and the Pacific Islands in particular.

This fine collection of essays, dedicated in his honor, is reflective of Archbishop Philip's prayerful and deliberate leadership of the Diocese of Melbourne in its mission to "make the Word of God fully known" over a period of more than thirteen years of episcopal oversight. Also present, rightly and powerfully, is the very profound importance of Indigenous spirituality and the Indigenous peoples of Australia in Archbishop Philip's own life and ministry and the manner in which this has been mutually enriching and sustaining. Further contributions are reflective of Archbishop Philip's significant role across Australia and Oceania and the many fruitful connections he has made as Primate of the Australian Church, as well as his lifelong support of the ministry of women.

I give thanks to God for the friendship and ministry of the Most Rev. Dr. Philip L. Freier, Archbishop of Melbourne and Primate of the Anglican Church of Australia. May God continue to bless him, and those to whom he is bound by the bonds of peace and love, and may God strengthen him to continue to make the wonderful gospel of our Lord as fully known as possible across the nations.

Introduction

Paul A. Barker and Bradly S. Billings

It was entirely coincidental that Archbishop Freier's birthday fell on the same day, in February 2019, that he presided over the ordination of twenty new deacons in the Cathedral Church of St. Paul in Melbourne. After some deliberation as to whether it would be appropriate or not, and the extent to which he may or may not appreciate the gesture, the fact of the Archbishop's birthday was ultimately acknowledged, and a joyous rendition of "Happy Birthday to You" was sung in the cathedral that day.

What the Archbishop made of it all, we do not fully know! What we do know is that one outcome of that gesture was the realization that the following year would mark the Archbishop's sixty-fifth birthday. In light of that, the idea for this book of essays was born. Given Archbishop Freier's long ministry in the church, his academic achievements, and his stature as a scholar in his own right, alongside the enormity of his contribution to the Anglican Church of Australia and the Diocese of Melbourne in particular, it seemed to us that a *Festschrift* was very much warranted. Everyone we subsequently approached about the venture wholeheartedly agreed, with the vast majority able to contribute willingly despite the tight timeframes involved and the many other demands placed upon each of them.

At the 2010 session of the diocesan Synod, Archbishop Freier unveiled a vision "to make the Word of God fully known" (Col 1:25) through the renewal of Christ's mission across "the whole area of the Diocese of

Melbourne." The stated aim of the vision was to achieve the sustainable development of mission across the diocese. The synod then undertook a number of decisions that have had the cumulative effect of reorienting the diocese away from "maintenance" and toward mission.

The inaugural vision was subsequently enlarged by the more comprehensive "Vision and Directions 2017–2025" and, more recently, by a Strategic Implementation Plan that identifies six key areas for resourcing and ministerial focus:

- Equipping archdeacons to be missional leaders in their geographical areas
- Developing the reach and impact of ministry in multicultural contexts and among clergy of a multicultural background
- Fostering the diocesan partnerships program
- Further resourcing and enlarging the parish mission resourcing portfolio
- People and culture, including the professional development and well-being of the clergy
- Establishing nine new Anglican ministries in areas of population growth where the church is not yet, or not adequately, present

All of this encapsulates a vision that will empower and resource the execution of the diocesan mission, "to make the Word of God fully known," into the future. This has been a particular triumph of Dr. Freier's time as Archbishop and represents a lasting contribution to the life of the Diocese of Melbourne. The clarity of vision brought by Dr. Freier is present in the unmistakable emphasis on ensuring the Anglican Church in Melbourne and Geelong be reflective of its community, which provides the missional context in which it seeks to execute its vision, together with the unquestionable imperative that the Anglican Church in early twenty-first-century Australia must, in fact, be church at mission. These emphases are evident throughout this volume of essays, reflecting the priorities and vision Dr. Freier has brought to the diocese, which will surely be one of the strong legacies of his time as Archbishop.

The essays in this volume are also reflective of the esteem in which Dr. Freier is held across the diversity of the Anglican Church, both nationally and internationally, and of the areas in which he has made a particular, and personal, commitment and contribution. The contributions are arranged thematically – Church and Mission, Indigenous Australians, Women, the Church in the World, and Theology and Personhood.

Over the course of his ministry, and certainly during his time in Melbourne, Dr. Freier has intentionally oriented the church toward mission in a variety of ways that are reflective of a number of contributions in this volume. That this vision has won the support of the Synod, and achieved resonance and commitment across the diversity of a large and complex diocese like Melbourne, is a testament to the persistence and gentle authority of Dr. Freier's leadership and the trust and respect he has accrued over the course of his time as Archbishop.

Both in his leadership of the Diocese of Melbourne and well before it, Dr. Freier's strong commitment to the ministry of women is evidenced and celebrated by contributions that provide a strong witness to this, complementing his active encouragement and support of the ministry of women, both in lay capacities, and in all three orders of the church.

Dr. Freier's strong and lasting commitment to the "common good," both at home and abroad, is present also in a number of essays on local and global mission, a contribution by his friend and colleague in New Zealand, Archbishop Philip Richardson, and his ongoing ministry as chair of the Brotherhood of St Laurence. In spite of many other national and international commitments, he continues to occupy and dedicate time to this role, thus testifying to the integrity of his own personal commitment to the church's ministry of care to the poor, needy, and vulnerable in our society.

Furthermore, no one who knows Dr. Freier or has heard him speak for any extended period of time could fail to grasp his enduring love for Indigenous Australians and his strong and ongoing commitment to Indigenous ministry. It is a commitment clearly evident not just in words but very much in deeds, in particular in his early life and career in teaching and ministry roles in remote communities, and more latterly, in his fostering of Indigenous vocations in the Diocese of Melbourne and across the Australian Church. Fittingly, a number of contributions in this volume are reflective of, and bear testimony to, the enormity and importance of this in the life of both Dr. Freier and his wife Joy, as well as their family.

We are each pleased and proud to have been able to collate and edit these essays, and to contribute an essay ourselves, in honor of Dr. Freier. As two of his four assistant bishops (with our colleagues Bishop Genieve Blackwell and Bishop Kate Prowd) in the Diocese of Melbourne, together with Bishop John Harrower, the Bishop assisting the Primate, who has also contributed an essay to this volume, we have had ample opportunity to observe first-hand the extraordinary energy and enthusiasm Dr. Freier brings to his various roles, the graciousness with which he deals with those under his leadership even in the face of enormous demands, and his steadfast dedication to the gospel of our Lord and to making that as fully known amidst his diverse leadership and ministry roles. Through working closely with Dr. Freier, we (and our episcopal colleagues) have also each experienced and known his unwavering friendship, support, and encouragement for us as colleagues in ministry and for our respective ministries. For all of this, we are profoundly grateful and thankful to God.

This modest volume, dedicated in his honor on the occasion of his sixty-fifth birthday, February 9, 2020, constitutes, we hope and pray, a fitting gesture of thanksgiving and appreciation to the ministry of the Most Reverend Dr. Philip L. Freier, Primate of the Anglican Church of Australia and Archbishop of Melbourne, and a lasting testimony to the large and important contribution he has made to the life of the Church in Melbourne, Australia, and across the Anglican Communion.

To the glory of God
Epiphany 2020

I

Making the Word of God Fully Known

Paul A. Barker

The motto that encapsulates the mission, goals, and directions of the Anglican Diocese of Melbourne under Archbishop Philip Freier is "Making the Word of God fully known." A suite of different goals and priorities for the diocese exists under this heading, and Archbishop Philip has led a mission-shaping strategic process over recent years to place mission at the forefront of the diocese's culture, priorities, and decisions. The motto is from Paul's Epistle to the Colossians, 1:25, and this essay aims to expound what it means to "make the word of God fully known."

The Word of God to Convert

Paul is writing to a church he doesn't know. As far as we can tell, he never visited Colossae. The gospel was taken there by his colleague, Epaphras, whom he references in 1:7.

Paul begins his letter giving thanks to God for the Colossian church because he has heard of "your faith in Christ Jesus and of the love you have for all the saints, because of the hope laid up for you in heaven" (1:4–5a). The three great Christian virtues of faith, love, and hope are evident in this church, to the extent that Paul, who does not even know them personally, has heard such positive reports of them.

As Paul expresses his thanks, he reflects on how these virtues have been produced. Intriguingly, faith and love appear to have been generated by hope: "because of the hope." We may not often consider that hope generates faith. Indeed, we probably consider faith to be the more foundational of the virtues. Yet Paul appears to be suggesting that at the heart of the gospel is a message of hope, and thus those who hear that message and welcome it come to faith as a result of the hope. As Moule says, "Precisely because it is stored in heaven, it is a potent incentive to action here and now."[1]

Paul goes on to say that these Colossians have "heard of this hope" in the "gospel," which is synonymous in this verse with the "word of the truth."[2] In turn, those expressions appear to be synonymous with "the grace of God" in verse 6. If it is right that "gospel" and "word of the truth" are also synonymous with "word of God" in 1:25, as seems to be the case, then at the heart of the word of God is a message of hope. The language of hope occurs later in chapter 1 in the famous statement, "Christ in you, the hope of glory" (v. 27). This expression takes further the description of hope in verse 5, "hope which is laid up for you in heaven."

What is important is that both references to hope in Colossians 1 are grounded in Jesus Christ. "Laid up in heaven" directs us to the resurrection and ascension of Christ, a theme developed further in chapters 2 and 3. "Christ in you" implies the Holy Spirit being given to Christians from Pentecost onwards, and thus the ongoing life of Jesus available for believers.

That Jesus is the center of hope—and thus faith and love—for a church and its message ought to go without saying. It is worth stressing nonetheless, as it is easy for a church to drift into other messages, as indeed the Colossian church was in danger of doing. In a motto for a diocese's goals, the significance is that our hope is not in management, a leader, finances, church structures, or adequate compliance. Our hope is in Jesus, grounded here in his resurrection, ascension, and Spirit.

We ought also to note this emphasis on the gospel being truth. In modern Western society, religion is regarded as a matter of personal opinion rather than a matter of truth or falsehood. When Christians succumb to that societal pressure, we will lose confidence in the gospel itself as truth, and thus we will be reticent to proclaim it at all.

The other synonym for "gospel" and "word of the truth" is "grace of God" in verse 6. The Colossians have heard and truly comprehended "the grace of God" (or "comprehended the grace of God in truth"). While grace

---

1. Moule, *Colossians and Philemon*, 50.
2. Moule notes that Masson takes "the gospel" as being in apposition to "the truth," and while Moule thinks this is unlikely, he notes the "meaning is scarcely affected" (*Colossians and Philemon*, 50).

is not here explained, Paul is clearly referring to a central part of the Christian message, that salvation is God's doing and not our right or just desert.

We ought also to notice that this word of the truth or gospel that the Colossians had heard through Epaphras has converted them. In the next paragraph, as Paul concludes his prayer for the Colossians, he gives reasons for joyful thanks, noting that God has enabled the Colossians to share in the inheritance of the saints, rescued them from darkness, and transferred them into Jesus' kingdom (vv. 12b–14). This has happened for the Colossians because they have embraced the gospel, the word of the truth, and comprehended the grace of God.

The implication of this is that the word of God is powerful. In a modern society and culture, it is easy to lose confidence in the power of the word of God to convert, to generate hope, faith, and love. A danger for any church or denomination is to seek to trust methodology, mission strategy, or programs, rather than the ultimately powerful word of God. A church that is missional will have to have confidence in the power of God's word or gospel to convert. Only then will it have reason and desire to make that word fully known.

The emphasis on the Colossians having "heard" (v. 6) underscores the importance of proclaiming, speaking, preaching, teaching the word of God. Such oral communication is essential. The idea of preaching the gospel without words, falsely attributed to St. Francis of Assisi, subverts the importance of speaking the gospel. While deeds of love and compassion back up the message and add credibility to the church and to the gospel, the message of Colossians, consistent with the rest of the New Testament, is that primacy of place is with speaking the gospel so people will hear it.

The Word of God to Bring to Maturity

So far, I have shown an emphasis on the word of God, the gospel, bringing people to conversion, to faith. However, conversion is not the full story. Paul reflects the importance of growing people to maturity of faith also through that same word.

In his prayer for the Colossians in 1:9–14, Paul prays they may be "filled with the knowledge of God's will" so that they lead lives "fully" pleasing to the Lord. Colossians does emphasis the language of fullness, which points to maturity or perfection. Paul's aim in ministry—in preaching, writing, or praying—is not simply conversion but maturity. His prayer expresses this idea, and he comes back to it in different words later in chapter 1. In verse 22, Paul expresses the goal of Christian life as being presented "holy and blameless and irreproachable" before Christ. In verse 28, Paul's labor is in order to "present everyone mature in Christ." The language of "present" is legal and used for bringing someone to court.[3] Paul is imagining bringing Christians before the divine judge on the final day to be found blameless.[4]

From these passages, notice that Paul prays for maturity, Christ died for maturity, and Paul labors for maturity. It would be fair to add that he writes this letter, among others, also for maturity in Christian faith and life. The means of this maturity is again the word of God, the gospel, the word of the truth. A focus on Jesus is central and essential.

At the heart of these references to maturity is the famous hymn-like passage of the supremacy of Christ, 1:15–20. Some argue Paul is quoting a hymn, others that Paul himself wrote it. The authorship of it is irrelevant for this discussion; nor is our primary focus its majestic theology. Rather, our focus here—and what is often overlooked by those preaching on this passage—is its function within Colossians.

In his prayer in verse 9, Paul prays that the Colossians will know the will of God. He does not define the will of God here, but it seems to me that the next paragraph serves the purpose of expounding God's will. The supremacy of Christ over the creation and re-creation is a statement but note the purpose clause in verse 18: "so that he might come to have first place in everything." The language is uncommon, and Moo translates this as "in everything he might have the supremacy." While many translate this as a clause expressing result, Moo argues this is rightly a purpose clause as not all things are yet under Christ's feet, and this clause thus expresses God's ultimate intention.[5]

The will of God is that Jesus takes first place in everything, not just some things, and this in effect matches Paul's prayer for maturity, that the Colossians fully please God in every good work. Similarly, note in 3:17 the injunction to do everything in the name of the Lord Jesus. "Everything" here and "every good work" in 1:10 are very similar to Jesus taking first place "in everything." Lucas points out that in writing such to a church, it must be possible for a church not to practice having Christ as its head. He suggests the new teachers infiltrating Colossae were perhaps claiming too much authority and displacing Christ as head.[6]

---

3. Lucas, *Fullness and Freedom*, 62, referring to Lohse.

4. O'Brien, *Colossians, Philemon*, 89, that Paul has the parousia in mind.

5. Moo, *Colossians and Philemon*, 130. Compare O'Brien, *Colossians, Philemon*, 51, who states that it is already the case that Christ has supremacy as a result of the resurrection.

6. Lucas, *Fullness and Freedom*, 52.

The hymn about Christ also serves the goal of maturity expressed in 1:22. Verse 21 applies the general language of the supremacy of Christ to the Colossians personally ("and you") and makes it patent that the reconciling death of Jesus was aimed at presenting the Colossians holy, blameless, and irreproachable. This work of Christ has been "heard" by the Colossians because it has been proclaimed (v. 23). Again, the word proclaimed or spoken is not only for beginning the Christian life but also for its maturity or perfection. Here "proclaimed" translates *kerysso*, almost always used in the New Testament where the subject of the verb is an authority figure, the context is usually a public one, and the message is almost always clearly Jesus and the gospel.[7]

Then finally, Paul's own labor and ministry to make the word of God fully known is emphatically focused on Jesus, the object of the proclamation preceding the verb: "Him we proclaim . . . " (v. 28). The "him" is Jesus, the Jesus presented in verses 15–20 not least. The verb translated "proclaim" here is *katangello*. Nicholls and Wintle suggest *katangello* is a stronger word than *kerysso*, though it is not clear this is the case.[8] The words appear to be relatively interchangeable. Griffiths argues that like *kerysso*, *katangello* normally has as its subject a person of authority, and the content is always Jesus and/or the gospel.[9] He goes on to argue that the inclusion of warning and teaching shows that Paul's proclamation is not simply an initial gospel presentation but suggests the "ongoing and systematic presentation of Christ as Lord."[10] Certainly, Paul sees making the word of God fully known as correcting and rebuking wrong belief, warning people against straying from the truth—something the modern Anglican church could be said to be weak in. This also fits the emphasis in this essay that making the word of God fully known is not for conversion alone but for maturity. He also points out that the mutual ministry of every believer described in Colossians 3:16 uses the same words, warning and teaching, so the mutual ministry of all Christians takes its lead from that of the authoritative figure, in this case Paul.[11]

My argument is that the hymn of 1:15–20 summarizes what the word of the truth, the gospel, the word of God, is. It is all about Jesus. Its function is for conversion, as the Colossians had experienced, but also for their maturity or perfection on the day of Christ. For now, that means living lives

---

7. Griffiths, *Preaching in the New Testament*, 31–32.
8. Nicholls and Wintle, *Colossians and Philemon*, 87
9. Griffiths, *Preaching in the New Testament*, 26.
10. Griffiths, *Preaching in the New Testament*, 35.
11. Griffiths, *Preaching in the New Testament*, 47.

fully pleasing to the Lord and looking to the future, to be holy, blameless, irreproachable, and perfect on the day of Christ.

So, making the word of God fully known is making the fulness of Christ known for the sake of people fully living lives pleasing to God. There is depth in this word of God, not merely a simple or trite message. At every level, this word is all about Jesus.

The Word of God for Everyone

There is another dimension of the word of God being made fully known that is often not stressed from Colossians 1:25. Moo translates the relevant phrase in verse 25 as "word of God in its fullness."[12] Lucas similarly concentrates on the full gospel being made known.[13] Nonetheless, as Moo observes, the language of verse 25 points to "fulfilling the word of God" and probably alludes to Paul's commission to the Gentiles (also mentioned explicitly in verse 27).[14] O'Brien speaks of "to complete the word of God" in the sense of "doing fully" or "carrying to completion" the divine commission, and likens this to Romans 15:19, which speaks of Paul bringing to completion the gospel from Jerusalem to Illyricum, a geographical reference. But, he notes, it is not simply preaching that fulfils the word of God but doing so dynamically and effectively.[15] So, while the fullness of the gospel itself is in mind, it is not to the exclusion of the breadth or extent of the gospel's aim, namely all people. This universality has been seen already in verse 15, referring to Jesus' supremacy over all things, and in verse 20, referring to Jesus' death bringing reconciliation to all things. Back in verse 6, Paul notes the gospel is "bearing fruit and growing in the whole world." It thus appears clear that making the word of God fully known involves not just conversion and maturity, the fullness of the gospel itself, but also the extent to which the gospel of Jesus is to go: to all people, through the whole world.

When this word of God was brought by Epaphras to the Colossians, they were likely pagans, worshiping presumably the pantheon of Greco-Roman gods. Some may have been from Jewish backgrounds; more likely the majority were pagan. Receptivity was not a criterion for deciding to whom to bring the word of God.

Again, the hymn of Christ establishes the foundation. Christ is supreme over all things. The hymn is at pains to emphasize that there is nothing at

---

12. Moo, *Colossians and Philemon*, 147.
13. Lucas, *Fullness and Freedom*, 70.
14. Moo, *Colossians and Philemon*, 154.
15. O'Brien, *Colossians, Philemon*, 82–83.

all outside the supremacy and lordship of Jesus Christ in the whole created world. The logical conclusion to draw from this is that because Christ died to reconcile "all things," then the word of God about and focusing on Christ is for the benefit of all things, not least people.

Not surprisingly, we see this reflected in Colossians 1. In verse 23, Paul says that the gospel the Colossians have heard has "been proclaimed to every creature under heaven." *Ktisis* here is the same word as in verse 15, tying in the proclamation to the whole world because Jesus is Lord of the whole world. Verse 6 also referred to the growth of the gospel in the whole *ktisis*. Presumably the statement is hyperbolic, as at that point of course there were large parts of the empire where the gospel had not yet reached. Paul's point is that the gospel is for every creature and it is being proclaimed by him, Epaphras and others, without discrimination to anyone and everyone. Moule suggests Paul means the gospel is proclaimed "in all the great centres of the Empire."[16]

In particular, Paul expands in verse 27 that the gospel of hope in the supreme Jesus is also for Gentiles. The message of Jesus was not only for Jewish people but for anyone. This had been a "mystery," not because it was beyond understanding but because it was only in the time of Jesus that the fulness of God's rescue plan for humanity was revealed. As we know from the Acts of the Apostles, it took a little time for the gospel of Jesus to be taken to Gentiles, and Peter needed a vision to convince him of this truth (Acts 10). Paul's conversion on the road to Damascus (Acts 9) led to his commissioning by God to be the apostle to the Gentiles.

Finally, we see in verse 28, a verse "remarkable for its emphasis on universality,"[17] the threefold mention of "everyone": "warning everyone and teaching everyone in all wisdom. So that we may present everyone mature in Christ." Clearly, "everyone" is emphatic. Paul is not meaning every person living in Colossae, or even more, living in the world, but "every person God brings into the scope of our ministry."[18] The word of the truth, the gospel, the word of God is unlimited in its relevance and object. Since Jesus is for everyone, and died to reconcile everyone and all things, then the word of God needs to be made fully known to everyone. As Moo comments, "Verse 28 elaborates what Paul means when he says at the end of v. 25 that he has been given the task 'to present to you the word of God in its fullness.'"[19]

---

16. Moule, *Colossians and Philemon*, 73.
17. Moo, *Colossians and Philemon*, 159.
18. Moo, *Colossians and Philemon*, 160.
19. Moo, *Colossians and Philemon*, 159.

The task of making the word of God fully known is described in verse 25 as "God's commission." Paul thus recognizes that it is not his ministry or his idea but rather a commission from God. We ought not consider this as limited to Paul. First, the wider sense of Colossians 1 suggests that making the word of God fully known is part of God's great plan for the whole creation, over which the Lord Jesus is supreme. Second, the phrase "God's commission" (*oikonomia*) actually refers more often to God's gospel plan than merely to a commission for Paul personally.[20] That commission or divine plan remains to all of God's church, not least his authorized ministers, to proclaim the gospel of Jesus fully, without reserve, to the world.

This challenges many church practices and expectations. Melbourne, a richly multicultural city but increasingly secular among its Anglo-Saxon population, needs the word of God about Jesus. While bringing the word of God to the city and suburbs is increasingly hard, and the soil harder than ever to penetrate, the church must not shrink back from making Jesus fully known. At times in the past, we have been prone to lament that there are "not many Anglicans in our patch," as if that is an excuse for a declining church and introspection.

However, since the days of Archbishop Penman in particular, but championed also by Archbishop Freier, a multicultural Anglican diocese is part of the goal. Currently there are numerous congregations meeting in various language groups: Mandarin, Farsi, Arabic, Dinka, Karen, Tamil, Malayalam, Māori, Bahasa Indonesian, Bari, Chollo, Cantonese and others. As strands of the church have sought to make the word of God fully known, then like the Colossians being rescued from darkness and transferred into the kingdom of God's Son, so too we see people rescued from Buddhism, Islam, Confucianism, Hinduism, Communism, and even secular humanism. This word of God being made fully known crosses not just language and religious backgrounds but socioeconomic boundaries. Traditionally, Anglicanism has been stronger in middle classes, but this motto from Colossians 1 challenges us to invest in ministry across all classes.

What we have seen, then, is that making the word of God fully known involves three dimensions: it's about bringing people to conversion or faith, it's about bringing people to maturity, and its extent is for anyone and everyone. We could express this as "the full gospel to the fullest extent of the world." So, the expression "make the word of God fully known" relates to both its complete message and the extent of its proclamation. As the

---

20. O'Brien, *Colossians, Philemon*, 81.

Lausanne Movement puts it, it's the whole church bringing the whole gospel to the whole world.[21]

Confidence in the Word of God

Colossians 1 ought to give the church pause to reflect if it has lost confidence in the gospel of Jesus. Perhaps too often, we are reticent to preach or proclaim Jesus and doubtful that an unbeliever might respond with faith. Given the scourge of past church failures with regard to children, it may seem presumptuous for the church to preach Jesus to its society. Christians are often regarded as bigoted and out of date and increasingly are mocked or vilified in Australia. Interestingly, in the 2019 Australian Federal election, with both the Prime Minister and Leader of the Opposition publicly professing Christian faith, the media pressed the party leaders about matters of belief—not least, following the sacking of Rugby player Israel Folau, their beliefs about eternal damnation. Christians are often on the backfoot in Australia these days. A result of that is the temptation to withdraw from the public proclamation of Jesus.

Colossians 1 ought also to challenge an increasingly pragmatic reliance on method or people for the future of the church. I have seen churches clutch desperately at Alpha or some other gospel presentation method or program, thinking it might save their parish or even renew and revive the parish. Good though many of these programs are, in essence they will not succeed if there is a lack of confidence in, and understanding of, the supremacy of Jesus. Content matters much more than method.

We see this confidence expressed by Paul in the transformation from verse 21 to verses 22–23. The power of the gospel has brought the Colossians from estrangement and hostility to God to reconciliation, from evil deeds to holiness. When we realize the plight of the unbeliever, we are provided the motivation to make the word of God fully known.

The sufficiency of, and thus the reason for confidence in, the word of God is implied further in verse 23 with the idea of continuing steadfast in the faith and not shifting from the hope. Paul is expressing here that the gospel of hope through the supremacy of Jesus Christ was not only sufficient for salvation but will remain sufficient throughout life. Christians are not to shift or "progress" from that hope to any other hope or gospel. It's possible that the false teachers in Colossae were urging the Colossian church to shift to some other teaching.[22] So, Paul is indicating that the word of God is suf-

21. Nicholls and Wintle, *Colossians and Philemon*, 83.
22. Lucas, *Fullness and Freedom*, 63.

ficient for one's whole life, and thus we ought to have utmost confidence in it and its power. Given that many Christians do move on to other teaching, making the word of God fully known will also include urging such people to return to the true gospel of Jesus' supremacy and his sufficient death for reconciling us to God.

Ironically, we can also see Paul's confidence in the word of God in his willingness to suffer for this gospel. He mentions his suffering in verse 24. While this verse has occasioned much debate over Paul's precise meaning about what is lacking in Christ's afflictions, for our purposes here it is sufficient to note his suffering. If Paul lacked confidence in the gospel, it is hard to imagine why he would suffer for it. Willingness to suffer reflects confidence.

The Content of the Word of God

Given that making the word of fully known at least involves the full gospel, it is worth summarizing the content of this word of God from Colossians 1. In doing this, we recognize that ways of summarizing the gospel will use different language, and indeed we see this in the New Testament itself. However, from Colossians 1, we note the following.

As mentioned in the opening to this essay, a major theme of the word of truth is hope. Hope derives from the resurrection and is made manifest in "Christ in you, the hope of glory" (v. 27).

In verse 6, Paul summarizes the gospel with the phrase "the grace of God." While he does not define grace here he does so elsewhere, emphasizing that salvation is not our own work or doing but a free gift from God.[23]

The end of Paul's prayer in verses 9–14 has a catalogue of aspects of the gospel content. God through Christ has done three things. He has:

- enabled to share in the inheritance of the saints in light (v. 12),
- rescued from the power of darkness (v. 13), and
- transferred into the kingdom of his beloved son (v. 13).

Each of these suggests something radical and powerful, a complete change of life. What God does in the gospel is not enhance an already attractive and pleasant life but fundamentally alter a person's standing and belonging. Note that it is the kingdom of Jesus into which believers are transferred, not merely God's kingdom. As a result of those three activities of God, there is a significant benefit: redemption, the forgiveness of sins (v.

---

23. See for example Ephesians 2:1–10.

14). Here forgiveness fills out what is meant by redemption. This is accomplished, as the next paragraph says, by Jesus' reconciling death on the cross.

The hymn of 1:15–20 is the fullest expression of the content of the word of God in Colossians. We cannot unpack the theology of this paragraph in full but attempt to summarize some key points.

The first half of the hymn extols the supremacy of Jesus over all creation. It is paradoxical that Jesus can be the image of something, or someone, invisible. In essence, we are being told that if we want to see God we are to look at Jesus. The centrality of Jesus is clear for any believer. There can be no downplaying the importance of Jesus for Christian faith and proclamation. While the phrase "firstborn of all creation" (v. 15), when taken by itself, has been open to various interpretations that diminish Jesus as simply part of the creation (such as that of the Jehovah's Witnesses), in context such interpretations cannot be valid. Verse 16 makes it clear that all things, without exception, were made in, through, and for Jesus. Thus, Jesus has an essential role in creation ("through him") as well as being its goal. An implication of this is that it is too simplistic to think of God the Father as Creator, God the Son as Redeemer, and God the Spirit as Life Giver. There is a much greater inherent unity in the Trinity, and therefore the role of Jesus, than this demarcation suggests. Everything is made for the glory and majesty of Jesus.

Note, too, the emphasis on "all things" or "everything" in these verses, eight times in total. That emphasis, as mentioned previously, undergirds the whole idea of making the word of God "fully" known to everyone. The word of God is all about Jesus.

The second panel of the hymn begins in verse 18, paralleling verse 15 with the repetition of "firstborn." Whilst this panel may look anticlimactic, it is not. If Jesus is supreme over creation, then by his resurrection he is also supreme over the new creation, that is, the universal church. Clearly the goal of God for this universe is achieved through the reconciling death (v. 20) and victorious resurrection ("firstborn from the dead") of Jesus. No gospel is complete if it does not lead to these pivotal and world-changing events. As firstborn, the implication is that others will follow him in resurrection. This is available for all things, for everyone, as verse 20 emphatically states. Verse 20 also stresses that the only means for reconciliation with God is through Jesus' death on the cross.

Reconciliation is an important theme in Australian social discourse. It is both right and important to seek reconciliation with our First Nations peoples, for example. But the gospel is not merely about human and racial reconciliation. It is primarily about reconciliation with God himself, and that is only through Jesus. Reconciliation with other people comes through being reconciled to God. Jesus is essential and supreme when it comes to reconciliation. Moreover, he is utterly sufficient as a universal Savior.[24]

We ought also pause here to note that verse 20 says "all things" and not merely "all people" are reconciled by Jesus' death. That phrase has occasioned much comment, but clearly Paul has in mind that this whole fallen world, subject to decay and groaning as he says in Romans 8:21–22, will be reconciled together and to God through Jesus. I recall a bishop saying at a General Synod meeting some years ago that "climate change is the gospel." While I disagree, for Jesus is the gospel, the reconciliation of the universe in harmony and renewal is what Jesus died and rose for, not merely human souls. Care of creation is the fifth mark of mission in the Anglican communion; however, I think Paul, in Colossians 1 and elsewhere, would argue that proclaiming Jesus is the primary mark of mission, not to the exclusion of the others, but certainly in pride of place.

For many years, there has been debate and division of opinion regarding the relationship between evangelism and social action or social justice. The Lausanne Movement, pioneered by Billy Graham and John Stott, has sought to bring these two themes together theologically. One way those two activities can be reconciled is to consider the goal of God at the end of verse 18, "that Jesus may come to have first place in everything." In all things, we need to put Jesus first. That will drive us in evangelism but also in acts of mercy and compassion. There is a fundamental unity when we think of Jesus first and do not pit evangelism against social action.

The supremacy of Jesus is not obvious in our world. In the West, with declining church attendances, we see that we are increasingly a minority, a quieter voice or influence, than in the past. That can be discouraging. Our brothers and sisters in other parts of the world have always known what it is like to be in a small minority, often in hostile environments. Church decline ought not lead us to a lack of confidence in Jesus or his gospel.

Paul wrote this letter because the Colossian church was in danger of drifting or being led away from the centrality of Jesus and the word of God. The same temptations exist today. There are competing gospels of varying degrees of inadequacy or heresy. The common theme in all is that Jesus is diminished, in his person or in the sufficiency of his death and resurrection. Colossians 1 ought to challenge us to ensure that what we preach, and how we live together as God's people, places Jesus first and extols his supremacy.

Here, I wish to make a further comment on verse 27, "Christ in you, the hope of glory." The mystery revealed in Jesus is that salvation is for Jew and Gentile, equally and together. Glimpses of this mystery can be seen in

---

24. Lucas, *Fullness and Freedom*, 57.

the Old Testament, notably in the call of Abraham in Genesis 12, when God begins his global rescue mission so that all the nations of the world will be blessed. By and large, Israelites and Jews had not understood this global salvation plan of God. Paul, though, grasped it, and so his life's goal was to make known the word of God fully, to anyone and everyone.

Verse 27 mentions "hope," used already in verse 5. In a world that yearns for hope, we have here an important statement for making the word of God fully known. Our message is not simply about the past, what Jesus did for us on the cross and in his resurrection. Rather, the aim of those past events is the hope of glory in Christ. We use the word "hope" weakly in our general conversation, hoping for our team to win or for good weather. Such hope is little more than wishful thinking, and it frequently disappoints us. But Christian hope is sure and certain, because it is anchored in and guaranteed by the death and resurrection of Jesus. The hope of glory is not a vain hope, a gentle wish, or personal preference. The hope of glory in Christ is certain and sure.

Thus, the only sure hope, and the best hope for our world, for all people and all things, is Jesus. That hope is laid up in heaven already (v. 5) and ensured by the living Christ now "in" us (v. 27).

Finally, in verse 28, Paul gives another summary of what this word of God is. His summary "is extraordinary in its conciseness . . . [and] can be put in a word, or rather a name; *him we proclaim*."[25] This matches the succinctness of the mystery—that is, the gospel—being Christ in you, in verse 27. As O'Brien says, Jesus "is the sum and substance of Paul's message."[26] So the word of God is all about Jesus: the Jesus of grace (v. 6), the supreme Jesus over creation, the Jesus whose death was totally sufficient for the reconciliation of all things to God (vv. 15–20), the Jesus who is able to bring people to maturity and blamelessness on the final day (vv. 22–23), the Jesus who guarantees our hope of glory. This Jesus is to be on our lips, proclaimed from our pulpits, and held onto steadfastly as we yearn for his glorious return.

Conclusion

Paul's life goal was to make this gospel of Jesus fully known. The word of God was to convert people, to grow people to maturity, and to be proclaimed to any and every person regardless of religious or racial heritage. The Lausanne Movement's slogan, "the whole church bringing the whole gospel to the whole world," fits well Paul's emphasis in this chapter.

25. Lucas, *Fullness and Freedom*, 73.
26. O'Brien, *Colossians, Philemon*, 87.

Paul labored hard for this gospel. He uses strong words for toil and labor in verse 29. We must not expect that making the word of God fully known will be easy or casual. We ought to expect hard work. Making the word of God fully known involves warning all people (v. 28), warning against false "gospels," and warning against false confidence, thus speaking grace (v. 6) but also speaking of the perils of ignoring Christ. It involves teaching (v. 28), suggesting time and depth.

In the end, the word of God, the gospel, the word of the truth is all about Jesus. As Paul says emphatically in verse 28, "Him we proclaim." Presumably the "we" includes Epaphras, Timothy and others. Jesus is whom we proclaim, the supreme Jesus over all creation, the Jesus who died to reconcile all things to God, the Jesus who is the firstborn from the dead by his resurrection, the Jesus who dwells in his people ensuring a sure hope of glory. This Jesus we are to make fully known, to see conversion, to see maturity, to see all people in Christ.

The future of the Anglican Diocese of Melbourne, and indeed the whole church, is found not in a method, style, program, or pathway. The future of our church is Jesus. That is why Paul prayed for the Colossians (1:9–14), why he wrote to them, why he suffered (1:24), why he preached (1:28), why he toiled (1:29) and why Christ died (1:22). Let us likewise labor and preach, and suffer if need be, so that the word of God may be fully known throughout our places.

Bibliography

Griffiths, Jonathan I. *Preaching in the New Testament: An Exegetical and Biblical-Theology Study*. NSBT. Downers Grove, IL: Apollos/IVP, 2017.

Lucas, Richard C. *Fullness and Freedom: The Message of Colossians and Philemon*. Bible Speaks Today. Nottingham, UK: IVP, 1980.

Moo, Douglas J. *The Letters to the Colossians and to Philemon*. Pillar New Testament Commentary. Grand Rapids, MI: Eerdmans, 2008.

Moule, Charles F. D. *The Epistles to the Colossians and Philemon*. Cambridge Greek New Testament Commentary. Cambridge: Cambridge University Press, 1958.

Nicholls, Bruce J. and Wintle, Brian. *Colossians and Philemon*. Asia Bible Commentary. Singapore: Asia Theological Association, 2005.

O'Brien, Peter T. *Colossians, Philemon*. Word Biblical Commentary. Waco, TX: Word, 1982.

2

A Diocese in Mission

Coaching and Parish Renewal in the Diocese of Melbourne

Richard Trist

Pastoral ministry within the contemporary Australian context is difficult. Church attendance is declining, and many clergy feel isolated and struggle with the demands of church leadership. Burnout of key leaders and the premature attrition of younger clergy continues to be an issue for most denominations as they seek to undertake effective mission in a period of rapid change.

In such challenging times, a program of coaching and parish renewal that commenced in 2011 in the Diocese of Melbourne has been remarkable in its impact, producing a renewed missional focus within the diocese. In the words of one observer, the program is "a great story [that] offers hope and good news in an age of church decline in Australia."[1]

My own interest in this effort to bring renewal to the diocese began in early 2010 with an invitation from Archbishop Philip Freier to join a small group looking at a new vision for growth in mission for the Anglican Diocese of Melbourne. The Archbishop was seeking feedback for his proposals,

---

1. Rietveld, *Coaching*, 17.

alongside assistance in knowing how to present the vision so that it might gain acceptance from Synod as well as budget appropriation.

After Synod endorsed the plan in October 2010, the Archbishop invited me to assist in some aspects of the establishment of the vision, particularly in the development of a pilot program to encourage growth in mission within twenty-five selected parishes. Although I was only able to engage in the development of the program for a short time, my interest in the diocesan plan for renewal continued, and it became an obvious focus for doctoral research.[2] I am pleased to have this opportunity to congratulate Archbishop Philip on the occasion of his sixty-fifth birthday and to tell the story of this missional initiative to a wider audience.

The Role of a Diocese in Church Renewal

What is the role of a diocese in the renewal of the church? According to the Constitution of the Anglican Church of Australia, the diocese is the center of its organization: "A Diocese shall in accordance with the historic custom of the One Holy Catholic and Apostolic Church continue to be the unit of organisation of this church and shall be the see of a Bishop."[3]

Although representatives of the twenty-three dioceses of the Anglican Church of Australia come together every three years as a General Synod to deliberate on matters of importance to the national church, ultimately each diocese is responsible, under the leadership of its bishop and governing council, to set the direction for mission and ministry in its local area. Through its economies of scale, it can impact a great number of people across a wide area. This gives it significant opportunities unavailable to most local congregations.

Bob Jackson, in his study on the growth and decline of churches in the Church of England, notes the way that diocesan strategies in the UK have made a difference to church life and health. He observes, from attendance statistics of the English church, the variations in trends between the different dioceses:

> If decline were inevitable due to a changing world, then it would be fairly uniform as the whole world changes together. But it is not. Some categories of church, and some churches in some denominations, areas and dioceses, are doing better than others. This means that parts of the church are performing differently in today's environment than are other parts. This in turn means

2. See Trist, *Report*, and Trist, *Two are Better*.
3. Anglican Church of Australia, *Constitution*, 4.

that some churches are finding answers to the question of how to grow. Perhaps those answers can be discovered and disseminated to help the rest of the church grow as well.[4]

Jackson describes the ways in which dioceses can work to either hinder or help the growth of the church. He suggests seven different operational modes:

1. Disapproval mode. This approach views with suspicion or hostility innovative parishes moving away from inherited traditions.
2. Disinterest mode. Rather than expressing disapproval to parishes with imaginative programs, dioceses in this mode simply show no interest. They seem only interested in receiving their proportion of parish income.
3. Permission-giving mode. Jackson suggests that many English dioceses are increasingly moving out of the previous two modes into this one. Parishes that are seeking to experiment and change in order to engage the contemporary world are permitted to do so. No diocesan help, however, is offered to support them.
4. Encouragement mode. In this approach the diocese encourages parishes to become more missional. Clergy and church councils come together for training programs. Parishes are invited to submit a "mission action plan" to the bishop.
5. Proactive mode. Greater effectiveness occurs as a diocese moves towards not just encouraging individual parishes into better practice, but to initiating its own programs for growth.
6. Policy mode. This mode involves a reshaping of diocesan practices and policies, particularly regarding financial and personnel deployment, towards the growth of the church. Larger parishes with effective outreach strategies are not penalized with ever-increasing diocesan payments. Parish appointments are made on the basis of missional impact rather than seniority.
7. Strategy mode. In this mode of operating, a diocese not only establishes appropriate policy but engages in long-term strategic thinking and coordinates policies and plans to achieve its goals.

Jackson's observations are equally as pertinent to the Australian Anglican church. In the 2006 report to General Synod, *Building the Mission-Shaped Church in Australia*, Alan Nichols notes the difference in church

---

4. Jackson, *Hope for the Church*, 15.

attendance rates between the two New South Wales dioceses of Armidale and Grafton. In the period 1991–2001, attendance in Armidale diocese grew by 2 percent, whereas attendance in Grafton diocese declined by 21 percent. Nichols suggests that this could not simply be due to population change, since in the same period the population of Grafton diocese grew by 4.9 percent and that of Armidale declined by 1.6 percent. He concludes that "different policies and leadership styles in different dioceses may well have contributed to the growth or decline." In the light of this, he proposes that "the Anglican Church in Australia is not powerless, and her dioceses are not irrelevant in the challenge of growth in the 21st century."[5]

In *Facing the Future: Bishops Imagine a Different Church*, Robert Forsyth concurs with this analysis and suggests four reforms for Australian dioceses, which could assist the church to arrest its decline:

1. Each diocese must refocus on the local congregation rather than the institution of the diocese itself. Most of the finances, time, and human resources of the diocese must meet the needs of congregations.

2. The diocese must serve the front-line parishes by providing mission-focused governance. Such governance involves defining the object and rules of the mission and holding the front-line leaders –both clergy and senior laity–accountable for the success of the mission.

3. The diocese must serve parishes by providing mission-focused resourcing. Such resourcing involves not only practical help in the area of insurance, property and compliance but more particularly the training and support of clergy and lay leaders.

4. The diocese must become more permission-giving and encourage new forms of church, church plants, and experimental ministries.[6]

Over the past decade, various dioceses in the Australian Anglican Church have taken up these challenges. New diocesan-based initiatives have been undertaken as expressions of missional proactivity. Notable among these are the Diocese of Tasmania's restructuring into a "Missionary" diocese, with the appointment of two missioner bishops as well as archdeacons becoming Mission Support Officers;[7] the Diocese of Sydney's "Connect '09" evangelistic program, with the distribution of copies of the Gospel of Luke to parishes, organizations, and Anglican schools;[8] and the Diocese of Bris-

5. Nichols, *Building*, 32.
6. Forsyth, "National and Diocesan Structures," 53.
7. Harrower, "A New Openness."
8. Nixon, "Connect 09: Final Report."

bane's promotion of Natural Church Development as a means of monitoring church health and vitality.⁹

These examples illustrate the variety of approaches that have been used. They indicate a growing recognition within the Australian Anglican Church of the need for support of congregations to become more missional in a time of national church decline. As will be seen, however, the program of coaching developed in the Diocese of Melbourne is distinctive in its approach and may well offer other dioceses and denominations a further model for church renewal.

The Archbishop's Plan for Renewal in Mission

In his 2010 address to the Synod of the Anglican Diocese of Melbourne, the Archbishop of Melbourne presented a vision that sought to promote an "outward focus" for the diocese. The key aspect of this was the role of the parish as "the central missional strategy of Australian Anglicanism":

> Parishes are a grid overlaying God's world, dividing up the mission field. For us the 210 parishes of the diocese provide a latticed network for organising mission across the more than 4 million people of greater Melbourne and Geelong, a mission that is as challenging for us today as it was for Charles Perry, our first Bishop. It follows that the parish is not the parish church, nor a congregation, but a defined area of the diocese with streets and lanes, paddocks and public places, schools and homes, medical centres and Anglican agencies. This calls for a paradigm shift in our thinking from parish as just congregation to parish as geographic neighbourhood and geographic mission field. Grasping a vision of parish in this way demands that we never just stop at our church door, no matter how comfortable, busy or thriving our congregations may seem. We need to be aware of the entirety of our parish.[10]

The Archbishop had realized early in his episcopacy that in such a large diocese "it is easy to become fully absorbed in the institutional work of the church." As a result, he had personally sought to move beyond the boundaries of the church by engaging the wider community through his "Prayer4Melbourne" quest and public "Breakfast Conversations" in Federation Square with well-known community figures.[11] He was now challenging

9. Bowles, "NCD Project Report."
10. Freier, "The President's Address," 6.
11. Freier, "A New Willingness," 213

his diocese—clergy and laity alike—to do the same by relating missionally with the local community in which they were located. The Archbishop described his vision as "to make the word of God fully known" (Col 1:25). He challenged the synod to witness to the world by words of proclamation and deeds of service in order to "break through the barrier of indifference with the message of God's love and of his Son, the risen Christ."[12]

The Pilot Program for Parish Renewal

A central aspect of the Archbishop's vision was the establishment of a pilot program to encourage growth in mission within twenty-five selected parishes over the following three years. This was a recognition that "congregations are key to the effective ministry and mission of the church throughout the diocese."[13]

In late 2010, the diocese advertised for a "Coordinator for the Implementation of the Vision and Strategic Directions," and Ken Morgan was appointed to the role.[14] Ken had extensive experience as a consultant, trainer, and coach to church planters, church ministers, and denominational leaders in a wide variety of church traditions across Australia. He was neither ordained nor an Anglican. This, in the minds of some, meant that in a diocese such as Melbourne, he was the ideal person for this new role!

The program commenced in 2011 with a decision to develop three cohorts of churches to participate in the program:

- 2011: fifteen pastoral-sized churches (average attendance of 70–120 per week)
- 2012: five pastoral-sized churches managing the transition to a program size (average attendance from approximately 150 to greater than 150 per week)
- 2013: five family-sized churches managing the transition to a pastoral size (average attendance from less than 50 to greater than 50 per week).[15]

---

12. Freier, "The President's Address," 8.

13. Anglican Diocese of Melbourne, *Making the Word of God Fully Known*, 3.

14. Mark Brolly, "Archbishop Freier Identifies Vital Signs of Church Life," *The Melbourne Anglican*, April 2011.

15. For a description of the term's family-sized church, pastoral-sized church, and program sized church, see Oswald, "How to Minister."

An application process for interested parishes was established with the following expectations:

- A commitment of clergy and Church Council (Vestry) to renewal and growth of the parish,
- The commitment of significant time and resources designed to bring about growth,
- A willingness to discontinue or change activities that did not facilitate growth,
- A willingness to set measurable goals or key performance indicators and report against them,
- The establishment of a Mission Action Team consisting of lay leaders or staff members to assist the vicar in the implementation of growth strategies, and
- The establishment of a prayer group that would commit to frequent and consistent prayer for the renewal and growth of the parish.

The key focus of the program was the monthly coaching of clergy face-to-face over a period of two years. Coaching was defined as "a one to one facilitation of the action-reflection model of learning. The coach assists the leader to focus more clearly on goals, gain a clearer perspective on their current challenges, assess options for progress and implement action plans."[16] The goal of the coach would not be to provide "advice or guidance based on knowledge and experience," but rather to "raise the awareness and sense of responsibility in the leader, and to empower the leader to take thoughtful action."[17]

In a series of articles in the diocesan newspaper *The Melbourne Anglican*, Morgan further described his coaching methodology:

> Coaching provides support and accountability to make learning "stick." As parish teams participate in training and develop action plans, coaching empowers the leader to implement, deal with the inevitable resistance, overcome obstacles and keep the change process on track. Coaching typically revolves around listening very closely, asking carefully crafted questions—questions that enable fresh thinking, or seeing familiar information with renewed clarity. Clarity leads to greater awareness and a realistic sense of responsibility—that for which the leader must

---

16. Morgan, "Strategy Paper," 2.
17. Morgan, "Strategy Paper," 2.

take responsibility, and (sometimes more importantly) those things for which the leader should not.[18]

And on common expectations of the program:

> Early on I felt some expectation to give "expert" advice and instruction. I'm guessing that some Vicars were bemused by my refusal to do so. It's my hope that the people of the parish will become the real experts on making disciples in their neighbourhood, so I've tried to keep away from directing parishes to "add this program" or "change that activity." Instead, I've sought to encourage people to think in new ways about everything the parish does.[19]

Linked to the coaching program was a series of training modules designed to assist clergy and lay leaders develop the "outward focus" that was the key emphasis of the Archbishop's vision. Each parish could determine which training modules were most appropriate for them based on their situation and needs. Training days were held in different locations, undertaken in workshop rather than lecture presentation style. The training modules were varied, but each aimed to assist parishes to pay more attention to developing a missional focus.

The most popular module was "Building a Parish Pathway." This training recognized that many congregations ran activities designed for their own members and had no intentional process to help those with little experience of church come towards Christ and his church. Through a series of exercises, clergy and lay leaders came to recognize "gaps" in their parish activities as well as areas where too many resources were committed. The seven stages of the pathways process were: making a potential contact, keeping in touch, developing a sense of belonging, embracing the gospel, following Jesus, serving in ministry, leading in ministry.

Following the training day, clergy and lay leaders met to plan a more coherent missional pathway for their congregation. The role of the coach in this process was to encourage follow-up and action. As Morgan explained:

> We've all been to training events and conferences where we've taken notes and brought home manuals. And most of these manuals go straight to the "manual shelf" where they remain, unexamined. A coach helps leaders to translate training into

18. Ken Morgan, "Giving Clergy the Opportunity to Reflect . . . and to Vent," *The Melbourne Anglican*, October 2011.

19. Ken Morgan, "Reflections On the Parish Pilot Program," *The Melbourne Anglican*, August 2013.

behaviour by helping them to develop concrete plans of action. Then they hold the leader accountable for implementation.[20]

In its early years, the pilot program garnered differing opinions and responses within the diocese. At the 2011 synod, one vicar spoke of their initial hesitations:

> We took the plunge, in faith, to enter this program, not knowing initially with what we might be confronted. Would this be just another one of those much-heralded programs of evangelism that wouldn't fit our parish, our tradition, our community? Would we end up being consumed by the pursuit of numbers, at the expense of that deep listening to the voice of God and the leading of the Spirit? Well, "no" to those concerns ... Working with Ken, guided by the Spirit, we examine ourselves and we plan our own directions; and we move at our own pace.... This is a stimulus to allow ourselves to try new ways of making the word of God fully known, to reform ourselves and to be open to the transforming power of God already at work in our midst.[21]

Some criticisms focused on the program's emphasis on church attendance numbers and a perception that it was primarily a "one size fits all" approach to mission. Other critiques were of the use of coaching as primarily about overcoming deficits rather than being about the provision of support and the development of potential.[22] These concerns were all valid and needed to be addressed. Research was required to explore the program and test its effectiveness.

Researching the Effectiveness of the Program

In 2011 the Archbishop, through the Bishop Perry Institute for Ministry and Mission, commissioned a research project to achieve the following goals:

- To establish a "baseline" of missional effectiveness for participating parishes as close as possible to the time and status of the parishes' entry into the program,

---

20. Ken Morgan, "Is Your Community Experiencing God's Love through Your Parish?" *The Melbourne Anglican,* February 2012.

21. Mark Brolly, "Pilot Parishes Greet Clearer View of Way Ahead," *The Melbourne Anglican,* December, 2011.

22. Ken Morgan, "Coaching Isn't Just for Those Who are Struggling," *The Melbourne Anglican,* October 2012.

- To evaluate the pilot program's efficiency and effectiveness in encouraging and facilitating improvement in missional effectiveness, and
- To report on practical outcomes of the pilot program, both intentional and unintentional, that could inform the improvement, expansion, and diversification of the program into the future.[23]

At the outset, a key issue for the design and conduct of the study was defining what was meant by "missional effectiveness." The approach taken was to recognize this as not just numerical growth but also changes in church health and vitality—the willingness of a church to engage with its local community. This broader approach was in line with contemporary missional thinking, which understands missional churches as those that embrace "a habit of mind and heart, a posture of openness and discernment, and a faithful attentiveness both to the Spirit's presence and to the world that God so loves."[24]

A longitudinal study was undertaken of six churches from different regions of the diocese representing different Anglican traditions—two Evangelical, two Anglo-Catholic and two Charismatic. Each was a pastoral-sized church managing the transition towards a program size (average attendance from less than 150 to greater than 150 per week). Each had its own set of challenges, including aging congregations and buildings, recent conflicts, and uncertainty about the welcoming and integration of people from other cultures.

It was decided to gather "before and after" data from each church. These included diocesan statistics relating to average Sunday attendance and data from the National Church Life Survey (NCLS) taken prior to, and after, the coaching program. A series of semi-structured interviews of the six clergy being coached was undertaken, alongside focus groups of over twenty-five lay people involved in the program as members of Mission Action Teams.

The following diagram illustrates the research plan:

---

23. A report based on the research project can be found at Trist, *Report*.
24. Van Gelder and Zscheile, *The Missional Church in Perspective*, 149.

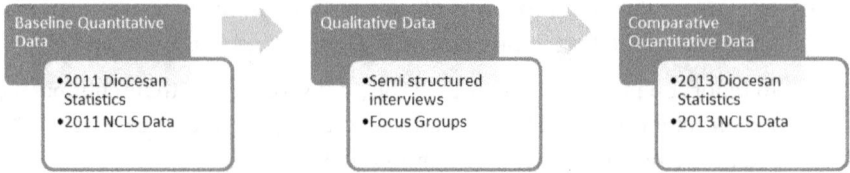

In coaching evaluation literature, validity, rather than reliability and replication, is the key criterion that ensures the integrity of the research. One means of achieving validity is the use of multisource data in which both participants and external observers are given a voice.[25] Another means of validity is the use of a longitudinal design with pre and post data collection. Such a design increases understanding of causal influences over time.[26] This was the approach taken in this research. What were its findings?

Research Findings and Discussion

The diocesan program was based on the premise that a coaching and renewal intervention over a two-year period would facilitate an improvement in the missional effectiveness of local churches. The research findings have overwhelmingly supported this.

(a) Impact on Clergy

All clergy interviewed found the coaching aspect of the program life changing, both personally and for their ministry. Many expressed that being coached was the most effective form of professional development they had ever undertaken. It gave them someone to journey alongside to whom they could be accountable and who could help them focus on the direction they were wanting to go. One participant expressed it like this:

> Having a personal coach, you're being kept accountable. "Well, what are you doing about this?" You know, and if you haven't done it, "It's okay, well you haven't done it, do you want to keep it on the agenda, or do you want to let it slide?" "No, I want to keep it on the agenda." "Okay, we'll keep it on the agenda." It isn't as though you've been beaten over the head, but you're really saying, "Well, is that important or not?" And yes it is, therefore I've got to keep working at it. And I may not get to it, but I'm

---

25. Ely et al., *Evaluating Leadership Coaching*, 596.
26. Bryman, *Social Methods Research*, 63.

being reminded I said this is important, therefore I've got to keep going.[27]

Meeting monthly with a coach helped these church leaders overcome the sense of isolation that many felt in trying to lead their parish towards growth but not really knowing how to do it. It encouraged them in the development of new skills and attitudes:

> I think it's helped me become a better time manager. I'm still working on all those, and there's still a whole lot of way I've got to go, but I think it . . . it's causing me to be more reflective, and that's been one of my big things, that I've got to become a more reflective leader. I think in the past everything is so urgent that you don't have time to sit down and reflect, and I realise that if I'm going to . . . move this church . . . I have to become a more effective leader.

The coaching sessions, as well as the recommended reading material, also helped clergy to rethink their leadership style and begin to shift from being a pastor to everyone to an enabler of others:

> I started to re-look at . . . what I should be doing as a priest . . . it's really made me understand the difference that a priest has to be, the different skills that a priest has to have in order to move the parish from below 200 to the over 200 mark . . . I'm moving from being a hands-on priest to being a priest that is ensuring other work is happening.

As well as all this, clergy expressed gratitude for the personal support and help they gained from their coach. As one priest expressed it:

> It has been an opportunity for reflection on my ministry . . . I've found I've taken the opportunity for personal growth in my ministry through vulnerability and just saying, "here's some things that I'm wrestling with," and so the coaching has extended beyond getting a job done to growing as a person in ministry.

These findings concur with other empirical studies, which show that the benefits of coaching are as follows: increased goal attainment; enhanced solution-focused thinking; a greater ability to deal with change; increased leadership self-efficacy and resilience; and a decrease in depression. There are several ways in which coaching may produce such benefits:

---

27. All participant quotes are from Trist, *Report*, 36–42.

- Talking through issues with someone in a confidential relationship helps with the relief of stress.
- The process of setting goals and purposefully working towards them fosters the enhancement of wellbeing and self-efficacy.
- Being supported while engaging in change processes encourages the development of resilience and self-regulation.[28]

(b) Impact on Lay leaders

As well as clergy finding the program useful, focus groups of lay leaders expressed benefits such as greater clarity of purpose, a growth in personal commitment, and the gaining of fresh energy and understanding. The training and readings they were given had helped them to understand more fully the changes that would be needed if they were to grow as a church:

> The book made a very strong case that you had to have a different paradigm for a different way of doing church . . . the *Two Hundred Barrier* book helped us recognise . . . blockages that you can ignore and blockages which are part of the process . . . And some of them are worth getting rid of, some of them are worth ignoring and going around, and some of them you just have to live with.

One person noted the new energy and ideas that flowed when they met as a team with a missional focus:

> Something that came out of the team itself was our Easter outreach. We've never had a context before in which to brainstorm . . . That idea came out of the brainstorming of the Mission Action Team, because we thought, what can we do differently this Easter as a public statement of the gospel, other than what we felt was becoming a bit tired.

Lay leaders also noted the positive changes they had seen in the clergy and the way such changes had begun to empower them for their service in the parish:

> From my position the biggest impact has been the positive impact on [the vicar] . . . it's helping [him] clear space in his head to more accurately identify how he can enable the church to grow where he's an enabler and a mover and a shaker and a leader rather than a doer to quite the same extent . . . I can see

28. Grant, *The Efficacy of Executive Coaching*, 4–5.

the release and the relief and the fire that's sort of in his belly now . . . and of course as he's been fired up and enabled, that's spreading to the leadership teams.

This change in clergy leadership style and the resultant growth in effective mission has been noted in other research.[29] It may be surmised that as clergy experienced a positive coaching relationship leading to new transformational leadership behaviors, they began to use the same approach in their own relationships in the parish, leading to the empowerment of lay leaders.

(c) Impact on Churches

Observation of the six churches studied indicated changes concurrent with their involvement in the program. New parish outreach initiatives such as Messy Church commenced, and evangelistic courses such as Introducing God and Alpha began. The intentional focus to connect with those on the fringe of the parish led not only to new programs but also to new strategies of welcoming those attending Sunday services, including those from other cultural backgrounds. In one parish this meant a relocation of the morning tea held after the main Sunday service. Another parish put effort into developing a specific area, a "welcome" desk, where newcomers could gather and find out more about the life of the church. The significant change for these parishes was not so much in finding a welcoming *location*, but rather in developing a new welcoming *mindset*, with church members looking after not just their own needs but also the needs of others.

A key driver for this new missional activity has been the Pathways training course with its emphasis on developing intentional welcoming and discipleship pathways. Activities not contributing to the growth of disciples have been discontinued and new activities begun. In the words of one lay leader:

> [It] helped us to think about how do we, for example, transition a young family who might have contact with the church through the playgroups . . . what path is there for them to become more involved in the life of the church? So how do we connect with them, help them to transition from non-believer, non-church goer into Warden or Vestry person, possible ordained ministry, committed Christian in their workplace, or whatever . . . the Pathways material has been incredibly useful.

29. See Rumley, "*Transformational Ministry.*" and Finn, "*Leadership Development Through Executive Coaching.*"

(d) Impact on Church Growth and Health

The study of Sunday attendance figures for the six parishes indicated that the activities of the pilot program had a positive impact on average Sunday attendance for all the parishes involved. This positive impact occurred in three parishes during the period of the program and in five parishes after the program. Of particular significance was the growth in Sunday attendance in two parishes that had previously been experiencing a decline.

As the diagram below indicates, overall average Sunday attendance of the pilot program parishes increased by 11 percent over the two years of the pilot program (from 164 to 191) at the same time that the average Sunday attendance in the diocese as a whole was static (from 98 to 102).

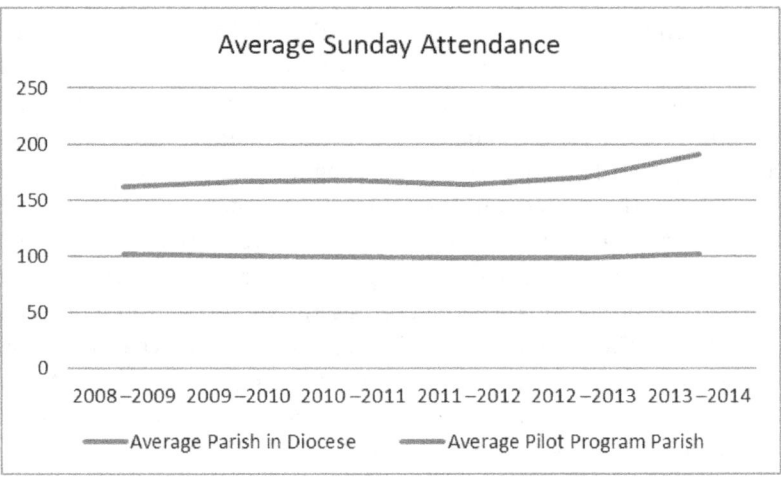

Unlike other programs for church growth and renewal, which rely on the importation of a model or program, it is likely that the contextual nature of the pilot program played a significant part in the transition that these parishes were making. The pilot program did not have a "one size fits all" approach but tailored the coaching and training to each context. Such contextualization enabled the parishes to become more missionally effective.

It was notable that most of those interviewed were able to specify new individuals or families who had joined their church over this period. For those parishes already on a growth trajectory, this was a challenge to ensure integration of the newcomers. For those parishes where attendance had been stable or declining, this was a source of great hope and optimism for the future.

A comparison of National Church Life Surveys before and after the program gives insight into this increase. Of the missional measures analyzed, there was a statistically significant increase in the percentage of church members who valued the church's priority on reaching the unchurched (4.2 percent), as well as a higher tendency to welcome new people (3.3 percent). These changes indicate that as a result of the parish renewal program the "DNA" of parishes had begun to alter, with changes in missional attitude as well as behavior.

The good news of these findings is that although local churches may be influenced by external factors, they need not be captive to them. Connection with the local community depends not only on the receptivity of the community but also on the openness of the church and its leaders to adapt to new ways of doing ministry and mission. Churches with a desire to change and grow can break out of patterns of decline or plateau. Involvement in an external support program such as coaching is one way in which parishes can do this.

One further significant finding is that the positive changes in missional effectiveness were seen in all the parishes, regardless of churchmanship. Although theological tradition has been shown to be a factor in church growth and vitality, the changes in all the parishes indicate that the diocesan program was successful in working with the different theological contexts of each parish.[30] This means that a program such as this is capable of being introduced across diverse contexts.

Conclusion

The Diocese of Melbourne Coaching and Parish Renewal Program has had, and continues to have, a positive impact on the life of this diocese. Thirty-eight parishes have now completed the two-year program, and another seventeen are currently involved. Since 2011, over one hundred clergy and ministry leaders have been coached, and another forty-eight trained by the Christian Coaching Institute to coach others. A new staff member, Carol Clark, was appointed in 2014 to oversee the growing coaching program. Those being coached continue to be positive about the program, speaking of new capabilities gained through it.[31] Parishes are still experiencing growth through new missional initiatives, and the program is evolving with the introduction of renewal retreats for church leaders and a new Archdeaconry-based cohort.[32]

30. Powell et al, *Enriching Church Life*, 113.
31. See Clark, "Coaching Program Survey."
32. Informal conversation with Ken Morgan.

In his study of the program, Rietveld suggests nine reasons why he thinks the model has been such a success:[33]

1. It builds on existing church structures and systems in a proactive, non-disruptive way. There is continuity with what exists already.
2. The process identifies and focuses on a model that can apply to all sorts of different churches, different sizes, locations, and traditions.
3. The process takes a long view. There are no gimmicks or quick fixes. The diocese is focused on going in the one missional direction.
4. The coaching training for each cohort is outsourced, bringing fresh language and input.
5. The program called for and required a commitment to the process. The commitment called for *from* participants is sustained by the commitment and support given *to* them.
6. The program is primarily "opt-in." This increases ownership.
7. There is an implementation of adult learning principles and a reciprocity of learning.
8. The model is at the same time a discipleship and a leadership development model. Leaders grow together in faith and skills.
9. The model is well implemented. Administration, follow-up, attention to details, encouragement, and creating options have enabled optimal participation.

He concludes:

> The model implemented in the Anglican Diocese of Melbourne is one that can be applied to various models of church . . . The dual focus of discipleship and leadership development breathes new life into weary clergy and tired churches and renews a focus on the Gospel. Christ will build his church, and the invitation to the Australian Church is to have the political will to seize the opportunity [and] the courage of faith to step up to God's call.[34]

In a recent synod charge, Archbishop Freier spoke of a growing "mission-shaped culture of hope" within the diocese, and of his personal encouragement at what has been achieved.[35] From its modest beginnings,

---

33. Rietveld, *Coaching*, 8
34. Rietveld, *Coaching*, 17.
35. Philip Freier, "Fostering a Mission-Shaped Culture of Hope," *The Melbourne Anglican*, November 2015.

this program has developed into an important feature of the missional life of the diocese. It has helped Melbourne to be a "diocese in mission" and may well be one of the most significant legacies of the episcopacy of Archbishop Philip Freier.

Bibliography

Anglican Church of Australia. *Constitution Canons and Rules of the Anglican Church of Australia 2010*. Mulgrave: Broughton, 2011.

Anglican Diocese of Melbourne. *Making the Word of God Fully Known: Vision and Strategic Directions 2011–13*.

Bowles, Ralph G. "NCD Project Report 2013: Annual Report to the PMC." Anglican Diocese of Brisbane, 2013.

Bryman, Alan. *Social Methods Research*. Fourth ed. Oxford: Oxford University Press, 2012.

Clark, Carol. "Coaching Program Survey." Anglican Diocese of Melbourne, 2018.

Ely, Katherine, et al. 2010. "Evaluating Leadership Coaching: A Review and Integrated Framework." *Leadership Quarterly* 21:4 (2010) 581–598.

Finn, Fran A. "Leadership Development Through Executive Coaching: The Effects On Leaders' Psychological States and Transformational Leadership Behaviour." PhD diss., Queensland University of Technology, 2007.

Forsyth, Robert. "National and Diocesan Structures." In *Facing the Future: Bishops Imagine a Different Church*, edited by Stephen Hale and Andrew Curnow, 53–63. Brunswick East: Acorn, 2009.

Freier, Philip. "A New Willingness to Connect." In *Facing the Future: Bishops Imagine a Different Church*, edited by Stephen Hale and Andrew Curnow, 213–21. Brunswick East: Acorn, 2009.

———. "The President's Address to the 50th Synod of the Diocese of Melbourne." Opening Address to Diocesan Synod. Melbourne, October 2010.

Grant, Anthony M. "The Efficacy of Executive Coaching in Times of Organisational Change." *Journal of Change Management* 14 (2014) 1–23.

Harrower, John. "A New Openness to Change." In *Facing the Future: Bishops Imagine a Different Church*, edited by Stephen Hale and Andrew Curnow, 203–12. Brunswick East: Acorn, 2009.

Jackson, Bob. *Hope for the Church: Contemporary Strategies for Growth*. London: Church House, 2002.

Morgan, Ken. *Pathways: Local Mission for All Kinds of Churches*. Melbourne: K.L.Morgan, 2017.

———. "Strategy Paper: Pilot Program." *Vision and Strategic Directions 2011–2013*. Anglican Diocese of Melbourne, 2011.

Nichols, Alan, ed. *Building the Mission-Shaped Church in Australia*. Sydney: Anglican Church of Australia, 2006.

Nixon, Andrew. "Connect09: Final Report from the Connect09 Management Committee." http://www.sds.asn.au/assets/Documents/synod/Synod2010/Supp Report2010/S04.Connect09.Rep10.pdf.

Oswald, Roy M. "How to Minister Effectively in Family, Pastoral, Program and Corporate-Sized Churches." In *Size Transitions in Congregations*, edited by Beth Ann Gaede, 31–46. Herndon: Alban Institute, 2001.

Powell, Ruth et al. *Enriching Church Life: A Guide to Results from National Church Life Surveys for Local Churches*. Second edition. Strathfield: Mirrabooka, 2012.

Rietveld, John. *White Paper: Coaching in the Australian Church*. Christian Coaching Institute: Melbourne, 2018.

Rumley, David D. *Transformational Ministry: Leadership, Church Growth and the Senior Pastor's Effectiveness*. Danville: Rumley Books, 2011.

Trist, Richard. "A Report on the Impact of the Pilot Program for Parish Renewal: 2012–2013." http://bishopperryinstitute.org.au/uploads/Report%20to%20Diocese%20-%20Final.pdf.

———. "Two are Better than One: The Impact of a Church Leadership Coaching Program upon Missional Effectiveness." DMin diss., Australian College of Theology, 2017.

Van Gelder, Craig, and Dwight J. Zscheile. *The Missional Church in Perspective: Mapping Trends and Shaping the Conversation*. Grand Rapids: Baker, 2011.

3

Cathedrals

Home Churches, Houses of Prayer for all People

ANDREAS LOEWE

WHAT IS THE PURPOSE of a Victorian cathedral in today's world? Archbishop Philip Freier's cathedral is possibly the most Victorian of them all: built at the height of Queen Victoria's empire and in the colony that bears her name, the Cathedral and Metropolitical Church of St. Paul may be truly said to be "doubly Victorian."

Melbourne's Anglican Cathedral stands the heart of the city of Melbourne in direct juxtaposition to the Town Hall, the main railway station, and the city's principal square, Federation Square. Named for the apostle to the nations, here is a little bit of England transplanted "unto the end of the earth" into the Southern Hemisphere. From the time of its completion in 1891, William Butterfield's cathedral, with its three soaring sandstone spires, has been a symbol of living prayer at the heart of Melbourne and a place of welcome for the people of the world's most livable city, Australia's fastest-growing city, and capital of Australia's fastest-growing state.[1]

---

1. Economist Intelligence Unit, "The Ten Most Livable Cities," *The Global Livability Report 2017*, 6. Accessed July 16, 2017. https://www.eiu.com/public/topical_report.

Pioneer Ministry in a Rapidly Growing Colony

St. Paul's Cathedral was built at the height of the Anglican Church's nineteenth-century revival, a time of liturgical, musical, and architectural renewal and sustained numerical growth. At the time in which the Church of England was renewing itself, the Australian colony of Victoria began to establish many of its own institutions. The church in Victoria grew organically alongside the colony; in October 1847, the founding vicar of St. Paul's Church Cambridge and Fellow of Trinity College, Charles Perry, along with his wife, Frances, sailed to Melbourne on the *Stag* to pioneer ministry in the new colony.[2] Consecrated bishop at Westminster Abbey at Petertide that same year and equipped with a modest grant of £500, Perry was sent to a vast domain. His letters patent defined the new see as "bounded by a line drawn from Cape Howe to the nearest source of the River Murray, and by the course of that river, until it reaches the one hundred and forty-first parallel of East Longitude," anticipating the terms of the separation, three years later, of the colony of Victoria from New South Wales.[3] The couple proved to be indefatigable in founding churches, schools, hospitals, and university and theological colleges during their thirty years in Victoria. The United Church of England and Ireland in Victoria grew alongside the roads that crisscrossed the colony, with the Perrys traversing much of their vast diocese on horseback from their Melbourne base.

The discovery of gold in the central plains and highlands of Victoria in the 1850s suddenly raised the potential of—and vision for—the new colony. The discovery of gold led to astonishing numbers of miners, diggers, fortune-seekers, and speculators migrating to Victoria from all corners of the earth, which made Melbourne and Victoria truly multicultural and multireligious communities. As these international teams of gold diggers flooded into central Victoria to extract gold, the colony's newly-found wealth enabled a building spree on an incredible scale. Where previously there had been tin churches, imported from England as self-assembly kits, now there were stone-built churches—as well as grand town halls, civic buildings, trams, railway lines, and other modern infrastructure.

The incredible wealth of the colony led to a population explosion: from 1870 to 1889 the population of Melbourne more than doubled. By the time Melbourne's first bishop retired home to England in 1874 (there to continue his work of founding centers of ministry and learning, establishing

---

aspx?campaignid=Liveability17

2. Robin, "Perry."
3. Robin, "Perry."

the Cambridge theological college Ridley Hall in his retirement), in a colony of some 700,000 inhabitants, "there were 125 clergymen, 27 lay readers, and 246 churches, accommodating 65,000 worshippers," *The Snowy River Mail and Tambo and Croajingolong Gazette* proudly stated.[4] Melbourne's population of 250,000 was young and diverse: the average inhabitant was twenty-three years old, and people from Aboriginal, British, German, American, Chinese, and French backgrounds made up the second largest city of the British empire.[5]

At the heart of this forward-looking, dynamic, youthful, and prosperous colony, the second bishop of Melbourne, James Moorhouse, envisaged a grand cathedral as a place to promote the Christian faith. In 1880, the Governor of Victoria laid the foundation stone for St. Paul's, "right in the centre of the city."[6]

A Cathedral for the "Queen City of the South"

St. Paul's Cathedral Melbourne was built in record time. Only eleven years after its foundation stone was laid, the cathedral was completed and consecrated. At its opening, the Australian press rejoiced in the beauty of "the cathedral of the 'Queen City of the South'":[7]

> The colouring of the cathedral is almost Oriental in its richness. The beautiful mosaic floor shows all the colours of the rainbow, blended into one harmonious whole. The banded pillars, showing alternately bluish-grey and light fawn colour, make a good setting for the burnished brass candelabra, shining like gold.[8]

The *Illustrated Sydney News* reported "by telegraph" how "the whole width of Flinders and Swanston streets . . . was packed with a crowd watching a long, white-robed procession . . . Even the tram-cars were stopped, and passers-by mounted on them . . . Melbourne's new Anglican Cathedral . . .

---

4. "Consecration of St. Paul's Melbourne," *Snowy River Mail and Tambo and Croajingolong Gazette*, January 31, 1891; Colonial Government of Victoria, *Census of Victoria, 1871*, 6, no. 17.

5. Colonial Government of Victoria, *Census of Victoria, 1871*, 8–9, 14, 15.

6. "Melbourne Letter," *Daily Telegraph*, September 20, 1880. At the time the site was acknowledged to be "well situated as regards the two great suburban railway stations," but felt inferior to the site of its Roman Catholic counterpart, "which stands out so nobly on the eastern hill."

7. "Melbourne Gossip. By Vita," *Sydney Mail and New South Wales Advertiser*, January 31, 1891.

8. "Melbourne Gossip. By Vita," *Sydney Mail*.

has at last been made ready for consecration."[9] The public interest was not captured merely by the opening of a new landmark building or the many dignitaries who had traveled to Melbourne for this celebration of faith. Rather, the consecration of St. Paul's Cathedral was a sign of hope: a sign of hope for the unity of the Anglican Church; a sign of hope for future unity of the five independent colonies that would, a decade later, form the Commonwealth of Australia; and a sign of hope for the unity of all Christians.

Press reports pointed out that the presence of the Primate of Australia and bishop of Sydney, Dr. William Saumarez Smith, "was a witness to the fact that the federation of the Anglican Church has long preceded the federation of the colonies."[10] The fact that leaders of all Christian denominations shared in prayer was seen as an important symbol of "the time, let us hope, when all the walls of partition will be broken down."[11] Above all, the consecration of St. Paul's Cathedral was a symbol of the hope that "this new Cathedral may be a centre of spiritual energy for the whole Colony."[12] The cathedral was to be a sign of unity as a nation, a church, and a community, and a place where all people might find a spiritual home.

An Icon of Lived Faith in the Heart of Melbourne

The journey from this grand aspiration to a prayed-through reality is lived out in the cathedral's vision to be a welcoming home church for the people of the Diocese of Melbourne and the Anglican Province of Victoria as well as a place of prayer for people from many cultural traditions and faith backgrounds. St. Paul's has an intentional ministry of welcome: clergy and parishioners from across the diocese are regularly invited to join the cathedral congregations for Choral Evensong on the day their parish is prayed for in the diocesan cycle of prayer, and members of the province of Victoria, led by their bishops and cathedral clergy, come together at St. Paul's every year to celebrate the establishment of the Anglican Church in Victoria. As parishes are invited to worship at St. Paul's, they are encouraged to inform the cathedral's prayer by their local concerns: every week, cathedral staff will engage with parish clergy, inviting them to offer prayer concerns to be shared right at the heart of the diocese.

9. "The Consecration of St. Paul's Cathedral Melbourne. (From Our Special Correspondent in Melbourne)," *Illustrated Sydney News*, January 31, 1891.

10. "The Consecration of St. Paul's Cathedral: By A Spectator," *Yea Chronicle*, January 29, 1891.

11. "Consecration," *Yea Chronicle*.

12. "Consecration," *Yea Chronicle*.

Both clergy and cathedral are deeply enriched by this partnership. For cathedral clergy, who frequently do not have the opportunity to visit parishes and ministries across the diocese, these prayers open a window into the challenges and celebrations of the rich patterns of ministry across Melbourne. For clergy and parishioners who often travel for considerable distances to be present at "their" Evensong, sharing in prayer means that their work has been recognized and validated at the heart of the diocese. A local incumbent recently wrote to me: "Thank you both for praying for us as a parish and also your invitation to join in the worship. Nine members of our congregation availed themselves of your kind invitation and we were particularly delighted by the use of our Parish Prayer in the service." Another local vicar wrote, "Thank you for this opportunity of our parish being made the focus of your intercessions. May God continue to bless you as you welcome the local population and overseas visitors."

While a cathedral's first care rightly is for its congregants and the people of the diocese it serves, our cathedrals are also buildings of great beauty that attract an incredible number of visitors and pilgrims. Year by year, more than 500,000 people, or 15 percent of the current total number of international visitors to Melbourne, will pay a visit to St. Paul's.[13] For comparison, more visitors choose to spend time at St. Paul's Melbourne than at all the National Trust properties in the state combined. Just as it was when it first opened in 1891, St. Paul's is "still the leading ecclesiastical attraction in Melbourne" as Victoria's most visited religious heritage building.[14]

There are a couple of reasons for this phenomenon: the cathedral is open every day of the year free of charge, and we succeed in telling its story and the story of our faith through the beauty of our historic heritage. At St. Paul's, we aim for tourists to become people who learn about the reason for the building and the faith that inspired it, in the hope that visitors might become pilgrims: in principal world languages, our volunteer guides provide tours and literature that introduce our building as a living place of worship, and they invite visitors to learn about the Christian faith. For the past four years, Mandarin-speaking guides have provided an introduction to the cathedral for the largest language group to visit the state, acquainting a culture that deeply values beauty and history with the living faith that inspired the creation of this magnificent Melbourne landmark. One of our guides told me, "It is a great privilege to welcome people from so many backgrounds

---

13. State Government of Victoria, Department of Economic Development, "Victoria's International Tourism Performance: International Visitor Survey Results for the Year ending March 2017," accessed July 16, 2019. https://www.tourism.vic.gov.au/research/international-research/international-visitation.html.

14. "Victoria," *Weekly Times,* January 31, 1891.

and languages to St. Paul's. I know that by sharing the faith that has made this building possible, many of our visitors are inspired to find out more about the gospel." With this in mind, guides offer introductions to the gospel stories depicted in the stained-glass windows, and so are able to literally bring to light the stories that have shaped our faith.

Our team of duty chaplains continue the ministry of our guides. Clergy from across the diocese of Melbourne choose to give a day a month to the cathedral and are trained as duty chaplains. They not only provide a visible presence and a listening ear to people seeking counsel or hoping to make their confession, but regularly invite visitors to pause and pray and, most importantly, to join the cathedral congregations in the daily rhythm of prayer. "Sharing what is the story of my faith, and listening to the stories of our many visitors, is a real honor. I hope that by my sharing in part of their journey, some of our tourists may turn into pilgrims," one chaplain told me about her motivation for taking time out of parish ministry to volunteer her time at St. Paul's.

At the end of the working day, tourists, pilgrims, and parishioners from across the diocese combine to worship at Choral Evensong. Together they may witness the cathedral's lived out proclamation of faith through Scripture, music, and prayer, led by our choir of boys and men or our girls' choir. Sharing in this living tradition of prayer can have a profoundly positive effect. Dick Gross, a columnist for Melbourne's *The Age*, notes:

> Choral Evensong is a quotidian calming. It is an opportunity for rest and reflection at the end of a day's travails. It would move the iciest atheistic soul as it indeed moves mine. When I sit in the cathedral, I see history, music and architecture paraded before me. One of the great duties of faith is to be the carrier of culture. Religions are the repository of our wonderful liturgical music and the majestic language of the King James Bible. The soaring architecture evokes images of both the Medieval roots of our European history and the Victorian English who, whether we like it or not, shaped much of the Australian persona... And the music is, for aficionados, deeply moving. Evensong is the total package.[15]

Gross's contemporary reflection echoes the hopes of earlier Victorians that St. Paul's would provide a haven for contemplation for the people. In 1891, "Churchman" wrote to the *Sydney Morning Herald*: "Melbourne churchmen [are] to establish a choral service, as at the more venerable St. Paul's in London, and in the grand old abbey at Westminster ... to throw

---

15. Dick Gross, "Apostates for Evensong," *The Age*, September 5, 2011.

open the doors of the Cathedral daily so that those who desired might retire from the streets of the bustling city for half an hour's rest and meditation."[16] The provision of a space set apart for a contemplative experience of timelessness is not only part of the cathedral's built-in heritage, but remains a lived-out presence. Particularly in times of conflict, or when faced with great national or international tragedies, the daily round of prayer at St. Paul's has provided a strong anchor that has enabled people to frame their commemorations through the lens of something greater than themselves. St. Paul's is the place at which the people of Victoria come together to celebrate and mourn: over the past three years, those acts of commemoration have become more frequent and more international, and frequently have involved leaders from other denominations or faith traditions. During the terror attacks in France, Belgium, Turkey, and Germany in 2016, for example, the cathedral offered a place for prayer for different national communities, led by their respective diplomatic representatives. Where possible, prayers were offered in the heart languages of the people affected: cathedral clergy led bilingual worship with the Melbourne French community following the terror attacks in Paris and Nice, in German with Melbourne's German Lutheran Church following the Berlin Christmas Market attacks, and in Arabic with the Coptic Community following the attacks on St. Mark's Cathedral Cairo.

At our daily Evensong, the stories of the past and the present coalesce and provide a powerful combination that, many tell me, helps them place in perspective the events marked by our commemorations. The timelessness of the stories of assurance from Scripture, the songs of shared suffering and hope told through the psalter, and the prayers and symbolic acts of the people, all framed in music and the liturgy of the *Book of Common Prayer*, have the capacity to reach across denominational and faith boundaries. Following the terror attacks in Istanbul and Ankara, the local Turkish diplomatic representative, a Muslim, requested that the events be marked with a commemorative Evensong at St. Paul's, at which readings and Christian prayers were led in Turkish and English, and the dead commemorated by shared silence and the lighting of candles. On other occasions, for instance following the loss of airliner MH370, the liturgy itself became a vehicle for expressing grief and sharing hope: as a spiritual home for many nations, the Christian prayer *requiem aeternam*, sung by the cathedral choir and the Jewish mourners' *kaddish*, chanted by a Jewish cantor, framed a celebration in which leaders of Melbourne's principal faiths read texts of hope from their scriptures and tradition. The people of Melbourne and the diplomatic

---

16. "Cathedral Services," *Sydney Morning Herald*, January 31, 1891.

community alike look to St. Paul's as the place where people from many nations may come together to honor one another, pray together for healing, and share in acts of community that model the aspiration to be nations where all may flourish and live peaceably with one another.

A Home Church for the People of Melbourne

The twenty-eighth governor of Victoria, Alex Chernov AC, reflects:

> There are many occasions when St. Paul's holds Services that embrace the broader community, whether these be the ANZAC or Remembrance Day observances that become a public focal point for worship at times dedicated to the memory of our fallen, or State Funerals and Memorial Services for leaders of the community, be they former Governors, Premiers, Ministers or other prominent Victorians, like Dame Elisabeth Murdoch... It was at St. Paul's where a moving Multi-Faith Service was held for those killed in the Malaysian Airlines Flight MH 17 disaster, and their families. Having spoken after the Service with a number of the bereaved relatives, I can say that the service helped them considerably in their time of grief.[17]

The fact that these commemorations occur, with increasing frequency, as a result of home-grown acts of terror only further demonstrates the need to strengthen the framework of communal prayer that is able to contain the unsettling experiences of the present in a prayed-through tradition. Chernov points to the cathedral as the place where prayer is made visible:

> St. Paul's has been part of Melbourne's DNA for over 125 years, and through its Services of worship and outreach has made a telling contribution to the life of Melbourne and Victoria. One cannot overstate the importance of St. Paul's Cathedral as a spiritual focal point for our wider community: its majestic structure is a reminder to all people of Christian values in today's increasingly secular and troubled society.[18]

It is from its own strong values base that St. Paul's is able truly to be a home church for the people of Melbourne. The lived-out understanding of Christian hospitality, coupled with an unashamed self-understanding as a place of Christian worship, proclamation, and prayer, enables St. Paul's to

---

17. Deutscher, *St. Paul's*, 7.
18. Deutscher, *St. Paul's*, 7.

offer a safe space where people may indeed make sense of the troubles of the day through the framework of faith.

This self-understanding has recently been captured in the cathedral's governance instruments. Over eighteen months in 2015 and 2016, the cathedral reshaped its Victorian foundation charter, the *Cathedral Act 1878*, into a modern governance instrument that, from its preamble onwards, captures the cathedral's purpose both in its function as "the seat of the Anglican Archbishop of Melbourne" and its mission as "the home church for Anglicans in the Diocese of Melbourne and the Province of Victoria."[19] By working with the Council and the Synod of the Anglican Diocese of Melbourne, the Cathedral Chapter was able, in October 2016, to legislate a modern governance instrument, in the form of the *Cathedral Act 2016*, that explicitly expresses its vision to be a home church for its people, a place of welcome for "the people of the Diocese around the Archbishop of Melbourne, celebrating our sense of belonging and our shared ministry in Christ," a place that "seek[s] to transform the City of Melbourne and the wider Diocese into communities where people can come to experience, know and love God in Christ Jesus" as well as affirming its role as "an iconic place of prayer, public celebration and commemoration in the City of Melbourne."[20]

It is this making explicit of the original intent of the cathedral's founders for St. Paul's to become a place of solace and peace for the people of Melbourne, coupled with the expression of the cathedral's contemporary mission as a place of welcome for people seeking faith and meaning in times of joy and sorrow, that ensures the continued relevance and popularity of St. Paul's in the hearts of the people of Victoria. Governor Chernov speaks for the wider Victorian community:

> We need St. Paul's. It is a key spiritual home of our City and State, that has served us for over a century and a quarter. In times when violence is escalating, when respect for religion and authority is diminishing, when sound traditions that have bound society for generations are disappearing, and when we are living increasingly in a spiritual vacuum, may this wonderful Melbourne icon continue to provide effective and compassionate guidance through its services and public outreach in our troubled society.[21]

The world inhabited by our Victorian forebears who created the space and enabled the tradition of prayer that still shapes our celebrations and

---

19. *Cathedral Act 2016*, Preamble A.
20. *Cathedral Act 2016*, 5: Mission of the Cathedral Community.
21. Deutscher, *St. Paul's*, 7.

commemorations was every bit as cosmopolitan and complex as it is today and witnessed as many conflicts and acts of terror as we do. I am not at all surprised that many of the hopes the founders had for the magnificent building they created still hold true today for this Victorian cathedral at the heart of the Victorian state capital.

In the more than 125 years since the cathedral's completion, the percentage of Anglicans in Victoria has halved.[22] Though just under half of the population of Victoria today still identify as Christians, the number of those professing no faith at all has increased dramatically, from 0.02 percent of the population in 1871 to 32 percent in 2016.[23] But in spite of this radical erosion, hundreds of thousands of people visit St. Paul's, and tens of thousands of people share in worship there, each year. The necessity for a place of prayer for people from all backgrounds at the heart of Melbourne clearly is just as acute today as it was when St. Paul's Cathedral Melbourne first opened its doors.

Contrary to expectations that "the novelty will soon wear off" for the many who flocked to St. Paul's in the days immediately following its consecration, the cathedral remains a much-loved beacon of faith in the heart of the city.[24] It may not have yet become the place where all the "walls of partition will be broken down," but it is well on the way.[25] Today, as then, St. Paul's provides a place of welcome and worship, inviting its tourists to become pilgrims who share in a tradition of prayer that enables and fosters the discovery of timeless faith amidst the "changes and chances of this fleeting world" and assists many to find peace, refreshment, and, we hope, meaning, at the heart of the world's most livable city.[26]

---

22. Colonial Government of Victoria, *Census of Victoria, 1871*, 21; Australian Bureau of Statistics, "2016 Census: Victoria."

23. Colonial Government of Victoria, *Census of Victoria, 1871*, 15–16: 20,000 out of 731,000 in 1871. Australian Bureau of Statistics, "2016 Census: Victoria": 1,876,738 out of 5,926,624 in 2016.

24. "Victoria," *Weekly Times*.

25. "Consecration," *Yea Chronicle*.

26. Economist Intelligence Unit, "The Ten Most Livable Cities,", 6.

Bibliography

Australian Bureau of Statistics. *2016 Census: Victoria.* Last updated June 26, 2017. https://www.abs.gov.au/ausstats/abs@.nsf/MediaRealesesByCatalogue/C508DD213FD43EA7CA258148000C6BBE?OpenDocument.

Colonial Government of Victoria. Census Office. *Census of Victoria, 1871.* Melbourne: John Ferres, 1871.

Deutscher, Robert, ed. *St. Paul's: The People's Cathedral.* Melbourne, St. Paul's Press, 2017.

Robin, A. De Q. "Perry, Charles (1807–1891)." *Australian Dictionary of Biography.* National Centre of Biography, Australian National University. Accessed October 9, 2017. http://adb.anu.edu.au/biography/perry-charles-4391/text7153.

4

The Changing Context of Ministry Through the Pastoral Offices

New Challenges and Opportunities for Traditional Ministry

Colleen O'Reilly[1]

THE ONCE FAMILIAR TERRITORY of Anglican rites for baptisms, weddings, and funerals is now an unknown and untraversed land for most Australians. Nothing signals the changes in the relationship of the Christians churches to Australian culture better than the decline in infant baptisms, church weddings, and funerals conducted by clergy.

This essay will reflect on the reality that what was once central to the Anglican Church's engagement with its members, nominal and committed, who made up a large segment of the population, is now an occasional encounter with a dwindling group in society. The new situation does not diminish the importance of Anglican rites. On the contrary, it provides new

---

1. I first met Philip Freier through a mutual friend who was studying with him in the same theological college in the early 1980s. Little did I imagine then, while the debate about women's ordination was raging, that I would one day be a senior priest in the diocese where Philip is Archbishop. It is always good to know that one's bishop has shared in the complexities and the joys of ordinary parish ministry before being made a bishop.

opportunities for meaningful connection to those who come seeking them. The change does, however, require clergy to have an informed understanding of the potential of their role in conducting rituals, since these are potent resources for shaping the lives of those who participate. They are also opportunities to present the stories, meanings, and values of the Christian faith as it intersects with significant moments in life. This is important not only for making contact with those who have minimal contact with the church but also as a valuable teaching moment in the lives of those with an active faith and participation.

The ministry of the pastoral offices is underpinned with the belief that "worship and liturgy care for us: God, through them, pays loving attention to us and we in turn are able to express the whole of our human experience to God."[2]

Our Rituals Express Our Identities

Nothing is more characteristic of humans than creating rituals. Nothing defines a people or a community more than its rituals. We humans look for meaning in the rhythms and patterns we observe in the natural world and in the events of our lives, both the anticipated and the unexpected. Anthropologically and historically, rituals have given expression to that universal sense that something or someone transcends us. It is both a universal and an ancient belief that through rituals we can effect changes in the world and in ourselves. The ubiquity of these practices in every known society points to the importance of rituals in giving order to the world and our place within it.[3]

When I was growing up in the 1950s in the suburbs of Sydney, there were basically three Christian "tribes" with their own distinctive rituals. People mostly identified with one, even if only nominally. So, some were Roman Catholics, most were Church of England, and almost all the rest were some kind of Protestant. There were some Chinese people and fewer Indians, whose religions were largely unknown and barely made it into view on the cultural landscape of a very homogenous "white" Australia. And like most white Australians then, I knew nothing of Indigenous spirituality or religious practices.

Tribal identities and religion were such that, being an Anglican child with an Irish name, I spent my childhood explaining our parents' decision to

---

2. Green, *Only Connect*, 2.

3. The work of anthropologists has influenced developments in liturgical theology. See, for example, Turner, *Ritual Process*.

raise my younger sister Maureen and me in our mother's Anglican Church, not our father's Roman Catholic one. We were told simply to tell anyone who questioned us that this was our parents' choice.

That world has now vanished. Australian society today is not just multicultural but diverse beyond the imaginings of previous generations. In the 2016 Australian Census, 30.1 percent of those responding to the optional question about religious affiliation said they had no religion.

People without religion still practice rituals, of course. Despite the unconscious assumption held by many people that rituals are not necessary, we all carry out many rituals every day in our secular society. Some are very clearly seen to be rites, such as graduation ceremonies or the swearing in of a new government; others are obscured by familiarity, such as the way we queue to board a bus or greet people we work with each morning when we arrive.

Australian poet Les Murray captured the ordinariness of ritual behavior in his short poem about two archetypal Australian farmers, *The Mitchells*. The poet sees two men who have just dug a post hole and now boil the billy—an old prune tin, in fact—and eat "big meat sandwiches," all the while having a conversation they have had many times before. Murray concludes with the line, "Nearly everything they say is ritual. Sometimes the scene is an avenue."[4] Although people do not consciously recognize it, so many of our daily conversations and exchanges with one another are ritualized. We cannot negotiate daily life without behaving, for much of the time, in ritualized patterns.

Clergy are still asked to conduct funerals and weddings, and to baptize infants and adults, but to a lesser extent than once was common. Given the changed context, and the evangelistic and pastoral opportunities these requests provide, it is now more important than ever that clergy understand their role and its potential when conducting these rites. It is also valuable to be able to give fresh expression to the purposes and meanings embedded in the texts being used.

Rituals provide a pathway through experiences than can feel chaotic or even threatening. By understanding baptism, weddings, and funerals as rites of passage, people can see how ritual effects a change of status in those taking part. For instance, a couple marrying one another have, perhaps without even fully appreciating the change, separated themselves from other single people when they make public their intention to marry. Families and friends begin to relate to them differently. They enter a time of liminality, when they are no longer single but not yet married. Of course, they may be living

---

4. Murray, "The Mitchells."

together and establishing a household, but they are not yet legally married. The English word liminal comes from the Latin *limen*, meaning threshold: they are on the threshold of married life, but so far only on the first step. The day comes for the wedding, and they enter as two separate people about to exchange vows of commitment to one another in the presence of at least two witnesses, but usually numerous family and friends, who agree to support their commitment and celebrate with them. In the exchange between the two, they marry each other. Clergy conduct the couple through the wedding service, pray for them and with them, and ask God's blessing on their married life, but the only two who can "change" their lives by their words and actions are the couple. When the couple depart for the festivities that usually follow, they are still two separate people but are now also a married couple. In law, and in the eyes of family and friends and all who will meet them from now on, their status has changed from single to married.

Funerals also confer a new status on the person who has died and on those who survive them. Pronouncing the dead to be dead is taken very seriously in traditional societies, which is a further reason Christians should never be shy about using the word, rather than a euphemism like "passed away." A funeral service moves mourners from grief to hope and enacts the departure of the deceased from this world and the resumption of life in their absence for the spouse or the children or the parents who have lost one they love. A Christian funeral that proclaims the hope of the resurrection to eternal life and at the same time enables mourners to give thanks for the person God gave them, but whom they now, in sorrow, entrust to God's care, has accomplished its purposes.

Clergy who understand these dimensions of rites and can see how Anglican pastoral practices can support people in crucial times—and even enable them to grow in faith and understanding—will find conducting rites a most fulfilling part of ministry. A deeper knowledge of the anthropological and the theological dynamics of these rites enables clergy to conduct them more effectively.

Only with a Fountain Pen . . .

I love writing in the parish registers, especially those that record what the 1662 *Book of Common Prayer* (hereafter *BCP*) calls "other rites and ceremonies of the Church."[5]

I have insisted that entries in all the registers of the parishes where I have been the vicar are made with a fountain pen. A biro pen just does

---

5. *Book of Common Prayer*.

not have the same gravitas to record baptisms, weddings, or funerals. These precious moments in people's lives are not just a record for future family and parish historians; they are the record of graced moments in individual lives through the ministry Christ entrusts to his church.

Clergy who conduct the pastoral services for those who come seeking the church's ministry are the harbingers of we know not what. Someone has baptized every ordinand, almost always without any idea of the vocation that eventually follows. Who can tell to what extent the couple coming to marry one another will "make their life together a sign of Christ's love in this broken world," as we now pray they will when using the 1995 *A Prayer Book for Australia* (hereafter *APBA*)?[6] Or, who can predict the effect of a funeral service that confidently and lovingly preaches the sure and certain mystery of bodily resurrection to those who live in a culture that believes anything about death except what the church proclaims?

The pastoral services of the church have been central to our engagement with the most faithful of parishioners as well as those who only come along when requesting these ministries. Anglican clergy have traditionally been very obliging, although I am aware that some hold strong views about not offering the pastoral services to people not closely connected with the particular parish or chaplaincy they serve.

Of course, the situation we are now in is very different to the sixteenth-century world of the *BCP*, when these pastoral services were first produced in the English language so that all participants could understand them. Previously the rites were in Latin, a language understood by the educated but not by the many more people taking part in sacraments and services. No doubt, people had notions of what was going on in these rites. We know many had primers to help them, but they lacked the comprehension we now take for granted when using languages understood by the rites' recipients.

The twenty-first-century context in which Australian Anglican parishes continue to provide services for the key "rites of passage," birth, marriage, and death, is radically changed from the times in which they were first developed. This is almost as true for the most recent rites as it is for the world of the English reformers. Some aspects of the changed context are well known and the result of historical and cultural factors beyond the control of anyone. In Australia, these include the pervasive secularity of public life and the decline in the percentage of the population who identity as Anglicans in the census.

---

6. *A Prayer Book for Australia*, 664. This is the most recent revision of its prayer book by the Anglican Church of Australia.

There has been a steady decline reported in the Census, from 39.7 percent in 1901 to 13.3 percent in 2016. The resulting substantial changes in values, beliefs, and ways of working and living have contributed to a further decline in religious practice as evidenced in Anglican parish records. The largest religious tradition in Australia now is Roman Catholic at 22.6 percent, while those who declare that they have no religion now make up 30.1 percent.[7]

The Pastoral Services

The pastoral services of the *BCP* have been the backbone of Anglican ministry for centuries. In addition to the daily worship through Morning and Evening Prayer, and the weekly worship through the Order of the Ministration of the Holy Communion, Anglicans have drawn on the forms and words of Baptism and Confirmation, the Solemnization of Matrimony, and the Burial of the Dead to give expression to their faith at key stages in life.

Parish registers record these services and the names of the individuals central to them. Once these entries were plentiful, as people sought the church's ministry in substantial numbers. Nowadays, many parishes hold very few baptisms, often one or two marriages a year at best, and only the funerals of those well-connected to the Sunday or weekday congregations. Some parishes have almost none. Others, normally older parishes with histories that embrace three or four generations of worshipers, continue to offer these ministries to people who look to a particular parish as "theirs" for such times. In my last year in Malvern, I conducted so many funerals that the Paschal candle was almost completely consumed.

One of the saddest circumstances to occur is when the elderly remaining parent, who has been a regular worshiper but is now in residential care, dies. The family, either through lack of instructions from the deceased, indifference to religious beliefs, or meeting their own needs for a secular occasion, sometimes arrange a funeral without clergy involvement. People who want a church funeral do well to leave their funeral instructions in writing. The funeral procession from their church is the most fitting last earthly journey for a Christian. A good funeral can be a compelling witness to mourners, who are often open to wonder and questioning at the time of a death.

This retreat from parish involvement in rites of passage is a dramatic change and has accelerated in the last decade. For over a decade, I was the incumbent of an older inner suburban parish in Melbourne, which still

---

7. ABS, "2016 Census Data."

retains connections across the generations in families, good links into the wider community, and is of a style that offers the traditional services still sought by people. However, in those years, I observed a slow decline in requests, particularly for weddings. I also became aware of how cultural changes were impacting the way people asked to celebrate these important services with images of celebratory events in mind.

Changed Times and Theological Tension

As stated earlier, there are a number of well-recognized and understood factors that have contributed to the situation we find ourselves in now. Among these factors is one that we have control of; that is, the so called "rigor" with which ministry has been offered. Perhaps this is always a perennial, though mostly unnamed, tension, between welcoming all who seek the church's ministry and maintaining the integrity of that ministry.

Some parish clergy decline to offer this pastoral ministry to people unknown to them, or who may not meet their particular requirements. During the time I was a member of Synod in the Diocese of Sydney (from 1978 to 1993), I recall a heated debate about the pastoral offices, precipitated by a motion about the "stole fees" associated with this ministry. The situation, where one parish refuses to, say, conduct the funeral of a person not a regular worshiper, but another will, and the second priest is paid the fee for putting on her or his surplice, is now quite widespread. It can be a factor in the reduction of pastoral ministry if those declined do not know to ask elsewhere. Stories of how ministry was refused persist in families for decades.

Many of the Sydney clergy spoke in that debate to justify their refusal to take such services for people unknown to them because they were not regular attenders on Sundays, and so their faith was judged to be in doubt. Others spoke of the extra workload they picked up as a result. It was my first experience of hearing that this attitude prevailed among many of those I mistakenly thought welcomed these pastoral opportunities. After some time, the Archbishop, Sir Marcus Loane, stood in his Presidential place and addressed the synod. I have never forgotten the impact of his words, nor the unusual emotion in his voice. The Archbishop spoke forcefully of his shame in listening to "his" clergy speak of the judgments they brought to bear on who was entitled to the church's ministry and who was not.[8]

Later, some people explained away his attitude as the "Erastian" accommodation of the church to the secular society—the first time I had come

---

8. Personal recollection, though I now do not recall what year. I was a lay member of the Sydney Synod from 1978 until 1993, when I left the diocese to move to Melbourne.

across this concept. I do not think that fully explains Archbishop Loane's plea that day. He was calling on clergy to offer Christ's ministry through the offices of the Anglican Church to those who came seeking with a sincere heart in a time of need or of major change in their lives. He was speaking against placing conditions upon people that become, in effect, barriers to ministry and to a further relationship with them.

The attitudes Sir Marcus was attempting to refute can appear at any time and place and are not limited to any one theological school of thought. There are those who seek to be hospitable and open to all comers, especially to all the baptized, while ensuring the ministry provided has integrity. On the other hand, there are those who believe they must only offer ministry to people they consider to be worthy or "fit" to receive it, usually demonstrated by active membership in the parish.

While no cleric should act against their individual conscience, can we ensure that those who ask for ministry are listened to respectfully and cared for appropriately? Rejection by the clergy echoes down the generations of a family just as surely as kindness is remembered.

Baptism

Parishes that still conduct weddings are more likely to attract parents bringing children for baptism. Parishes with ethnic congregations or associated with tertiary chaplaincies are likely to have more adult baptisms.

The baptism of infants continues to attract controversy among Anglicans despite the *BCP*'s provision of a rite and the even longer church tradition, assumed to date to the days of the Book of Acts. Some clergy refuse unless the parents are regular attenders, and even then, they may encourage a dedication service rather than baptism. The anecdotal evidence is that some baptisms are barely "regular," with only the pouring of water in the name of the Trinity being from the rite, the rest being testimony and hopes expressed by the parents. This suggests an uncritical adoption of cultural sentiments about the birth of a child rather than the intention to raise a child in the church, which must be expressed by parents and godparents in the authorized rites. Anecdotal evidence suggests that some Anglicans, if the family is known to the clergy, will dispense with some requirements, such as a credal confession of faith in the service. This indicates a need for better teaching and formation for those who administer this sacrament. It is likely that there will be more adult baptisms in future, as those not baptized as children come to faith and choose to belong to the church.

A generous approach to requests gives parishes the opportunity to follow up a baptism with invitations to take part in parish life that have the potential to build a real relationship with families, as difficult as this proves to be in practice.

Some civil celebrants offer naming ceremonies and indicate that "godparents" should be chosen. Certificates, and sometimes the giving of a candle, are included, and religious readings may be used.[9] This inevitably impacts on the understanding in secular society of the real significance of the rite of baptism.

Marriage

Marriage is a most malleable social institution. Consider the shifts in relationships between women and men since the 1960s and 1970s to appreciate how readily marriage adapts to new economics and social dynamics. For the most part, theologians have yet to take seriously the dramatic changes in sexual behavior, and in marriage, which result from reliable, safe, and now widely accepted forms of contraception as well as from women's wider participation in the workforce. The reality is that marriage, sexual relationships, and child rearing are no longer connected or sequential in the way they used to be. It is possible to have sex without children and children without sex. Until relatively recently, this was unthinkable.

The meaning of marriage is also changing, as women no longer need to marry to have a secure economic life or to have children. Of all the couples marrying in Australia now, over three quarters are already living together.

When Anglicans debate marriage, we are also fighting over differing views of human sexuality. Some conservatives place the emphasis on marriage as an order of creation, a gift of God to all peoples in which, some argue, the woman is subject to the greater authority of the man. Other conservatives place the emphasis on marriage as a sacrament of the church, though this is a small minority, and may even oppose marriage following divorce if the former spouse is living. The Anglican Church resolved the question of whether a divorced person may marry a second time by passing a General Synod Canon, provisionally in 1981 and finally in 1985. The canon must be adopted in a diocese to have effect but is now a widely accepted practice when the circumstances accord with the canon.[10]

---

9. ABS, "2016 Census Data."

10. Marriage of Divorced Persons Canon, 1981; Canon 7, 1985: "A canon to regulate the practice and procedure of this church with respect to the marriage of divorced persons."

The Anglican Church is now grappling with the reality that both the meaning and the practice of sexual relationships have changed in a society where reliable contraception is readily available and used almost universally, cohabitation without marriage is recognized in law as "de facto" and is almost the norm, and Commonwealth law now provides marriage for same-sex couples.

The fundamental disconnect is that marriage is no longer primarily about children, as important as that remains to most couples, but nor is it primarily a sexual relationship. Whatever we may think of the new reality, this is the brave new world we inhabit. Now, couples who cohabited before marrying are more likely to marry in a civil ceremony than those who lived apart.

Civil Celebrants

The introduction of civil celebrants, with authority to conduct weddings in any setting and use any words that conform to the legal requirement that the couple commit to an exclusive and lifelong relationship, has dramatically changed the context, not only for weddings but for other rites of passage.

The Attorney General's Department registers and regulates celebrants only in relation to marriages. Anyone may conduct a funeral service or a naming ceremony for a child. There are approximately 9,000 civil and 23,000 religious celebrants in Australia. There is a code of practice concerning professional standards for civil celebrants. However, once registered, Australian civil celebrants may do almost anything they and their clients want within the legal requirements for marriage, which they must state (and do); and they may blend any religious sources into any ceremony they conduct.

The proportion of marriages performed by civil celebrants has increased over the past twenty years, with the majority of marriages now being overseen by civil celebrants. The proportion of civil marriage ceremonies increased to 78 percent of all marriages in 2017.[11] In 2012, of the 34,613 marriages performed by ministers of religion, the most common rites used were Catholic (31.8 percent) followed by Anglican (16.2 percent).[12]

In European countries, all marriages are civil and only those who choose it have an additional religious ceremony. The delineation is clear and, I consider, much better than the largely unregulated blurring of boundaries in Australian law and practice, which risks being sentimental and ill informed. In the UK, civil wedding ceremonies require the attendance of

11. ABS, "Marriages and Divorces."
12. ABS, "Marriages and Divorces."

a registrar, who may not necessarily conduct the ceremony but *must* be present. It is also possible to marry in the registry office and have a civil ceremony elsewhere with any "celebrant" the couple chooses. The ceremony in the registry can include readings, songs, or music, but must not include anything that is religious, such as hymns or readings from the Bible. There is clearly an intention to separate a civil celebration from a religious one in a way not required in Australian law.

Clergy are licensed to conduct the marriage of the members of their own churches, using only the rites approved by those bodies. The trend is downward, and the anecdotal evidence confirms fewer forward bookings than ever, even in the most photogenic churches. As someone asked of Anglicans some time ago, "Are there any breeding pairs?" What a pity if Cranmer's wonderful wedding words become only infrequently heard or relegated to the arcane consideration of that other dying breed, liturgists.

The "Wedding Industry"

There is little doubt the wedding industry both responds to, and sets trends in, wedding ceremonies. Emphasis on "the bride's big day" and the expectation of the perfect day, along with the trend of using a wedding as the big celebration when a couple become serious about children, renovate the "forever house" for their growing family, all indicate changed attitudes and customs around marriage. Some things remain, of course, and I find that couples still want a long and happy marriage that fulfils the expectation of mutual comfort and support that Cranmer so winsomely added to the purposes of marriage.

The wedding industry is large and lucrative. Couples (and their parents and guests) are sold, usually at inflated prices, perhaps a destination (sometimes overseas) and/or a venue, accommodation, maybe a theme for the ceremony, a choice of celebrant, purchase of wedding rings, musicians for the ceremony and the reception, stationery, clothing, hair and make-up styling, catering and a cake, flowers, cars, photography, setting up a gift registry, bubbles to blow, rice or confetti—all in pursuit of a perfect wedding day.

Wedding Services

Cranmer's wedding service has proven remarkably enduring. The *BCP* rite was based on the Sarum rite from Salisbury Cathedral, which had a long history of theological, liturgical, and cultural influences. Cranmer moved the whole rite into the church building. Previously, marriages had taken place in homes, and later in part at the church door. Marriage was made an occasional office and did not need to take place in the worshiping congregation but only in the presence of the family and friends of the bride and groom. Over the centuries, it has been modified, most significantly with the 1928 revisions of the Preface to exclude reference to entering marriage in order to "satisfy men's carnal lusts and appetites, like brute beasts that have no understanding."[13] This revised form was used for the Royal wedding of Prince William and Kate Middleton in 2011.

The form for the Solemnization of Matrimony in *BCP* contains some of the most ancient words in the English language associated with marriage. The Anglican wedding service is replete with words and phrases once widely known in English-speaking cultures. Along with the funeral rite, the wedding service may well be (or have been) more widely experienced than the central acts of Anglican worship: Morning and Evening Prayer and Holy Communion. This cultural knowledge persists to a greater extent with the wedding service than with funerals.

In 1977, the General Synod approved the first completely revised book in the Anglican Communion, which became *An Australian Prayer Book*, adopted throughout the Australian dioceses. The marriage service was little revised, except that provision was made for a form in more contemporary English, which meant that two orders for marriage were now available to clergy and couples. There was strong Evangelical opposition to the omission of the wife promising to "obey" the husband in the Second Order.

In 1995, debate within the Liturgical Commission preceded the protracted and bitter disputes over the new book in the General Synod of that year, when the word "honor" was substituted for "obey" in a First Order in *APBA*. By 1995, the equality of spouses in marriage was widely accepted among most Anglicans; moreover, it is the legal situation and the widely held community expectation. With the revisions approved in *APBA*, more extensive changes were made to one of the two forms of the marriage rite. Controversy focused on the inclusion or omission of the word "obey" in the woman's vows. Since 1995, the Diocese of Sydney, which never approved the 1995 book for general use, has created a "Sydney only" marriage rite, which includes the woman promising to "submit" to the man. This form of service is authorized only by the Synod of the Diocese of Sydney and includes a prayer for the woman that she be given the "unfading beauty of a gentle and quiet spirit in submitting to her husband."[14] It remains to be

13. "Preface to the service Of Matrimony," *BCP*, first occurring in the 1549.
14. "Services for Marriage."

tested whether this Sydney only book sets a precedent for other dioceses to produce liturgical resources for their local use. Could a diocese authorize a rite for same-sex marriage? The return to locally recognized rites would be a return to the pre-Reformation situation in England, from which multiple resources Cranmer and others crafted *one* book of common prayer for use in England.

The next big challenge for Anglicans, both locally and nationally, is what to do now that the Commonwealth has legislated for same-sex marriage. Debate has already been fierce and is likely to become even more divisive in the next few years. The range of options includes complete opposition and rejection of such marriages, in much the way we used to treat the second marriages of divorced people; acceptance of a form of blessing following a civil same-sex marriage; or, most radically, provision of a service for such a marriage with clergy acting, as now, as agents of the state as celebrants.

Cultural Shifts in Funerals

While many customs and practices in the wedding service have not changed dramatically in their externals, funerals are another matter altogether. Cranmer's burial service is now, to contemporary sensibilities, far too severe and fails to mention the deceased by name. Its theological focus is on judgment following death, and it lacks any note of the celebration of life now expected by mourners.

The Funeral Service in BCP

Cranmer and other reformers truncated funeral rites, in part as a reaction against the excesses of multiple masses for the dead, the doctrine of purgatory having undermined the church's earlier assurance in the face of death. Cranmer provided for a service in two locations: the office in church and the burial at the grave. The reactive Protestant reformers were even less willing to take the corpse into the church. The *Westminster Directory of Worship* permitted prayers only at the graveside, and no eulogy except acknowledgment of the achievements of the deceased.[15] This strikes me as the seed of the secular funeral in that the religious component is stripped to the barest influence possible but it does not exclude reference to the person's accomplishments in this life.

---

15. *Westminster Directory of Worship.*

As already noted, in *BCP* the deceased is not referred to by name, but only as "our sister/brother." The service is not to be used for the unbaptized, the excommunicated, or suicides; there is no provision for eulogies or "family tributes," and the reading of chapter fifteen of the first letter to the Corinthians in its entirety is required by the rubric. There is no sermon.

Cranmer's provisions for the funeral seem particularly spare and comfortless to our sensibilities, but twice in over a decade of my ministry in Malvern, families specified that the *BCP* rite be used, despite the clergy pointing out what would not be included, and that the deceased being cremated was something Cranmer would never have imagined proper for a Christian.

Funeral Services Now

More commonly now called a "thanksgiving for the life of . . .," the contemporary funeral service has multiplied into a variety of texts and alternatives in a world where the meaning of death has changed, even for the majority of Christians. The funeral has become a celebration, in contrast to the display of grief and concern for the salvation of the deceased of previous generations.

Funeral celebrants, who unlike civil wedding celebrants need no authorization to call themselves that, conduct civil funerals. In my limited experience of attending such funerals, they have no shame in borrowing from religious sources and blending these with secular sentiments. People in my parishes sometimes told me they went to a civil funeral and "it had no shape" or it was "without any hope."

Attending to the dead has also changed markedly. It was once women's work. Families were involved in all aspects of the process, but with refrigeration and embalming this work was taken over by professionals, who could afford the new technology. It is work that is now in the hands of large corporations or local businesses, not families. Funerals are held in commercial parlors, because in the past the deceased would have been kept in the front parlor of the home and taken from there to the church for burial in the churchyard. Now these matters, along with most aspects of illness and dying, are handed over to the professionals. As good as they are, they do have a pecuniary interest in providing the venue and celebrant if mourners do not specify religious ceremonies. Furthermore, commercially driven time constraints may add pressure to keep the service short, especially at the crematorium. I have the greatest respect for undertakers. I consider it is holy work to care for the dead and for mourners, and I have only ever found them compassionate and professional. But in the end, they are conducting a service and a business and will fill the vacuum of religious beliefs and practices with secular customs unless asked to do otherwise.

In the past, in England, the burial of paupers was a charge on the local parish, and many parishes kept a coffin with an end that opened to allow the body (it would have been called the corpse, as in *BCP*) to slide out into the grave. Most churches no longer have churchyards for burials, but many have memorial gardens for the interment of cremated remains. Parishes are often the only place the dead are now remembered by name in public when names are read on the anniversary of death, or at celebrations in All Saints' tide.

Funerals are now tailored to reflect the individual who has died and the personal choices of those making the arrangements. Provisions include a rite for reception of the body into the church, the placing of symbols of Christian faith when appropriate, a gathering rite that names the purpose of the funeral as giving thanks to God for the life of the person, time for mourning and honoring them, the laying to rest of their mortal body, and provision of support for one another in grief. It also includes acknowledging that we face "death and judgment," and refers to the Christian belief that those who die in Christ share eternal life with him.

Following the *BCP* pattern, sentences of Scripture are read, suitable passages of Scripture are to be read, preaching is expected, there may be a celebration of the Holy Eucharist, and the prayers are adapted to include qualities of the deceased and prayers for mourners. The funeral service may now be used for suicides, there are prayers for use when a child has died, and a separate service is provided for the interment of ashes. The additional liturgical resources now available in *APBA* are valuable in acknowledging the particular circumstances of each death in response to our changed cultural sensibilities surrounding death.

Closing Remarks

The occasional offices are the "bread and butter" of daily parish ministry. We underestimate their value to our cost. Each is a rite of passage functioning anthropologically to serve human need, and each has its own internal structure that changes the status or standing of people within the human and faith community. Each confers a new identity on the person and encapsulates in the rite the dynamics of a significant transition in life.

Each also offers possibilities for growing in faith and understanding or at the very least creates a foundation for future participation in the life of the church. Clergy and communities who understand these patterns are better able to conduct these rites and proclaim the invitation to ongoing conversion or growth in faith that each stage of life may enable.

Attitudes and customs have changed over the centuries since the *BCP* was first devised, and the church has adapted the rites to accommodate many of these. The most dramatic social changes in our time are in the area of marriage. The introduction of same-sex marriage is causing deep and possibly irreconcilable division among Anglicans in Australia and in other parts of the Communion. It is not clear at the time of writing if Australian Anglicans will be able to live with differing practices in dioceses or if this issue will be "the line in the sand," as some are calling it.

Faithful exercise of these various ministries accompanies regular public worship as a primary purpose of Christian community. Such moments can be missional if clergy and parishes understand the opportunities each provides. In the Anglican way, this is normally in parishes that live within particular historical and social horizons, open to both the past and the present. These ministries must also be understood, valued, and critiqued, so that Christ's ministry may be exercised thoughtfully and hospitably and the gospel brought to life for each generation. Engagement with people at the precious moments in their individual, familial, and communal lives can be one of the most demanding, yet rewarding, dimensions of parish ministry.

Bibliography

Australian Bureau of Statistics (ABS). "2016 Census Data Reveals "No Religion" Is Rising Fast." Media Release, AUSSTATS website, June 27, 2017. https://www.abs.gov.au/AUSSTATS/abs@.nsf/mediareleasesbyReleaseDate/7E65A144540551D7CA258148000E2B85.

——— "Marriages and Divorces, Australia, 2017." Media Release, AUSSTATS website, issued November 27, 2018. https://www.abs.gov.au/ausstats/abs@.nsf/mf/3310.0.

An Australian Prayer Book (1978). Liturgical Resources, authorized by the General Synod. Sydney: AIO, 1978.

The Book of Common Prayer and Administration of the Sacraments and Ceremonies of the Church according to the Church of England together with the Psalter or Psalms of David pointed as they are to be sung or said in Church and the From or manner of making, ordaining and consecrating of bishops, priests and deacons. 1662. London: Eyre and Spottiswood, n.d.

Green, Robin. *Only Connect: Worship and Liturgy from the Perspective of Pastoral Care*. London: DLT, 1987.

Murray, Les. "The Mitchells." In *Anthology of Australian Religious Poetry*, selected by Les Murray, 45. Blackburn, Vic: CollinsDove, 1986.

A Prayer Book for Australia (1995). Broughton Books: Sydney, 1999.

"Services for Marriage: Form 2." In *Resources for Gospel Shaped Gatherings*, Archbishop of Sydney's Liturgical Panel, 76–80. South Sydney: Anglican Press Australia, 2012.

Turner, Victor. *The Ritual Process: Structure and Anti-Structure*. Ithaca, NY: Cornell University Press, 1969.

Westminster Directory of Worship, 1644. Grove Books: Bramcote, 1980.

5

Ministry and Mission

Considerations for Parishes Urban and Rural

ANDREW CURNOW

IN RECENT TIMES THE parish system, which has been the mainstay of the pattern for ministry and mission in the Anglican Church of Australia, has been under the microscope. Questions have been raised about its sustainability and applicability in both urban and rural Australian contexts. Is it an antiquated model, and does it need drastic surgery?

This essay explores the situation in our nation at the present time and argues that the parish model has much to offer us by being more creative in advancing the kingdom of God. But to be more creative requires some significant new ways and means of making that possible. I am delighted to offer this essay in recognition of the leadership of the Most Rev. Philip Freier, who has served the Anglican Church of Australia with commitment and vision. Philip has been a good friend for over twenty years and has given me significant encouragement in my own leadership in this church.

Then and Now

I am part of a rare breed these days. I am a cradle Anglican, and I was ordained a deacon at twenty-two (by special faculty). Today, most ordinands are over the age of thirty; I was placed in charge of my first parish at the age of twenty-five and have had the privilege of serving in the ordained ministry for over forty-six years.

At the time of my becoming ordained, the Anglican Church was still experiencing the glory days of the baby boomer period in Australia. Sunday Schools were well-attended, youth groups were burgeoning, and most parishes offered a whole range of clubs to belong to, many events to attend, and a wide offering of Bible study groups and Christian education programs. The parish at which I was assistant curate, St. Alban's West Coburg with St. George's Pascoe Vale South, even had a football team, cricket team, and tennis club. Life was hectic, and the parish was at the heart of the community. True, not everyone who was involved was in church every Sunday, but there was a connection with a great many people across the two suburbs, and I was warmly welcomed into people's homes and lives. Visiting and maintaining a wide range of contacts was at the heart of the parish's pastoral life. There was, on average, a funeral at least once a week, baptisms were held as part of the main Sunday service at least once a month (and it was often bedlam), and there were weddings on most Saturdays in Autumn and early Spring. There was even a robed choir with choir practice every Thursday, a strong Mother's Union group, a youth group of 120 and a never-ending parish diary that was full of activity. In 1964, a new War Memorial Hall had been built, and it was seen as the best public venue in the area.

My first parish was in northern rural Victoria amidst a mixture of dairy and dry land country. Many were farming livestock—cows, sheep, cattle and pigs—and growing crops, mainly wheat. There were two rail lines that traversed the parish. It was quite different to suburban Melbourne in geography, population, and community feel, as the parish was made up of four distinct towns and areas in between. But in common with the urban parish, the church was at the heart of the community. My first Christmas there, I found the experience of "the community Christmas Tree" a unique and exciting event. A local gravel contractor made available his semi-trailer gravel truck, and Santa went around the community with a ladder so the children could climb in the truck. Can you imagine this happening today within our risk-averse environment?

How things have changed! I can get nostalgic, but that time has gone, and society and the church have dramatically changed over the past fifty years. Much has happened in the world, our nation, and the church.

Computers used to be the size of a house, and now I hold one in my hand with a mobile phone. When I reflect on the past, I recognize that I and many others did not anticipate the move away from the church being at the heart of the community and the subsequent impact on congregations. Back then, I could never have imagined that we would be dealing with a shrinking and ageing church in the way we are now.

The Challenge of Change

The changes in the churches did not take place overnight; there were signs of decline as far back as the 1980s, with rural populations decreasing and our metropolitical areas beginning to outgrow the resources of the dioceses to keep pace with urban sprawl. The word multiculturalism began to appear, and with the Whitlam government in the early 1970s much legislation was introduced that would change the face of our nation.

In response to considerable societal change, the church began to struggle with how to understand, interpret, and theologize about it. Differences that had been part of the Anglican scene in Australia since the 1850s began to emerge with more force and feeling: issues such as remarriage of divorcees, the nature of the ordained ministry, the role of the Bible, the governance of our church, and, more recently, human sexuality.

During General Synod in 2014 and 2017, the Anglican Church of Australia received reports from the Viability and Structures Taskforce. These highlighted the challenges dioceses across Australia, both urban and rural, are facing in sustaining the long-term ministry and mission of the church.

In large urban areas, the main issue is rapid population growth and the inability of dioceses to keep pace with that, coupled with decline in attendance across the board. Rapid growth of population and the explosion of new housing areas and suburbs has led some urban dioceses to address this with a strategy of establishing more Anglican schools. These schools, often offering lower fees, have in some places been combined with the establishment of new parishes. However, there is little evidence that this strategy has led to any increase in numbers of committed worshipers. Another strategy has been to allow or encourage the establishment of associated congregations such as ethnic churches or "fresh expressions" congregations. Many of these initiatives are more of a "gathered congregation" approach and have moved away from the traditional Anglican pattern of parish ministry being available to all in the local community. In the end, no capital city diocese has been able to keep pace with urban growth.

In rural areas, population decline has led to a decline in church attendance and stretched resources. Many rural dioceses struggle to achieve the critical mass that would enable them to be well resourced with both people and finances. At the same time, there are creative things happening in rural dioceses as they come to terms with the context in which they are ministering.

The Anglican Church, like all churches in Australia, is struggling with mission and the future shape and direction of the church. In addressing the future, we need to be mindful of some considerations.

Considerations for Ongoing Mission and Ministry

"Local" Comes Before All Else

First, we must heed the importance of place in ministry. This is particularly true of rural churches, where people identify with a strong sense of place, but increasingly this applies also to urban dioceses, where numbers in congregations are declining in the midst of an isolating urban environment. Missiologist Bishop Lesslie Newbigin, writing in *The Gospel in a Pluralist Society*, argues:

> In a situation of declining numbers the policy has been to abandon areas where active Christians are few and to concentrate ministerial resources by merging congregations and deploying ministries in places where there are enough Christians to support them. Needless to say, this simply accelerates decline. It is the opposite of a missionary strategy, which would proceed in the opposite direction . . . The task of ministry is to lead the congregation as a whole in a mission to the community as a whole, to claim its whole public life, as well as the personal lives of all its people, for God's rule. It means equipping all the members of the congregation to understand and fulfil several roles in the mission through their faithfulness in their daily work. It means training and equipping them to be active followers of Jesus in his assault on the principalities and powers which he had disarmed on the cross.[1]

Newbigin's understanding of mission is timeless, but the challenge is, how do we organize the church to be more effective at mission in the suburbs, towns, and districts of our nation? Newbigin would argue that the formula for vigorous local churches is context, connection, and community.

---

1. Newbigin, *Gospel*, 235

History shows us certain things:

- Few parish mergers or amalgamations work. People seem to be invariably lost in the process.
- A huge turnover of clergy in rural areas has, over time, weakened the missional training and leadership of rural congregations.
- Mission is not solely about numbers in the congregation. It is about developing a mature faith and a well-equipped laity for leadership and ministry.
- The large urban areas of cities present challenges in simply trying to relate to community and build the church.
- Over time across Australia, the proportion and participation of Anglicans in rural areas is stronger than that of metropolitan areas. The 2016 Census reveals that the number of Anglicans across metropolitical dioceses averaged 18.5 percent and in rural dioceses 23.1 percent. All dioceses declined in real terms.

Having these things in mind, "local" does not mean that everything should stay the same. It is a matter of bringing people with us as we seek to address the mission of the church. What Newbigin has highlighted is that we need to understand our contexts; the unique nature of local communities needs to be grasped and engaged with. So often in ministry, clergy think it is their task to bring Jesus to communities. No; Jesus is already present. It is the task of the whole people of God to discover Jesus in their midst and make that known. Ministry is of the people, for the people, and with the people!

Leadership is Paramount

At the heart of becoming a missionary church lies leadership: the leadership of laity, clergy, and bishops. Such leadership must take the following realities of mission, highlighted by Bosch in *Transforming Mission*, into account:[2]

- The church must be a missionary church in its own context, and all members must begin to see mission as a state of mind as much as a way of action. It is about purpose, the ordering of goals, and the way the church's ministry is formed, organized, and delivered.

---

2. Bosch, *Transforming Mission*. These points are taken from pages 2–10.

- The church is going through a period of disturbance, crisis, and transition, but why should it be any different? God can speak to us as much through the storm as in times of calm.
- There are no easy answers, no series of major events that are going to turn the ship around. Each church and congregation must begin by looking at who they think they are and where they think they are going. The theology of mission must be the compass to show the church the way forward.
- The church is a pilgrim on a journey and must remain faithful to its calling and, at the same time, be engaged and present in its context.

Leadership in the Anglican Church is exercised by a multitude of people, lay and ordained, in a variety of roles and callings—and it all begins with Christ. Croft writes:

> Any understanding of leadership and ministry within the church which is to be a Christian understanding cannot be derived directly or simply either from the society around us or from the Old Testament images and models. Rather, a Christian understanding of what it means to exercise leadership within the church must take account of, be mediated and integrated with:
> - Our understanding of Jesus and his mission
> - The gifts of the Holy Spirit to the church and
> - Our understanding of the church as the "Body of Christ."[3]

This is where we begin, and this grounding of leadership will be reflected in the thoughts, words, and actions of those leading in the church. But how is this reflected in the practice of leadership?

I want to suggest four key elements to the practice of leadership in the church:

The Message

And the Word became flesh and lived among us (John 1:14).

Christian leaders have a huge gift when it comes to the message we bring: The Old and New Testaments, the great story of faith, of God, Jesus, and the Holy Spirit. As Gardner says, "A leader must have a central story or

---

3. Croft, *Ministry*, 38.

message . . . Stories should not only provide background, but they should help people to frame future options."[4]

The message must be lived out and reflected in the life, actions, and values of the leader. Authenticity is a key criterion; leaders must resist pressure to conform to an organization but rather behave with an integrity and consistency that is communicated through their behavior and speech. People have high expectations of Christian leaders, and the recent Royal Commission into Institutional Child Abuse in Australia has left the credibility of much leadership in our churches with a cloud over it. Although many church leaders have been very quick to inform the media that the church has changed, the community is not so sure. There is still a significant gap between the message and the behavior of the church.

The Context

> After some days Paul said to Barnabas, "Come let us return and visit the believers in every city where we proclaimed the word of the Lord and see how they are doing" (Acts 15:36)

The church is people, and all people come from a place, a local community. They can work, belong to a host of other organizations and clubs, and have a wide variety of interaction with other people. All of this is part of knowing the context, the place, for the practice of ministry.

From the very beginning of white settlement in Australia, the Anglican Church has tended to follow the English parish model as the way to establish place for ministry and mission. It is essentially a geographic model for organizing the church; the aim, over time, was to see all of Australia divided up into parishes. This was aided by the creation of dioceses and the appointment of bishops. Given the size of this country, the aim of establishing parishes to see that all people could be ministered to was largely achieved, except for in the remotest regions,

At the heart of leadership in this model was a strong identification with context. The aim was to make the church available, part of the local community, and involved in the day to day lives of people and their cities, suburbs, towns, districts, and communities. Bishops, clergy, and lay leadership were intimately involved with knowing their local communities, parishes, and dioceses, and this a great support to effectively making the gospel known. Where the church's leadership is seen as being remote and coming from outside, it quickly creates a barrier to communication. A strength of

---

4. Gardner, *Leading Minds*, 290.

Paul in his apostolic leadership of the early church, as his letters in the New Testament reveal, is that he knew the early Christian communities inside out and upside down.

The importance of this remains true for today. It is harder in larger urban conglomerations, but this is where the ministry and leadership of regional bishops, clergy, and lay people come to the fore. In London, the test for getting a taxi license is called "The Knowledge." It is about knowing the geography and locations of London. In ministry and mission, leadership must know the people and the local area in depth. A great example can be seen in the Diocese of St. Arnaud, which was established in 1927 and existed in North Western Victoria for fifty years. The first bishop was Melville James. He never drove, but remarkably, given the distances he had to traverse, he knew just about everyone across the diocese. How? He traveled everywhere by train or buggy or was driven by parishioners who had cars. Particularly in his train travel he was known to speak to everyone, and he soon became a well-known character across the Mallee. Those days have gone, but the power of church leaders who know their contexts intimately stands forever.

Relationships

> This is my commandment, that you love one another as I have loved you. No one has greater love than this, to lay down one's life for one's friends (John 15:12).

No leader in the church can effectively lead without relating to the people they are accountable to or responsible for. If real estate is about position, leadership in the church is about relationships.

These relationships can be at many different levels of depth and complexity. Ministerial and administrative leadership involves relating to people in a diversity of roles, and these need to have clear boundaries and be at the highest level of professional conduct. Leadership in the church is not a solo role but has to be undertaken collaboratively in a spirt of genuine co-operation and goodwill. As Croft says,

> Leaders often find themselves living in a paradox. The more responsibility we carry, the more advice and help we need in a complex, ever changing role. But the more responsibility we carry, the harder it becomes to listen to that advice and help. Trusted companions, external perspectives, humility and open ears are essential to discover what is not working and to mend it. At each stage of the leadership task, there is a danger that the

essential tasks of leadership will be overwhelmed by the details. In those moments as leaders we need an external perspective, fresh eyes. Those eyes will help us to see the essential things we need to do and those which can be delegated to others.[5]

So, bishops need to be not loners, but team players, open to advice. The same can be said of all holding leadership responsibilities in the church.

Ultimately, the nature and importance of relationships begins with our relationship with God and the way that is expressed in relationships with those around us. This requires good self-knowledge, an openness to mentoring and regular appraisal, and the ongoing development of one's theological understanding and skills for ministry.

Values

> For we are what he has made us, created in Christ Jesus for good works, which God prepared beforehand to be our way of life (Eph 2:10).

Undergirding all leadership is the leader's value system.

As we know, the Scriptures are laden with values that have been the mainstay of civilization for thousands of years. The ministry and leadership of Jesus built upon this and established the Judeo-Christian value system. Jesus' opening to the Sermon on the Mount (Matt 5:1–12) and Paul's list of the fruits of the Spirit (Gal 5:22–26) are explicit examples of values that are to be embodied in Christian leadership. Those involved in ministerial and missional leadership must be able to articulate and communicate the core values of the Christian faith, and they must be translated into the everyday life of the church.

But more than that, they must be lived out authentically. Leaders must behave with an integrity and consistency that is communicated in speech and behavior. We cannot verbalize values and not live them out. As Steven Croft says,

> Jesus turns the values of human society upside down. The least important in society is the most valued in the Kingdom of God: little children, lepers, tax collectors and sinners. The meek, not the strong and powerful, are to inherit the earth. The values of the kingdom are to apply especially among the community of

---

5. Croft, *Gift of Leadership*, 46.

faith, the church, where there is to be a completely different attitude to leadership.[6]

We also need to be mindful that the church is not a company or a government agency, and we need to be careful about adopting leadership models that fit the management style of large corporations. We can learn from them, but our value base is different in the church, which is a unique community of faith, hope, and love, called by Christ to be the light of the world and the salt of the earth. In the current circumstances that we face, dioceses and large parishes are all too readily tempted to emulate contemporary management models and strategies in the hope that they will make the church a more effective organization. There is nothing wrong with being effective for the glory of God, but we need to be careful as to how we do it. Strong morale is vital in the administration and delivery of ministry, and this will be assisted with a clear set of values that reflect gospel values, such as the following statement.

In the name of Jesus as the Lord of the church, we value:

- People—as individuals and communities
- Partnership—laypeople, clergy, and bishops
- Diversity—in the church and wider community
- Openness—welcoming to all
- Freedom—in speech, worship, and society
- Integrity—upholding the highest ethics in service
- Generosity—in spirt and in giving
- Safety—an environment which is a safe space

I am sure one could add more or make your own list, but a list of values like this, set down clearly and transparently, are a good starting point for the church at all levels. Values should be about developing a culture of trust and mutuality in order to build communities that have a clear purpose and understanding of who we are as the people of God. They communicate to the faith community and wider society that we are accountable. They also help to build in parishes and across dioceses a culture of integrity, authenticity, and trust.

Effective leadership is critical for the future of the church, and that leadership needs to be delegated, collaborative, and consistent.

---

6. Croft, *Ministry*, 36.

The Pastoral Can Be Missional

Many larger churches today operate, or aspire to operate, in programmatic or corporate models of organization. Such churches offer a diversity of programs for different age and interest groups, and there is often a staff team that enable this to happen. Worship is spread across a range of services: a more traditional service, a family service, and a young adult service in the evening, for example. Staff are usually recruited to concentrate on one of the congregations. Such churches are often gathered congregations with members coming from a number of areas and attracted by the programs, worship, and style of church. Many of these churches have been effective in their mission and ministry, though they ebb and flow over time. They have in many places been seen as the way of the future for the local church. Smaller parishes have been encouraged in many dioceses to adopt such a programmatic or corporate approach as the way forward.

However, after thirty or forty years of restructuring and reimagining the practical mission of the church, even to the point of questioning the future of the parish system, the question of the future shape and provision of ministry and mission remains.

What is required are not more initiatives, particularly from diocesan headquarters, but a more searching analysis of the social and cultural factors that are working against living a full and faithful Christian life within the church. Whatever way we read the statistics or crunch the numbers, it seems that the strategies in themselves are not enough to halt, let alone reverse, the decline in church membership or, alternatively, to attract new members. Over many years, I have seen diocese after diocese launch ambitious and well-resourced programs to motivate the laity to evangelize. Many have had only limited impact and are a misunderstanding of the way to engage people. The dioceses and senior clergy who often initiate such programs may feel they have done their bit by setting them up, but I am not convinced that these programs reflect where people today are at in their own journey of faith.

Welsh singer and radio and television presenter Aled Jones, who regularly comperes *Songs of Praise,* has stated, "I am a modern Christian. I don't need to go to church."[7] I am sure that there are more and more people like this in Australia. Even the 2016 Census reports that over 65 percent of the population still believe in God. But do they believe in the church? If this is the state of our nation's belief, I would argue the parish system has great

---

7. *Compass*, ABC1 Television, 5 May 2019.

potential to reengage us with the diaspora from the church as well as those who do not know Christ or the church.

In Anglicanism, at the heart of the parish system is a pastoral church. From the early days of Anglicanism, the *Book of Common Prayer* provided a range of pastoral offices. As Stanley Hauerwas has argued in a recent article about the strength of pastoral care, there "is a clear sense the difference Jesus makes for our care of one another, and how that difference makes a life of joy possible."[8]

The pastoral offices of the *Book of Common Prayer* were founded on a village way of life, and the evolution of urbanization has produced a new context for them, but every sociological study one reads about urban Australia tells us that people crave to belong: they want to be part of a village experience. The popularity of television reality shows such as *Escape from the City* and *The Real Seachange* highlight the search of many people living in our large cities who want to experience a place where they feel they belong.

As a child, I grew up in a large regional city in Victoria with three churches—the Roman Catholic, Methodist, and Anglican churches—all having a well-developed parish system. We lived close to what was called the Quarry Hill Methodist Church, which subsequently became part of the Uniting Church. In recent years, due to the decline and aging of the congregation, it was sold to a local community group and rebadged as "The Old Church on the Hill." For a church that was at death's door, it has had an amazing revitalization and has become a hub in the local community. "The Old Church provides a place where people are valued and community can grow. The site is home to a community garden, feast space and kitchen, recreation hall, and the renowned Old Church itself."[9]

The Old Church does not state a specific Christian purpose, but Christians are very actively involved with it, and it is the heart and center of the local community and thriving, providing:

- A community pantry
- Community Garden Social club
- Sustainability Group
- Neighborhood Pizza Night
- Regular community musical evenings

8. Stanley Hauerwas, "Being with the Wounded: Pastoral Care within the Life of the Church," opinion piece, ABC Religion and Ethics Report, ABC website, January 11, 2019. https://www.abc.net.au/religion/wounded-pastoral-care-within-the-life-of-the-church/10708802.

9. www.theoldchurchonthehill.com

The Old Church on the Hill shows what could happen with many local churches if they were really well-connected and engaged with their local communities, rather than just being a small community of the faithful. I believe what they are doing is an embodiment of much of the parish/pastoral model of church in a twenty-first century expression.

Not everything about what is regarded as the traditional approach of being church should be discounted. There is still much that can be done to be a missionary church using the parish/pastoral model, but it needs to be totally integrated into the life of the local community. The key to this model is to engage people in what interests them, to share in their significant life moments, and to be with them in all the ups and downs of contemporary life. Traditionally, this often happened through the administration of what were called the "occasional offices" for births, marriages, and deaths. This way of contact has declined in popularity, so there are challenges to build bridges into the community.

Sandra Millar writes:

> In research with clergy and lay ministers we discovered a great deal of anxiety about whether our services and our facilities are alienating people, and therefore a lot of expectation that fixing things like premises and service books would be the key to changing the way we meet to engage with us. However, a clear pattern emerged that showed that it is the way we build relationship that makes the biggest impact. Or to put it another way, it's the "soft stuff," not the hardware that matters. Having a warm building, comfortable seating and the highest quality presentation will not draw people back, unless these aspects are accompanied by genuine smiles and interest. Over and over again, the research revealed the central importance of welcome and hospitality, and this is something that is the ministry of the whole people of God. . . . This can seem quite challenging when many life event services take place away from the church building, as with a funeral at the crematorium. Yet a pattern emerges that shows that when people meet people, when they discover the potential for friendship at church, this can be the key in helping them to want to find out more.[10]

The following things are crucial to the pastoral approach:

- *Connection:* Establishing contacts with people across the local community. The church has to go out beyond the immediate community

---

10. Millar, *Life Events*, 16.

of faith. Worship and ministry only come alive when relationships are established.

- *Flexibility:* Second, the minister needs to know the texts, services and structures that the church provides, even if on occasion only to depart from them. There needs to be some generosity on the part of the church to work with people distant or detached from it.
- *Awareness:* Third, one must always be aware of the prevailing stereotypes about the church and its representatives, for example, the impact of the Royal Commission.
- *Acceptance:* People approach the church for a variety of reasons, not all of which are the "correct ones." Get over it and use the fact that they are there at all as an opportunity to inject a bit of God into their lives. Don't tie yourselves up in knots over whether to baptize babies. Use the opportunities!
- *Perseverance:* Don't give up. You may or may not see the fruits of your labors; that is of no importance in God's economy. You may never know. =

The church has in many ways turned in on itself, and everything in mission and ministry is based on a premise of bringing people into the tent. We need a mind change to go out of the tent and get involved with where we live and move in the name of Christ.

All of us in the church need to get back onto the road to Emmaus (Luke: 24:13–35). As Brendan Byrne writes,

> The account of Jesus' appearance to the two disciples on the way to Emmaus is Luke's masterpiece. Rich in suspense, irony and play upon emotion, it offers a paradigm of the Christian life and mission. The Church goes on its pilgrim way, instructed, nourished, companioned by its Lord. The Church learns from him who walked with the two disciples."[11]

Jesus is encountered out on the road in an ordinary everyday situation. Today, it is no different as to how and where Jesus can be encountered. As followers of Jesus, we have become too rigid about where the interaction with people can take place to enable the sharing of stories so that "eyes are opened" (Luke 24:31). In other words, we need to think about mission and ministry beyond the confines of our buildings.

Similarly, I have always been attracted to another post-resurrection passage:

---

11. Byrne, *Hospitality*, 186–90.

> When they had gone ashore, they saw a charcoal fire there with fish on it, and bread. Jesus said to them, "Bring some of the fish that you have just caught." So Simon Peter went abroad and hauled the net ashore, full of the large fish, a hundred and fifty-three of them; and though there were so many, the net was not torn. Jesus said to them, "Come and have breakfast." (John 21:9–12)

The experience of the disciples and the invitation to come and have breakfast with Jesus has strong eucharistic overtones, as in partaking of the meal, they know "it is the Lord" (John 21:12). The gospel again gives the church a model, a way by which people experience the hospitality of God and encounter the living presence of Jesus.

The pastoral ministry of the church must recapture this same generosity and openness and not limit Jesus to the obedience of rules and regulations or declare that being part of the church is entirely on the terms that the church and the congregation or the parish declare. In recent years, whether intended or otherwise, the church has put up huge barriers to belonging, with the result that people just stay away or feel excluded. When Jesus gave the invitation to come and have breakfast, he did not cross-examine the disciples but simply said, "Come." He had earlier given them an instruction to cast the net on the right side of the boat, but that was to help and encourage them, not to draw lines or give the impression you will not qualify for the invitation.

Despite various attempts by the church to be more welcoming, one continues to hear in conversations with many people on the ground that it is just not happening. Lay people frequently tell me of couples approaching local parishes about baptism and being given a list of requirements to enable a baptism to happen. No wonder so many couples with babies respond to ads in local newspapers for naming ceremonies offered by civil celebrants. "They are more welcoming and straightforward to deal with, and we can have it in our own home." This trend is difficult for the church and challenges a lot of our established pastoral practice, but at the moment we are shooting ourselves in the foot. I am not in any way abandoning the pastoral practice of the church or trying to break it down, but I am arguing for the church to return to its pastoral heart as embodied in the Scriptures and to act with generosity and a genuine spirit of welcome.

Again, Sandra Millar writes,

> Ministering to those we meet through one of life's big moments is also where those who are already on their faith journey and active in the local church can grow their faith as they pray for

all involved and commit to being part of showing warmth and welcome. That may be within the context of church services and activities, or in a more specific ministry such as baptism or marriage preparation, toddler groups, bereavement support, pastoral visiting and other ways of serving.[12]

More and more in the church, we are limited by our imaginations. We need to think outside the box and know deeply and intimately the communities in which we are ministering. I heard of an Anglican rector in a country town who had a gift for evangelism. In Sydney, he had been a colorful Hyde Park corner speaker. However, trying to engage people in the main street of a country town was misplaced and showed a limited understanding of rural life. No wonder local people got to the point of ducking into local shops to avoid him. It was a type of evangelistic frontal attack that few people will respond to in a positive way. A more effective way, long term, would be to get to know the people. Visit them, spend time with them, let them know they are valued, and journey with them through life events. Pastoral care can grow churches.

Training Is Essential

In the earlier part of my ordained ministry, Christian education and training had prominence in the Anglican Church of Australia. Major dioceses all had a Christian Education Unit, and they often served across dioceses to assist in the mission and ministry of the church. Then they all came tumbling down and were disbanded as resourcing issues hit the church. It has left a great gap in the church's ability to train and enable an effective laity.

We are now dealing with the consequences. At present, the church is spending a lot of time and resources on Safe Church Training—and so it should—but the overall training of the laity has largely been left to those parishes or clergy who have the time, motivation, or resources to do it. Many parishes put all their eggs into running Lenten programs, which are largely focused on spiritual renewal, but there appears to be very little in actually training and enabling laity in mission. In some parishes there has been training for programs like Alpha, but they tend to be a one-off activity. The task of systematically training laity seems to have been abandoned, unless individual laity take themselves off to some event or course.

But the problem is bigger than that. I am no longer sure that Anglican theological colleges know what sort of church they are training their

---

12. Millar, *Life Events*, 181.

ordinands for. This will produce a howl of reaction from the colleges, but do they understand the context in which the church is now operating in in this country? The sustainability of stipendiary ministry is disappearing rapidly; we have a need, not for specialist clergy, but for more clergy who may have to sustain part of their income from other work. New models of formation and training need to be explored. These comments in no way imply an abandonment of core theological subjects, as indeed we need a well-trained and theologically literate clergy who can deliver mission and ministry across this land.

Concluding Reflections

So, what is the role of Anglican churches in Australia for the future? Dietrich Bonhoeffer reminds us that "Christianity means community through Jesus Christ and in Jesus Christ."[13] This central aspect of the gospel is increasingly lost in our culture, with its overemphasis on individuality. Recovering a profound sense of community is one of the major tasks of mission in this land and will involve local parishes and churches adopting these features of their life and mission:[14]

1. *Incarnational*: Christ became flesh and lived among us. A church must be involved in and be contributing to its local community, listening to the people, and responding to their real needs and concerns.
2. *Unifying*: Christ took down the barriers that divide. The local church is not just another interest group; it must be welcoming and open to all, not a closed group with a defined membership.
3. *Open-doored*: It cannot be a private club that is not able to adapt to change and new circumstances. People need to feel that it is welcoming and good to belong.
4. *Celebratory*: The church must provide opportunities for people to mark significant events of both personal and community life, including life events, local events, and festivities. Build bridges.
5. *Light on structures*: Streamline administration. It is not possible to do everything in every parish or church congregation. Identify your strengths and weaknesses.

---

13. Bonhoeffer, *Life Together*, 10.
14. Adapted from Hopkinson, *Seeds in Holy Ground*.

6. *Comfortable enough:* Buildings should be taken seriously but as a means to an end. A well-looked after and welcoming building is a great witness to the glory of God and our faith, but if it becomes the most important thing in parish life, it negates mission.

7. *Nurturing:* a church should provide opportunities for people to grow and develop in understanding their faith, local community and mutual responsibility for the world in which we live.

8. *Spiritually alive:* The church should be a spiritually growing people, with prayer, a knowledge of the Scriptures, and worship of God the Trinity at their heart.

The mission and ministry of the church is God-given, and it grows by following the example of Christ and being nourished by the working of the Holy Spirit. It is not simple or straightforward but requires commitment and perseverance over a significant period of time. Fundamentally, the mission and ministry of the church must first and foremost relate to the community in which it exists and seeks to serve and make Christ known. I long recall some words from missiologist, Lesslie Newbigin:

> The relation between the Church in a "place" and the secular reality of that "place" is intrinsic, not extrinsic. It is not just that it happens to be located in that spot on the map. It is *the Church of God for that place*, and that is because the Church does not exist for itself, but for God and the world which Jesus came to save.[15]

The Anglican Church of Australia has some formidable challenges in the years ahead. To survive, and thrive, it needs to be united and purposeful, returning to the basics of good leadership and pastoral care and working with a new intentionality in local communities.

---

15. Weston, *Lesslie Newbigin*, 133. Italics original.

Bibliography

Bonhoeffer, Dietrich. *Life Together.* Translated by John W. Doberstein. London: SCM, 2015.

Bosch, David. *Transforming Mission: Paradigm Shifts in Theology of Mission.* New York: Orbis, 1991.

Byrne, Brendan. *The Hospitality of God, A Reading of Luke's Gospel.* Strathfield, NSW: St. Paul's Publications, 2000.

Croft, Steven J. L. *Ministry in Three Dimensions,* London: DLT, 2008.

———. *The Gift of Leadership: According to the Scriptures.* London: Canterbury Press, 2016.

Gardner, Howard. *Leading Minds: An Anatomy of Leadership.* Glasgow: Harper Collins, 1996.

Hopkinson, Jill. *Seeds in Holy Ground: A Workbook for Rural Churches.* London: Acora Publishing for the Archbishop's Council, 2005.

Millar, Sandra. *Life Events: Mission and Ministry at Baptisms, Weddings and Funerals.* London: Church House, 2018.

Newbigin, Lesslie. *The Gospel in a Pluralist Society.* Grand Rapids, MI: Eerdmans, 1989.

Weston, Paul. *Lesslie Newbigin: Missionary Theologian. A Reader.* Cambridge UK: Eerdmans, 2006.

6

Aspects of Multicultural Mission in Melbourne

Len Firth[1]

Mission has been central to Archbishop Philip Freier's vision and strategy for the Anglican Diocese of Melbourne. This vision has been, to a degree, responsive. The context of the Australian church, particularly in Melbourne, has been profoundly impacted by the arrival of significant numbers of refugees who have seen themselves as Anglican Christians. The church has needed to respond to this important reality and to think carefully about how to be missional in a way that is consistent with being followers of Jesus Christ.

This essay will seek to describe the global and local factors that are in operation in the Melbourne context and to detail some of the diocesan response under the Archbishop's leadership. I will also seek to give, as a case study, an area of my own involvement, the theological education of those from refugee backgrounds, which is a part of the ministry of Ridley College.

---

1. A significant portion of this essay was originally contained in my paper, *Accidental learning: Issues in teaching theology to African refugees in Australia,* presented at the Harvest Bible College 2016 Research Conference, "Can Theology be Practical?" on August 25–26, 2016.

Global and Local Factors Contributing to Multiculturalism

The motto for the Anglican Diocese of Melbourne's articulated vision springs from Colossians 1:25: "Making the Word of God fully known." In his charge to the synod meeting in October 2016, Archbishop Freier went on to make this comment: "It has been good to sit with a biblical text—in this case Colossians 1:25—as a concerted point of reflection over the period of our Vision and Directions journey."[2] He went on to comment on the wider context of the verse in Colossians 1:24–29. This process evidenced the need for the diocesan vision to be firmly rooted within the Christian Scriptures so as to be aligned with the mission of God and the gospel of Christ.[3]

The need for the church to be "mission focused" has been a consistent theme for the Archbishop. In his synod charge, he defined mission in this way:

> When I . . . use the word "Mission" I mean doing the things that Jesus sent us as his disciples to do. We proclaim the coming reign of God by telling people about the saving works of Jesus and bringing others to the knowledge of Christ as Saviour and Lord.[4]

The *Vision and Directions 2017–2025* document articulates four strategic directions:

1. Be a compelling and outward-looking Christian presence in our communities
2. Reach across boundaries of human division to serve our communities and proclaim Christ
3. Be open to the Holy Spirit in transforming lives to be mature in Christ
4. Use all the energy that God powerfully inspires to better manage our human and capital resources.[5]

A specific strategy to come out of this, as a subset of the second strategic direction, is that "10 new multicultural congregations (either language

---

2. Philip Freier, *The President's Address, 2016*, 4. See also Anglican Diocese of Melbourne, *Vision and Directions*, 5.

3. I originally intended that this essay would also lay out the need for a biblical theology to undergird the multicultural focus for the mission of the Australian church and the diocese in particular. However, I could not do this within the constraints of the project.

4. Philip Freier, *The President's Address, 2016*, 4.

5. Anglican Diocese of Melbourne, *Our Journey: Vision and Directions*, 2.

or ethnic specific) are initiated by 2022."[6] This focus is an appropriate response to the arrival of significant numbers of refugee Christians in Australia during the period of the Archbishop's ministry in the Anglican Diocese of Melbourne. It must be noted, of course, that not all culture and language specific congregations are from refugee backgrounds. Others, such as the Chinese language congregation at St. Matthias North Richmond or the Māori congregations also significantly contribute to the multicultural landscape of the diocese.

Dr. Freier was installed as Archbishop of Melbourne on December 16, 2006. The previous year had seen the first wave of refugees from Southern Sudan arriving in Australia. This group had escaped the ravages of more than fifty years of civil war by fleeing to neighboring countries.[7] The 2006 Census recorded 19,050 Sudan-born people in Australia, an increase of almost 300 percent from the 2001 Census.[8] They arrived as humanitarian refugees, principally from Kenya, Uganda, and Egypt.[9]

At the same time, another community began to become a significant presence in several Anglican churches. Karen refugees arrived from camps on the Thai-Burma border. Many Karen had been forced to migrate after decades of war, with a 2004 estimate that 160,000 refugees from Myanmar, mostly Karen, were living in refugee camps on the Thai side of the border in 2004.[10] International Organisation for Migration statistics (2006–2009) detail over 6000 resettlements to Australia from these camps.[11] These figures include family reunion and national migration. In 2011, the Karen global diaspora population was estimated to be approximately 67,000.[12]

The number of refugees admitted to Australia reflects the record global refugee numbers. The UNHCR's annual *Global Trends* study reported that at the end of 2018 a record number (70.8 million people) had been displaced as a consequence of persecution, conflict, violence, or human rights violations. The previous year's report commented, "The past decade has seen substantial growth in the global population of forcibly displaced people. In

---

6. Anglican Diocese of Melbourne, *Our Journey Continues . . .* , 2.

7. The first and second Sudanese Civil Wars are reckoned to cover the period 1956–2005. (see BBC's South Sudan profile—Timeline http://www.bbc.com/news/world-africa-14019202).

8. Hatoss and Huijser, "Gendered Barriers," 152.

9. Some stories are told in Alan Nichols, *From Every Nation*.

10. See TBBC, *Programme Report*, 6.

11. TBBC, *Programme Report*, 9.

12. Thawnghmung, *"Other" Karen*, 84.

2007, this population numbered 42.7 million; over the last 10 years, this figure has increased by over 50 per cent."[13]

This trend continues. The Internal Displacement Monitoring Centre (IDMC) is the leading source of information and analysis on internal displacement worldwide.[14] Director Alexandra Bilak commented in the 2019 GRID, "The number of people living in internal displacement is now the highest it has ever been. Unresolved conflicts, new waves of violence and extreme weather events were responsible for most of the new displacement we saw in 2018."[15]

In the 2016 Higher Education report, Not There Yet: An Investigation into the Access and Participation of Students from Humanitarian Refugee Backgrounds in the Australian Higher Education System, the authors graphed the year of arrival in Australia of students from refugee backgrounds. The graph demonstrates the dramatic increase in arrivals, particularly in the years from 2004 to 2012.[16] This correlates with data from other sources, such as with the graph of the number of permanent settlers arriving in Australia from Sudan and South Sudan each month since 1991.[17] The 2011 Census recorded that the greatest number of those born in South Sudan were living in the state of Victoria.[18]

---

13. UNHCR, *Global Trends 2017*, 4.

14. The Internal Displacement Monitoring Centre (IDMC) is the leading source of information and analysis on internal displacement worldwide. Since 1998, our role has been recognized and endorsed by United Nations General Assembly resolutions. IDMC is part of the Norwegian Refugee Council (NRC), an independent, non-governmental humanitarian organization.

15. See http://www.internal-displacement.org/global-report/grid2019/. For more detail, consult *Global Report on Internal Displacement 2019*.

16. Data sourced from Terry and Naylor *Not There Yet*, 23–24. The authors comment, "In terms of arrival in Australia nearly 78 percent of students from refugee backgrounds reported that they entered Australia between 2006 to 2009."

17. Source: https://en.wikipedia.org/wiki/South_Sudanese_Australians. Accessed 29 July 2016.

18. Australian Government Department of Immigration and Citizenship, *Community Information Summary: South Sudan-born*, 1. The information in this summary is based on data sourced from the Australian Bureau of Statistics Census of Population and Housing.

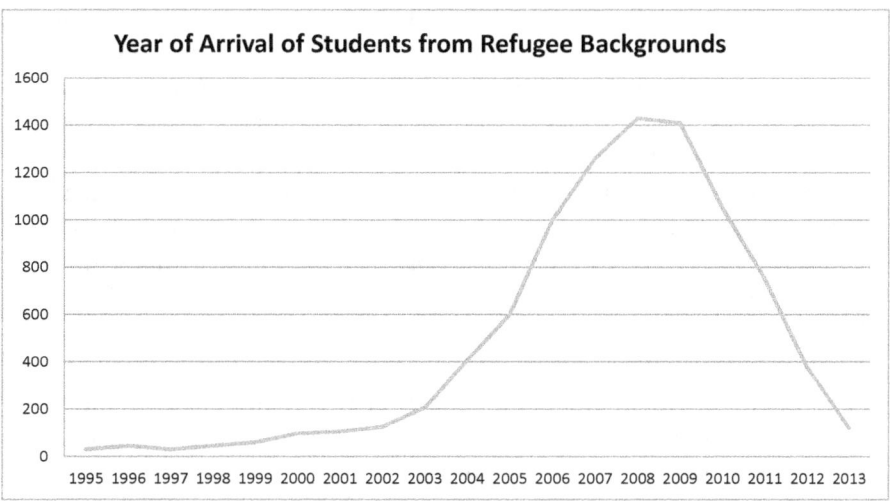

Year of Arrival of Students from Refugee Backgrounds

Increased refugee intake numbers have not always been received positively. Xenophobic political rhetoric has been decidedly unhelpful. Media reports of "African Crime Gangs" have a powerful negative impact on whole communities.[19] A former Archbishop of Melbourne, Dr. David Penman, once commented that "cultural pluralism is now a fact of Australian life, uneasily accepted by many who have forgotten their own migrant ancestry."[20]

Models used to help settle newly arrived residents have been slow to adapt. The process observed in the first decade of this millennium seemed to mirror that used to resettle post-war European migrants. Six months' language education was hardly sufficient from those learning English from European languages. It was nowhere near enough for those seeking to add English to their existing languages when their mother tongue was an African, Asian, or Middle Eastern language.

Teenage migrants from refugee camps often suffered from significant educational disadvantage. African students looked different and did not easily integrate, and many became disengaged. A communal social structure is a strong element of their worldview. The word "gang" became easily applied to gatherings of young people who felt a strong need for mutual support. Social problems soon emerged.

Many Southern Sudanese arrived, strongly identifying as Anglican Christians. They had come to faith in the context of a powerful movement of God's Spirit and the endeavors of committed evangelists in the south of

19. See, for example, Bernard Lane, "East African Crime in Melbourne," *The Australian*, November 19, 2018.
20. Penman, "Australia: A Multicultural Society?" 4.

Sudan. These preachers had ministered in the face of many tribulations and dangers. One influential evangelist was Bishop Nathaniel Garang Anyieth. Marc Nikkel summarizes his ministry: "For six years, from 1985, Bishop Nathaniel Garang has traversed the land on foot, like a threadbare prophet behind the battlelines, proclaiming the gospel."[21] The ministry of these evangelists was often accompanied by miraculous healing and deliverance from evil spirits. The victory of Jesus by his death and resurrection spoke powerfully to a people in the face of absolutely appalling atrocities. Those who turned to Jesus Christ often commented on their experience of God's help during those difficulties. They saw the power of God, and the church grew dramatically.[22]

In the emerging Episcopal Church of Sudan, there were, however, almost no trained church leaders. It is impossible to maintain a theological training program in a war context. In fact, a functioning school of any description was a rarity. Christians who could read and had a Bible and a prayer book were often judged as qualified for ordination and church leadership. Clergy and other leaders had little by way of resources.[23] Parts of the Bible (principally the New Testament), Christian songs and hymns, and Anglican prayer books were available in some languages.[24]

A strong oral culture also served the church well. Old Testament stories, for example, were faithfully taught and repeated. Song and dance played a big part in communicating the Christian message.[25]

Classical Anglican understanding sees theology as vitally inculcated through worship.[26] This is reflected in thoughtful Bible-based liturgies, the provision of homilies or sermons, and the use of credal confessions. Thus, the translated Anglican prayer book served these emerging churches well. The prayer book, hymns, and public reading of the Bible were the primary

---

21. Nikkel, "Look Back upon Us," 152.

22. Some would describe this as revival, but technically revival is a bringing back of spiritual vitality where this has been lost.

23. This was communicated by a number of Southern Sudanese clergy, such as Rev. Peter Ayor Alier Jongroor.

24. There is a great diversity of ethno-linguistic and tribal groups in Sudan. Those who were formally educated were taught in Sudanese Arabic, the national language during the period of the civil wars.

25. On a 2016 Ridley study tour to Israel, which I co-led, Dinka members of the tour would occasionally burst into song as we visited places mentioned in their songs.

26. Ashley Null argues that the introduction of English language homilies into Sunday services was the first great reform of Thomas Cranmer. These homilies are theological treatises and they are seen as an essential part of worship. See Null *Cranmer's Doctrine of Repentance*.

theological educational tools. No other resources or theological books were available.

In South Sudan, church gatherings were a whole-day activity. Many walked to church over long distances, and they would participate in every aspect of the gathering. Therefore fellowship, worship, and teaching were integrated.

When this community began to arrive in Australia, language and culture specific congregations soon came into existence. The leaders of these congregations desired to be equipped for church leadership and ministry. Anglican standards for licensing clergy likewise demanded some theological education. There was also great hunger to deepen their understanding of the Scriptures. So, the incentives to enter theological study were significant, but almost none could meet the standard entry requirements of any of the Australian College of Theology courses. Their educational background demanded a different methodology than that used in our usual college programs.

The Anglican Diocese of Melbourne identified a need for ministry training and needed to begin with the leaders who were presenting themselves. Waiting for new leaders to emerge who had a stronger educational base was not an option. Non-African Australians who had training in theology and ministry saw the task of learning language and culture as too difficult. There was a pressing need for the provision of ministry in this new community in their own languages. Southern Sudanese pastors and clergy were the only group who could minister to these churches.

Case Study: A New Learning Community

In 2005 and 2006, I found myself thrust into this new learning context. At the time I was working as the principal of a missionary training college.[27] This role involved preparing Church Missionary Society—Australia (CMSA) and other cross-cultural workers before they left for mission in a diversity of locations. Many who came to St. Andrew's Hall were expecting to serve as Bible teachers in Africa or Asia. My own cross-cultural mission experience had involved teaching theology and Bible in North Australia with Indigenous groups, in Hong Kong detention centers with Vietnamese refugees, and with Chinese students in an Anglican seminary after Hong Kong was returned to Chinese sovereignty.[28]

27. The Church Missionary Society Australia (CMS-A) training College, St. Andrew's Hall, Parkville. I held this position until late 2007.
28. SKH Ming Hua Theological College (香港聖公會明華神學院).

Archdeacon Graeme Sells and Melbourne Diocese cross-cultural ministry coordinator Dr. Irene Donohoue-Clyne requested that I become involved with training leaders from these African congregations. My background in missiology was of great assistance as I sought to develop an appropriate course that would address the needs of this group.

The Need for New Methods

An African proverb suggests that if you "close your eyes to facts, you will learn by accident." The assumptions of traditional Australian methodologies for theological education and ministry preparation are challenged by this new learning community. Some learning was definitely accidental as we came across various problems and issues and tried to address them. A major lesson for me was that traditional Australian methods did not best serve this group.

Traditional Africans are holistic thinkers.[29] Western education is generally analytical and compartmentalized. In Australian theological education, New Testament, Old Testament, historical theology, systematic theology, biblical theology, preaching, and ministry practice all command their own departments and course codes. Classes can become siloed from other subjects.

For African refugees, compartmentalized subjects did not make sense. The question arose, "How can Bible and theology be taught holistically?" Let me give an example. One teaching day, the class chose the topic of death and funerals. Motivation was already high, because the class had chosen the topic. They could see its relevance, so engagement was strong.

Our learning engaged a number of questions.

- What does the Bible teach about death and resurrection? About grieving and the Christian hope?
- How could we prepare a funeral, the service, and the sermon in such a way that the gospel is proclaimed and the people ministered to in their grief?
- What are the differences we can observe between African practice and Australian practice surrounding death and burial?
- Does the Bible and Christian thinking challenge any aspect of either culture?

---

29. For example, Njoroge states that "because of the nature of the gospel any curriculum must have a holistic character" ("Ecumenism and Theological Education in Africa," 90).

- How can we be equipped to pray for families and communities in times of grief?
- What else would be helpful for us to think further about on the topic of death and funerals?

One interesting issue we engaged was the custom of sending the bodies of those who die back to Africa for burial. This costly practice impoverished a community with limited financial resources but was seen as important because, as one ordained priest in the class observed, "those back in Sudan would find it hard to believe the person had died if they could not see the body." But we found the pastoral principle articulated would not operate in reverse, such that a relative who died in Africa would not have their body sent to reassure the Australian relatives. Did this practice owe more to traditional culture than to the need for others to see the body? Like the Indigenous peoples of Australia, there is a strong sense of connection to country, and it is seen as "right" for a person to be buried in their own traditional lands. Some biblical justification for this practice was quoted. Joseph and other patriarchs were buried in their ancestral lands (Genesis 25:9–11; 35:27–29; 50:24–26; Exodus 13:19; Hebrews 11:22).

During the session, one student asked: "What biblical justification do Australian Christians have for burning the bodies of their family members when they die?" This reference to cremation demonstrated awareness of their new Australian cultural context and a willingness to apply the Scriptures to exploring that culture. The question surprised me, but it also encouraged me as it indicated theological reflection on a cultural practice.

Our topic of death and funerals led to an exploration that strongly engaged in the Bible texts and was theological and practical. A holistic approach has proved very effective in engaging participants in studying the Bible and theology and seeing it applied in a ministry context. A holistic approach also opened my eyes to the importance of relevance and how theology can be applied. This is an issue for students from all backgrounds.

As Harris, Spark, and Watts observe, young people from refugee backgrounds "arrive in Australia with high aspirations for educational achievement."[30] Since 2013, our cohort of African students has been enrolled in an ACT Diploma of Ministry program. The course requires units in Old Testament introduction, New Testament introduction, Church History, Theology, plus Old and New Testament exegesis, Ministry and Practice, and elective units. This structure is more atomistic than holistic, but we sought,

---

30. Harris et al., "Gains and Losses," 371.

as much as possible, to make learning relevant and applied, while encouraging an increasing level of academic rigor.

One way we seek to integrate learning is by reflecting what we learn in a time of praise and worship. Our evenings begin with chapel, and the Bible reading and sermon are on a topic related to the theme of the class to follow. In class, we seek to have discussion about applications to life and ministry in mother tongue small groups.

The Issue of Language

This brings us to the issue of the language of instruction. In the context of global mission, a cross-cultural educator would be expected to learn and use the language(s) of the host culture. However, this can be complicated by the limited resources available in tribal and national languages and the dominance of global languages in higher education. Many postgraduate students in an African context desire an internationally-recognized Master or Doctoral degree. Often these qualifications are sought in a Western-based tertiary institution.[31] Also, many missionary theological educators struggle to acquire the language level required to engage in theology in a local language. This was my own experience in teaching New Testament to Chinese students in Hong Kong.

For the Southern Sudanese students, the language of their new Australian context was English, and therefore this would be the language of the next generation. This would also be the language of the future for the Southern Sudanese congregations. So, the only option that seemed viable was to use English in teaching Bible and theology.

The expectation of a high level of English competence would create a hurdle that denies training to leaders of these culture and language specific congregations. This would clearly be to the detriment of the church. It is a matter of justice that church leadership is not denied to these communities because of language barriers. The usual IELTS scores required for international students could not be assumed or easily achieved. These students are not international students; they have become Australian residents and citizens.

---

31. This is despite the known problems associated with people returning home to teaching roles after a Western degree. Their acquired theological language and frameworks do not easily relate back to their context of origin. Bediako Kwame was the African theologian who has articulated this issue most clearly. Andrew Walls describes Bediako's key themes as the "vernacular principle in Christianity, the significance of theological expression in the mother tongue, and the capacity of African languages to illuminate biblical concepts" (Walls, "Kwame Bediako," 188–93).

The challenge in teaching theology to this constituency is to engage in complex ideas while using a simple level of English. Simple, but not simplistic! As noted already, young people from refugee backgrounds have high hopes for educational achievement. However, significant appropriate support is required for such aspirations to be enabled. The mission of the church needs to be mindful of this need.

Teaching a group from a non-English speaking background (NESB) often encourages good teaching practice. For example, ideas frequently need to be stated more than once and in slightly different ways. Narrative is easier to understand than theory, so the use of stories in illustration is important. A lecturer is required to read his or her class to gauge comprehension. Questions and feedback are vital means of assessing student understanding. Over my time with this NESB group, some have improved greatly in English language competence, but not all.

Adapting Assessment Tools

A significant associated area where traditional teaching needed adaptation is that of assessment. Assessment is a challenge: many forms of assessment are also a measure of English linguistic competence. As Strauss suggests, those with a lesser standard of academic English "might well be heavily penalized by those evaluating their work."[32] This is unhelpful for this cohort, so we have sought to develop ways of evaluating learning that are not primarily filtered through a high level of written English competence.

Several of the assessment instruments used are oral in nature. For example, we adopted oral exams.[33] These are very similar to written exams, except the students give their answers verbally. These exams are conducted by two examiners to enable a less subjective grade.

Oral assessment tools have two distinct advantages. First, most ministry is oral. Preaching, responding to questions from church members, Bible studies, and pastoral care are all delivered orally. The assessment therefore fits the outcomes sought in training and equipping theological students for ministry. This is also true for non-Africans and so should be considered in framing assessments in our mainstream courses.

Second, oral exams give teachers instant feedback. It has become plainly evident to me that a topic has not been understood by most students when they are unable to give clear responses to an exam question.

---

32. Strauss, "Academic English," 321.
33. Examples are available for those who are interested and request them.

In most other ways, an oral exam achieves similar educational outcomes to a written exam.[34] The major exception to this is in the area of moderation. We complete an oral exam assessment form for each question, which can be reviewed by an external moderator.

Another oral mechanism is the use of classroom presentations. These give students practice in public presentation skills as well as forming a basis for evaluating engagement in the area of theological learning.

One of the gifts of African refugees to the Australian church is their passionate spirituality. Teaching that is not passionate will rarely connect with this community. The vital faith that sustained these Christian refugees through the fires of war and conflict and years in refugee "camps" is not abandoned on arrival in a new country. This has challenged me to reconnect with that aspect of my own Christian faith. Likewise, this community has enlivened the mission and ministry in a number of parishes.

This learning community has a strong belief in biblical authority. They are passionate in this belief. This works positively in teaching in Old and New Testament, but also most other subjects. There is a strong motivation to engage with the Scriptures. Students arrive with this motivation; the teacher only has to connect with it.

Multicultural Ministry and Diocesan Response

A comparable program to that which began with the Southern Sudanese was developed for the Karen ministry based at Werribee/Hopper's Crossing. However, a significant difference was that this group shared a common language and culture. This allowed an approach that involved the use of translators.

More recently, the Ridley College diploma class has included students from a variety of language and culture backgrounds. A developing community of Persian background believers in the diocese and, potentially, future and current leaders from the Arabic-speaking ministry are likely to be represented in this learning community.

Another helpful diocesan response to this newly arrived community has been the welcome that Anglican churches have given. One very noticeable example is the 2013 banner which continues to hang from St. Paul's cathedral. Its declaration, "Let's Fully Welcome Refugees," has proclaimed a significant counter-message to more negative voices. The Dean of St. Paul's, the Very Rev. Dr. Andreas Loewe, commented about this banner:

---

34. For example, students have to revise their course learning for both oral and written exams.

> Looking out for those who are less well off than we are stands at the heart of the Christian gospel. Jesus' command, 'what you have done to the least of these my brothers and sisters you have done to me' extends to displaced persons and refugees. This is why St. Paul's Cathedral and the Brotherhood of St. Laurence have joined in partnership to promote a full welcome to refugees. . . . St. Paul's Cathedral has partnered with the Brotherhood of St. Laurence in this awareness campaign because we already work with asylum seekers and refugees. We exercise a ministry of welcome to them through our successful English as a Second Language Program. Twice a week, recent arrivals to our shores meet at St. Paul's. Our program enables them not only to improve their understanding of Australia and English, but also provides a platform for them to share their stories of past hardship, and to give voice to their hope for a better future.[35]

Canon Robert Vun, in a presentation at the CMS Victoria summer conference in 2015 reported that in the year 2000 the Anglican Diocese of Melbourne had three official non-English congregations, though the number was more likely around six. In 2015 there were fourteen languages in thirty-four congregations, and culture and language specific ministries made up more than 20 percent of diocesan Sunday attendance.

Multicultural ministry had been a very important aspect of the leadership of Archbishop David Penman. Much of the foundational work which developed during Penman's leadership in Melbourne is found in the book, *A Garden of Many Colours: The Report of the Archbishop's Commission on Multicultural Ministry and Mission*, which was presented to the synod of the Anglican Diocese of Melbourne in 1985. However, much of the visionary agenda laid out in that document had not been developed more fully. Financial constraints have meant that priority is given to other aspects of ministry and areas of concern.

Concluding Remarks

From my own reckoning, during Archbishop Freier's time in Melbourne, almost fifty clergy from diverse cultural backgrounds have been ordained and licensed to ministry roles in the diocese. This number does not include those who have substantial ministry experience in another cultural context, such as the Rev. Canon Farag Hanna, who leads the thriving Arabic Anglican congregation at Holy Trinity Coburg, or the Rev. Peter Ayor Alier

---

35. See https://cathedral.org.au/2013/08/08/lets-fully-welcome-refugees/

Jongroor, who came to the diocese from Egypt to support Sudanese ministry and now leads the Casey Dinka congregation based in Melbourne's South East. Nor does it include those bicultural clergy who have completed a mainstream theological qualification and gone on to serve curacies and ministries in English-speaking parishes and placements. By any measure, this is a huge cohort of multicultural leadership that has been recognized and prayerfully appointed.

From a preliminary analysis, I estimate that there are more than thirty-five congregations in the Anglican Diocese of Melbourne that could be defined as culture and language specific, that is, congregations that primarily use a language other than English and/or operate for the gathering of a community for a specific ethnicity or culture.

However, this is far from the sum total of multicultural ministry. The Anglican agencies such as Anglicare and the Brotherhood of St. Laurence have substantial connections with those refugees who have come to Australia during the last decade. Schools and specific groups like the Asylum Seeker Centre founded and facilitated by David Spitteler, all make a substantial contribution. Many parishes have become a Christian family for the newly arrived and those who have recently become Christians.

Colleges like Ridley and Trinity need also to adapt their programs to the new reality of multicultural mission and ministry in the church. No-one can be properly equipped for ministry in twenty-first-century Australia without the expectation that they will find themselves ministering to a diverse community and to a church that consists of members from many different cultures and languages. This reality is in fact the ultimate direction of the age to come when, as depicted in the vision of Revelation 5, there will be a great celebration of the Lamb: "for you were slaughtered and by your blood you ransomed for God saints from every tribe and language and people and nation; you have made them to be a kingdom and priests serving our God, and they will reign on earth" (Rev 5:9–10).

If this is the calling and ultimate direction for God's people, then Archbishop Freier's missional call to his diocese rightly includes a mission which acknowledges those from other lands who have come to call Australia home. A ministry for the future must engage with the reality of a multicultural church and community.

> We will foster the growth of multicultural ministry by ensuring that cultural diversity is affirmed across the diocese, building resources and opportunities and equipping leaders for ministry.

Bibliography

Anglican Diocese of Melbourne. *Our Journey: Vision and Directions 2017-2025.* Melbourne: Anglican Diocese of Melbourne, 2016.

Anglican Diocese of Melbourne. *Our Journey Continues . . . : Vision and Directions 2017-2025.* Melbourne: Anglican Diocese of Melbourne, 2017.

Anglican Diocese of Melbourne. *A Garden of Many Colours: The Report of the Archbishop's Commission on Multicultural Ministry and Mission.* Melbourne: Diocesan Registry, 1985.

Freier, Philip. "Presidential Address." Delivered to the 52nd Synod of the Diocese of Melbourne, October 19, 2016. Melbourne: Anglican Diocese of Melbourne, 2016.

Harris, Anne, et al. "Gains and Losses: African Australian Women and Higher Education." *Journal of Sociology* 51/2 (2015) 370–84.

Hatoss, Aniko, and Henk Huijser. "Gendered Barriers to Educational Opportunities: Resettlement of Sudanese Refugees in Australia." *Gender and Education* 22/2 (2010) 147–60.

Njoroge, Nyambura J. "Ecumenism and Theological Education in Africa." In *Theological Education in Contemporary* Africa, edited by Grant LeMarquand and Joseph D. Galgalo, Eldoret, 83–104. Kenya: Zapf Chancery, 2004.

Nichols, Alan, ed. *From Every Nation: Stories of Faith and Culture Struggles by Melbourne Anglicans who have Been Refugees.* Melbourne: Anglican Diocese of Melbourne, 2012.

Nikkel, Marc R. "'Look Back upon Us': The Dynamism of Faith among the Jieng." In *"But God is Not Defeated!" Celebrating the Centenary of the Episcopal Church of the Sudan, 1899–1999,* edited by Samuel E. Kayanga and Andrew C. Wheeler, 149–58. Nairobi: Paulines Publications Africa, 1995.

Null, Ashley. *Thomas Cranmer's Doctrine of Repentance: Renewing the Power to Love.* Oxford: Oxford University Press, 2000.

Penman, David. "Australia: A Multicultural Society?" *International Review of Mission* 68 (1979) 4–11.

Strauss, Pat. "Academic English—Who Sets the Rules?" *Research and Development in Higher Education: Reshaping Higher Education* 34 (2011) 320–29.

Terry, L., et al. *Not There Yet: An Investigation into the Access and Participation of Students from Humanitarian Refugee Backgrounds in the Australian Higher Education System.* Melbourne: University of Melbourne, 2016.

Thai Burma Border Consortium (TBBC). *2010 Programme Report January to June 2010.* https://reliefweb.int/sites/reliefweb.int/files/resources/873E627E341A8BF7492577A6001CFDA1-Full_Report.pdf.

Thawnghmung, Ardeth Maung. *The "Other" Karen in Myanmar.* Lanham, MD: Lexington, 2011.

UNHCR report. *Global Trends: Forced Displacement in 2017.* Geneva: UNHCR, 2018.

Walls, Andrew F. "Kwame Bediako and Christian Scholarship in Africa." *International Bulletin of Missionary Research* 32/4 (2008) 188–193.

7

Towards an Australian Anglican Ecclesiology

Bradly S. Billings

Dr. Freier's tenure as Archbishop of Melbourne has been one of significant change in the way the church, and especially the parish, has been conceived, particularly in regard to the collective mission of the church. This has not been coincidental by any means, and can be seen clearly in the passage of Synod legislation over the course of Dr. Freier's leadership of the diocese, several items of which have gone to the heart of our understanding of the church as the vehicle of God's missiological activity in the world, both at a macro (diocesan) and micro (parish or communal) level.

When Dr. Freier was installed as Archbishop of Melbourne in December 2006, the prevailing diocesan culture viewed the parish as the primary vehicle both for organizing the ecclesiastical affairs of the church and delivering its ministry and missionary endeavor. In light of the long hegemony of the parish in Anglican polity, this is unsurprising. There were one, and possibly two, extant examples of what would today be known as an "Authorized Anglican Congregation" (AAC), although neither were ever actually authorized as such. Chaplains in both educational and other institutions regularly complained about being omitted from diocesan communiques, which spoke inevitably of parishes and their clergy. Examples of what we would now call "church planting" were evident, but somewhat rare, and even more rarely spoken about, let alone advocated or legislated for.

Since Dr. Freier commenced his tenure as Archbishop, all of that has changed significantly, even if the pace of the change has been either too slow, or too fast, for the comfort and liking of some. One need only look to the legislative initiatives introduced under Dr. Freier's tenure as President of the Synod, and assented to by him as Archbishop, to gain an insight into how our understanding of the church has been codified in "mission-shaped" legislation. These include:

- A thoroughgoing reorganization of parish governance in the provisions of the *Parish Governance Act 2013*, which has facilitated not just administrative functions but missional activity like ministry sharing and intra-parochial cooperative arrangements;
- The adaptation of what was the *Authorised Anglican Congregations Act 2004* into the *Parish Governance Act* in a form that made it fit for purpose in respect to church growth in the early twenty-first century, as evidenced by the immediate, and continuing, utilization of the legislation;
- The introduction of the conceptual framework of an "Anglican Ministry Presence," which has as its imperative the facilitation of new ministry initiatives of an experimental and entrepreneurial ("pioneering") nature.

Notwithstanding the more recent introduction of the "authorized congregation" and "ministry presence," the origins of the Anglican Church of Australia in the Church of England, bequeathed an essentially parochial system of church organization and governance, although the Church of England in Australia commenced, of course, in the form of a military chaplaincy. Even so, as Bruce Kaye notes, "it is indisputably the case" that the system inherited from the Church of England by the Australian church was overwhelmingly parochial in terms of its organization and local in character.[1] This is assumed in the *Parish Governance Act 2013*:

> The parish is the geographical unit for organizing the mission of God throughout the Anglican Church within the Diocese of Melbourne. The boundaries of each parish are those approved by the Archbishop in Council. The Anglican Church within the Diocese is constituted of clergy and lay people committed to building up the body of Christ under the leadership of the Archbishop (*Parish Governance Act 2013* s 5).

---

1. Kaye, *Church Without Walls*, 155.

Nonetheless, both the "Authorized Anglican Congregation" and the "Anglican Ministry Presence" are present in the same legislation, providing a legislative framework intended to assist the church in responding missionally to the rapid expansion of greater Melbourne and Geelong. The authorized congregation, although in most expressions lacking a church building, administratively functions as though it were a parish (in that most of the *Parish Governance Act* applies to it as though it were a parish). The "ministry presence" is intentionally relieved of an obligation to put in place the administrative architecture of a parish in its formative stages. This is so that its focus can be firmly on ministry and mission, with the resources at its disposal orientated all but exclusively to the praxis of ministry.

Although neither the authorized congregation or ministry presence are, in any tangible sense, parishes, both are overtly, and intentionally, Anglican. This raises the broader and somewhat fascinating question of how, and in what way, congregations, new church plants and pioneer ministries (all of which might be used to describe "authorized congregations" and "ministry presences" in the Diocese of Melbourne) are to be understood in respect to Anglican polity—and, perhaps more potently, what place they occupy in Anglican ecclesiology.

This goes to the heart of how we understand and speak of "the church." For Anglicans, many of whom have known only the parish system, such questions can present something of a challenge. The reality is, however, that the missional imperative for more flexible and agile ministry initiatives along the lines of the authorized congregation and the ministry presence will only grow in the Diocese of Melbourne (and across the Anglican world) into the future. We can expect to see more such initiatives with a range of purposes, be it to reach a specific subculture, language or ethnic-specific group, or discrete geographical area, or whether the motivation is simply a ministry unencumbered by physical buildings and infrastructure or a desire to "try something new" in a locality where there is not currently any tangible Anglican presence.

There are ways in which none of this is new; much of it represents a journey "back to the future" in that all existing parishes had a beginning at some point in time, and many began life in a community hall, with a greenfield site, or in a cleric's living room. Additionally, there have always been expressions of Anglicanism other than the model of "church building plus priest serving a defined locality." And there have always been Anglican ministries to schools and other educational institutions, agencies, and organizations, to branches of the military, police, and emergency services, and to workplaces and just about any social entity one can think of—just as there are Anglican religious orders, missionary agencies, and multiple parachurch organizations, none of which are parishes.

All of this, together with the manner in which the Diocese of Melbourne has sought to respond institutionally to the missional imperatives it has faced under Dr. Freier's leadership, indicates that a new, robust, and possibly reinvigorated understanding of Anglican ecclesiology is vital. For if we can locate ourselves in the infrastructure of Anglicanism—whether a parish priest, school chaplain, the leader of a house church, a pastor to a migrant community bound by a common language and culture, or other—then our mission and our ministry can only be enhanced by a common cause and collegiality, and the legislative facilities in place will be increasingly looked upon as both legitimate and life-giving by all Anglicans, whether directly affected or involved or not.

To achieve this, we will need to examine what it means both to be "church" and Anglican in the context of twenty-first-century Australia. The goal will be to reach an understanding of the essential qualities, values, and characteristics of Anglican ecclesiology, and of the things that make and define us as Anglicans and as the Anglican Church.

In short, the quest on which we now embark is one of boundaries. If our own legislation in the Diocese of Melbourne has tested and stretched our previously settled understanding of what the Anglican Church is by expanding the possibilities of authorized ministry beyond the traditionally received categories of parish and chaplaincy, then it will be necessary and valuable to establish just where the boundaries are and what the limits of Anglicanism, in terms of its ecclesiology, may be. It is to that task we turn.

Biblical and Theological Considerations

The term used most frequently in the New Testament to describe what we today call "the church" is *ekklesia*, meaning (succinctly) "the called-out ones." The *ekklesia* is comprised of those called out of "the world" by profession of faith in Jesus Christ. Frequently, the *ekklesia* is defined geographically—for example, the *ekklesia* in Corinth, the *ekklesias* in Galatia, and so on. As a term, and like most words, *ekklesia* is in itself incapable of capturing the fullness of the theological meaning of the church as it emerges in the Scriptures. A variety of additional metaphorical imagery—examples of which are the Body of Christ, the Temple of God, the Bride of Christ—are employed throughout the New Testament to express what it means to be the "called out" and "assembled" as the people of God.

Sometimes in the New Testament, the imagery associated with the church is universal—of all Christian people expressing allegiance to Christ—and sometimes it is localized. The English word church (like its Greek antecedent) is capable of being used in both senses. From the very beginning, the followers of Christ met to "break bread" and to experience Christ as in some way present with them (Acts 2:43–47). This central act is called by St. Paul (1 Cor 10:16) "communion" (*koinonia*). Communion may describe both the fellowship of Christian people vertically, with Christ, and horizontally, with each other. *Koinonia* is capable, then, of giving expression to the fullness of the Christian understanding of the church, in terms of both its essence and praxis. For this reason, the term "community" is used of the *ekklesia* by Karl Barth through the course of his volume on ecclesiology in the *Church Dogmatics* (Vol. IV, Part 3.2): "From the very outset Jesus Christ did not envisage individual followers, disciples and witnesses but a plurality of such united by Him both with Himself and with one another . . . He places them in His community . . . the communion of saints."[2]

Robert Warren, drawing on (then Archbishop of Canterbury) Rowan Williams's succinct definition that "church is what happens when the impact of Christ on a situation brings two or more people together," takes us away from the traditional model of "Church = Building + Priest + Sunday Services" by positing a communion-centered definition: "Church is essentially a community of people drawn together by faith in and encounter with Jesus Christ as Lord, which leads them to take action in the whole of life, living by a different set of values from what would otherwise have been the case."[3]

There is nothing explicit in the New Testament to suggest that the Christian community called into existence by Jesus Christ was commenced with the threefold order of bishops, priests, and deacons, nor with a system of geographical organization (although the communities in which the church had its locus were geographically defined entities). As Kevin Giles points out, "This means that the church is not defined by its ministerial structures; it is defined by its communal existence given by God in Christ, and by the presence of the Spirit who provides the leaders needed."[4]

From the beginning, in the apostolic age and in the pages of the New Testament itself (especially the Pastoral Epistles), there is, however, evidence of internal organization, together with a process of institutionalization, that crystallizes in the geographically defined structure of communities gathered

---

2. Barth, *Church Dogmatics*, 681–82. This is consistent with the practical exposition, by Dietrich Bonhoeffer, of the church as being lived together, in community: see Bonhoeffer, *Life Together*.

3. Warren, *Healthy Churches Handbook*, 83, 85.

4. Giles, *What on Earth is the Church?* 187.

around a local *episkopos* (bishop). This is already present by the time of Ignatius (early second century AD):

> See that you all follow the bishop, even as Jesus Christ does the Father, and the presbytery as you would the apostles; and reverence the deacons, as being the institution of God. Let no man do anything connected with the Church without the bishop. Let that be deemed a proper Eucharist, which is administered either by the bishop, or by one to whom he has entrusted it. Wherever the bishop shall appear, there let the multitude of the people also be; even as wherever Jesus Christ is, there is the Catholic Church.[5]

Thus, the tradition, very early in the apostolic age, bequeaths the structural concept of the church as a community gathered around its *episkopos*. The somewhat bold claim of the Ordinal accompanying the *Book of Common Prayer* is, "It is evident unto all men diligently reading holy Scripture and ancient Authors, that from the Apostles' time there have been these Orders of Ministers in Christ's Church; Bishops, Priests, and Deacons."[6]

The Scriptures further speak in much broader terms of the church as being comprised not only of all of the baptized in a particular locality but of all the baptized everywhere, transcending even time and space, and crossing even that barrier between life and death. Anglican ecclesiology gives expression to this by recognizing that the church is manifest on multiple levels—that there is, at the same time, a church transcending earth itself, a universal (or catholic) church consisting of all the baptized on earth; that there are within this also national and denominational churches, of which the Anglican Church is itself one; and that within the Anglican Church of Australia there are distinct geographical units, the diocese and the parish. When the parish is referred to, it is the geographical area that is meant, not the worshiping congregation or congregations therein.

Further, as the fundamental declarations of the Constitution of the Anglican Church of Australia make clear in their provisions, for Australian Anglicans it is the diocese, not the parish, that is the primary organizing principle in Anglican polity.

> When they are thinking ecclesiologically, Anglicans do not think of the gathered congregation as the fundamental unit of the Church, but of the diocese as the local church, comprising all the parishes within which the clergy exercise a ministry of

---

5. Ignatius, *Letter to the Smyrnaeans*, 8.
6. Preface to the Ordinal, *Book of Common Prayer*.

word, sacrament and pastoral care that is commissioned and overseen by the bishop.[7]

The structure of parochial organization within the unit of the diocese, together with the necessity of episcopal leadership and oversight, has direct relevance to mission. Paul Avis explains: "The Church's mission is to all. Anglicanism can never be a sect. The Church of England is a territorial church and embraces all within its parishes who do not refuse its ministry. Its ethos is essentially inclusive, not exclusive." [8] Richard Giles agrees: "Under the direction of its parish priest, every parish church has an apostolic commission to share the good news of Jesus Christ with the people God has put in their patch. This is a great privilege."[9]

The calling, and gathering, of individual believers into community has, then, both a pastoral and a missional purpose: "The Christian community exists as called into existence and maintained in existence by Jesus Christ as the people of His witness, bound, engaged and committed to Him . . . Called out of the world, the community is genuinely called into it."[10] What's more, "To be a parish church, a church must find a community and locate itself within it, incarnating the life of God there in ways that are both local and catholic."[11]

This manner of ecclesiological organization, in which the geographical entity of the diocese consists primarily of a patchwork of parishes, might be summarized as the "traditional" Anglican understanding of the church. And with good reason. It has served the church well over many centuries and continues to be the fundamental way the Anglican Church of Australia is organized both administratively and operationally to the present today, as evidenced both in the Constitution of the Anglican Church of Australia and in Diocese of Melbourne's *Parish Governance Act 2013* section 5, and in multiple other ways.

There is, however, more to be said ecclesiologically, as indicated by the definitions proposed by Dr. Rowan Williams and others above, and by the language of Article XIX, *Of the Church*, which declares that the Church of Christ exists wherever "the pure Word of God is preached, and the Sacraments duly administered."

---

7. Avis, *Anglican Understanding of the Church*, 84.
8. Avis, *Anglican Understanding of the Church*, 45.
9. Giles, *How to Be an Anglican*, 48.
10. Barth, *Church Dogmatics*, 752, 764.
11. Percy, "Many Rooms in my Father's House," 14.

Fresh Expressions and the "Mixed Economy"

Looking back over its long history, the Church of England, via the compilers of its "Mission-Shaped Church" report, understand the development of the parish system to be the appropriate historical response to the situation of the ancient and medieval church.

> The missionary advance of Christianity has always involved the crossing of cultures and developing skills of translation . . . A church which has grasped this principle actively seeks ways to embody the gospel in ways of life, service and worship which are locally appropriate. Their primary concern is to embody Jesus (to be the body of Christ) within the local culture or cultures. [12]

Recognizing that the existing structures were now insufficient to meet the missional priorities of the early twenty-first century, the Church of England (in England), under the leadership of then Archbishop of Canterbury Rowan Williams, introduced the notion of the "mixed economy" church: "It was a view echoed by the Australian General Synod in 2004 (see Resolution 67/04). The mixed economy is essentially a church comprised of any number of forms or expressions."[13]

In the same year, the Diocese of Melbourne adopted the *Authorised Anglican Congregations Act 2004*. The Act, in section 4(1), required that an authorized congregation not be synonymous with the congregation of an existing parish, be led by a licensed priest, and "worship as an Anglican congregation."[14]

The advent of "fresh expressions" of church, though vital and important, does not, however, announce the end of the traditional parish system of church organization. Archdeacon Bob Jackson, in his influential *Hope for the Church*, argues for a "both/and" approach, which seeks to combine the best of both the "parochial" and the "gathered" church models.

> For centuries, Christians have argued about whether the church should be a gathered community of faith or an organism with no real membership boundaries committed to the care of all . . . However, perhaps this debate has now run its full course and needs to be laid to rest. What has happened, as much by default as design, is that each side has recognized the strength of the practice and argument of the other and has adjusted its own

---

12. Cray, "Focusing Church Life," 66.

13. Nichols, *Building the Mission-Shaped Church*, 2.

14. The *2004 Authorised Congregations Act* was subsequently repealed, and its provisions inserted into the *Parish Governance Act 2013*.

> practice accordingly. Today there are few "gathered" churches that do not have a clear sense of calling to be involved in and to serve the communities around the church. Equally, even Anglican churches with a strong sense of their civic role have a sense of coming together to be nourished in the faith as a loving community of believers . . . An exclusive emphasis on either "gathered" or "parish" is seen as odd or unhealthy.[15]

In publications as diverse as Bob Jackson's *Hope for the Church* and his subsequent *The Road to Growth*, the Australian General Synod's *Building the Mission-Shaped Church in Australia*, and the Church of England's *Mission-Shaped Parish: Traditional Church in a Changing Context*, the traditional entities of the parish, the diocese, the minster, and the cathedral are each recognized as valued instruments of the mission of the church, alongside the need for ongoing transformation by the Spirit.

> The parish system of England, which was in place at the birth of the Anglican movement, was a mission response to the cultures of its day. And in holding fast to the parish system as part of its life, the Church of England has built on a mission foundation. Commitment to the parish system is commitment to mission; there is no theological room in it for the idea that the Church is just there to chaplain its own . . . There is no doubt that as a mission narrative the parish system has served the Church of England well. We build on it still, and we should.[16]

Thus, while "fresh expressions" of church at one level might appear to threaten the very existence of the parish church, at another level it may in fact be the savior of the parish, by complementing the practice of parochial ministry with an emphasis on mission, and by establishing new, extra-parochial faith communities, supplementary to that of the parish, to assist with the shared mission as a vital act of the transformative Spirit of God. From this standpoint, a dual focus or "mixed economy" of church is required for the future, at parish, diocesan, and national levels.

> In this picture of the contemporary Church it is an aeroplane struggling to stay aloft with only one wing, spiraling downwards and widely expected to crash out of control. The one wing it has is the traditional, inherited model of church—a proper liturgy in a proper building with proper clergy at the proper time on the proper day. The wing it is lacking is the "fresh expressions" wing of new styles and concepts of church suited to the variety

15. Jackson, *Hope for the Church*, 58.
16. Hayes et al., *Mission-Shaped Parish*, 17.

of people and life-styles in the postmodern world. The task today is to construct the other wing in mid flight before the plane crashes.[17]

Accepting that this imagery is a helpful and accurate measure, then the Diocese of Melbourne, under the leadership of Dr. Freier, is well on the way to performing this feat, both administratively, as evidenced by the passage of the legislation already referred to, and operationally, as the burgeoning examples of new congregations and fresh expressions of church that have been facilitated by it bear testimony.

The theological reality is expressed well by Ian Mosby, who notes that the different ecclesiological approaches—fresh expressions or traditional parish—often result from the place one begins: with the context of our shared mission in and to the world, or with the people of God and the organized church.[18] The dichotomy is, however, a false one. It was false at the time of the early church and in the early Middle Ages, when the "minister model" was widely utilized, and it is false in today's "mixed economy" church. Thus, it is important to examine just what the recognition—and dismissal—of this false dichotomy might mean for Anglican ecclesiology.

Towards an Australian Anglican Ecclesiology

As Tom Frame states at the beginning of his *Anglicans in Australia*:

> The Anglican Church of Australia is not a newly created or fashioned stand-alone religious entity. It is descended directly from the Church of England, which has claimed historical continuity with the teaching and mission of Jesus Christ and the undivided Christian Church of apostolic antiquity. Understanding "Australian Anglicanism" is impossible without some knowledge of the conflicts and challenges that gave the Church of England its organizational architecture and corporate ethos, two things that have given outward form and inner substance to the Anglican Church of Australia.[19]

The Anglican church arrived in Australia initially in the form of a military chaplaincy with the first penal settlement. It did not take long, of course, for the instruments of the "established church" to be rapidly transplanted from England, and for the parish system to be replicated in Australia. As the

17. Jackson, *Road to Growth*, 78.
18. Mosby, "Afterword," 170.
19. Frame, *Anglicans in Australia*, 23.

colonies expanded and grew, so too did the Anglican presence. Nonetheless, the Church of England in Australia was never established by law in the same way as in the United Kingdom; and as Stephen Pickard further notes, the Anglican Church of Australia has always struggled to develop an ecclesial outlook consistent with the antipodean context ever since the establishment model of the English Church was transplanted into "a tough colonial world."[20]

Similarly, Bruce Kaye claims that, having adopted the parochial system uncritically from its English origins, "the question of the development of an appropriate model for ecclesiology in a plural and non-ecclesiastic society such as Australia has been a continuing theme in the history of the Anglican Church of Australia."[21] In his influential *A Church Without Walls*, Kaye argues strongly for a "church in society" or "incarnational" ecclesial model. While acknowledging that we tend to act locally and think missiologically in terms of the parish, Kaye does not, however, equate the incarnational model necessarily with the parochial structure, but argues for something more fluid than this.[22] Although writing before its advent was being fully realized, he seems to point inexorably in the direction of fresh expressions and the mixed economy of church.

Three Essential Features of Anglican Ecclesiology

As we have noted, the inheritance of the Anglican Church of Australia is that of a parochial system embedded in a local community and exercising an "incarnational model of ministry."[23] The parish has, however, always been complemented, both in England and in Australia, by other equally valid models and forms of ministry. These include a range of chaplaincies, social agencies, monastic communities, and (in more recent years) multicultural communities and fresh expressions of church, some embedded in existing parishes and some not.

As we have seen, since 2004 the Diocese of Melbourne has legislated for "authorized congregations" that are not parishes in a geographical sense, but retain through legislation the rights and obligations of parishes; more recently, it has enabled pioneer ministries in areas of strategic growth and importance that require very little administrative infrastructure. Thus, there is in the Diocese of Melbourne (and across Australia in general) already a

20. Pickard, "Many Verandahs, Same House?" 196.
21. *A Church Without Walls*, p. 65.
22. Kaye, *Church Without Walls*, 198–220.
23. Kaye, *Church Without Walls*, 198–220.

somewhat well-established "mixed economy" of church. This mixed economy must be understood with reference to the Constitution of the Anglican Church of Australia.

Although there is a sense in which the missional strategy of the Diocese of Melbourne in respect to the mixed economy of church and the emergent fresh expressions therein is simply to get out of the way and let them happen, this does not mean that anything goes, or that anything carrying the label "mission" goes! This is evidenced by the very fact that there is a legislative framework imposing conditions and limitations, and by the use of the word "authorized," and in multiple other ways. As with the parish, chaplaincy, and any other established expression of Anglicanism, a ministry carrying the authorization of the Anglican Church and its episcopal oversight must be, in fact, Anglican.

To this end, the "Fundamental Declarations" of the Constitution (sections 1–3) identify the Anglican Church of Australia as part of the "One Holy Catholic and Apostolic Church of Christ" and affirm the threefold order of bishops, priests, and deacons. The "Ruling Principles" (section 4) further state that:

> This Church, being derived from the Church of England, retains and approves the doctrine and principles of the Church of England embodied in the *Book of Common Prayer* together with the Form and Manner of Making Ordaining and Consecrating of Bishops, Priests and Deacons and in the Articles of Religion sometimes called the Thirty-Nine Articles.

Reading the doctrine and formularies of the church in conjunction with the theological import of the New Testament, together with the received tradition as mediated through the Church of England, it is possible to distill therein three essential characteristics of Anglican ecclesiology, each of which were reflected in the 2004 Authorized Congregations Act, which required an authorized congregation to (i) be a distinct ecclesial community, (ii) be led by a licensed priest, and (iii) conduct its rites of public worship in the Anglican liturgical tradition.

The three essential features of Anglican ecclesiology, are then:

(i) Community (Koinonia)

Both Article XIX (*Of the Church*) and the Ordinal (*The Making of Priests*) speak of the church as being "a congregation" of the faithful, but there is nothing, of course, to determine whether that congregation may be contained within a predefined geographical area, a school, a hospital or nursing home, the armed forces, a monastic order, a fresh expression of church meeting in a local pub, or any other place where people may form Christian community.

In the New Testament, the church is to be found where the people of God come together in corporate expression of their fellowship or communion (*koinonia*) in Christ. The basis of Anglican ecclesiology is, thereby, the same as that of the New Testament. It is found in, and experienced in, community. Well might the poet and Anglican convert, T. S. Eliot, have written in *The Rock*, 1936:

> What life have you, if you have not life together? There is no life that is not in community. And no community not lived in praise of God.

(ii) *Authorized Leadership*

This community is not any community of Christian people, but one in which there is a duly "set apart" (ordained) and authorized (licensed) leadership. The bishop's charge to the newly ordained priest in the Ordinal is, "Take thou Authority to preach the Word of God, and to minister the holy Sacraments in the Congregation, where thou shalt be lawfully appointed thereunto."

Anglican community is thereby further defined by the presence of a "lawfully appointed" (licensed) minister (of one of the three orders of ordained ministry, or an authorized lay person).[24] This minister is to have the "cure of souls" and exercise a leadership in that community that is at the same time in partnership with and accountable to the responsible bishop, who alone makes the "lawful" appointment.

(iii) *Common Prayer*

Anglican community requires an authorized and lawfully appointed leadership for it is a community in which "the pure Word of God is preached and the Sacraments duly administered" (Article XIX). The ministry of Word and Sacrament is, furthermore, not conducted according to any rite and pattern, but a prescribed form—that of the *Book of Common Prayer*,

---

24. In his chapter on "Generous Episcopacy," Stephen Conway is "careful" to leave open the possibility that authorized leadership in a community may be provided by a lay person. Conway, "Generous Episcopacy," 25.

or another lawfully authorized form, and none other (so the Constitution, section 4). This is expressed most potently by the form and manner for the making of oaths and declarations, undertaken by all clergy in the Diocese of Melbourne (in accordance with the *Oaths Affirmations Declarations and Assents Canon 1992*) at the point of ordination and licensing to a new office or role, whereby the cleric to be licensed declares: "In public prayer and administration of the sacraments I will use the form prescribed in the *Book of Common Prayer, A Prayer Book for Australia* or another lawfully authorized form and none other." This preserves, insofar as is possible, the now greatly fragmented concept of "Common Prayer" together with the Anglican doctrinal touchstone *lex orandi est lex credendi* (which approximates to "the law of what is to be prayed is the law of what is to be believed").[25]

In light of these three essentials, the fundamental elements of an Anglican ecclesiology become clearer. The Anglican Church is a Christian community, an expression of the universal church of Jesus Christ, particularized and given its Anglican identity by the presence of a leadership authorized by, and exercised in partnership with, the responsible bishop, in which there is exercised a ministry of Word and Sacrament that is conducted according to a lawfully authorized form of liturgy, whether the *Book of Common Prayer* or other duly authorized form, and none other.

Summary and Conclusion

As we have seen, the Anglican Church of Australia has always arranged itself geographically into diocese and parish and inherited from the Church of England the instruments of parochial governance, ministry, and incarnational mission. The traditional model of the diocese comprised of parishes is the most ubiquitous and instantly recognizable expression of Anglican ecclesiology. But it is not the only one.

Anglican ecclesiology has in the past, does now, and can into the future bear many other ways of forming and nurturing Christian community, be they monastic congregations, fresh expressions, educational institutions, and so on. The historicity of the parochial system, its long and deep roots in the tradition inherited through the Church of England, together with the manner in which the present-day church assumes this structure, warrant the architecture of the diocese comprised of parishes being considered the foundational unit of Anglican ecclesiological organization, upon which other fresh expressions of Anglican ecclesiology arise and are built.

---

25. Burnham, *Heaven and Earth in Little Space*, 2.

It is not the case, however, that the parish is the primary organizational unit in the Anglican Church of Australia, for in the constitution of the church, this vests in the diocese. And the diocese is comprised of much more than parishes, typically including a multitude of ministries to communities other than parishes in a variety of ways.

Several possibilities for an ecclesiological model emerge. The Anglican Church in Australia may be described as a community conceived and comprised of:

1. All those living in a geographical area who do not refuse Anglican ministry (the parish model), or
2. The sum total of those who gather in an institution or organization (the chaplaincy model), or
3. The congregation that gathers and meets in a certain place (the fresh expressions or gathered model).

This is not, however, just any community, but one in which:

1. There is present a leader duly authorized by the responsible bishop, and
2. The pure Word of God is preached and the Sacraments duly administered, and
3. The liturgy of the church being at that time authorized is used.

Such an understanding of Anglican ecclesiology validates a "mixed economy" church. This is one in which there may well be (and indeed in the Diocese of Melbourne already are) within the geographical area of a single parish a "traditional" parish with its church building and vicar, a school community served by a chaplain, a congregation meeting in a community center hall whose stated mission is "to reach young professionals," and a group comprised of recent arrivals worshiping in a primary school hall in a language other than English. To expand on the image a bit, just down the road there is a new housing estate rising on land that was until recently used for the agistment of horses, that is technically still within the geographical area of the same parish, and in which an enterprising young cleric has obtained the requisite permission and some funding to try and establish a new Anglican ministry, initially in the front room of the family home.

All of the ministries in this example are properly, and rightly, "Anglican" in their ecclesiology, and all are seeking to serve God and his church in their own way and as a part of the one Anglican family. All are now administratively possible in the Diocese of Melbourne—and indeed already evident, with some well-established. That a commixture of expressions of Anglicanism has become evident and received legislative legitimacy is no small achievement in the context of a hierarchical ecclesial structure with a long tradition firmly rooted in the parish model.[26]

On several occasions in the Synod, Dr. Freier has cited the proverb "the rising tide lifts many boats" in relation to our shared mission as Anglican Christians. In doing so he has pointed to the truth inherent in the "mixed economy" understanding of the church, that the rapid fragmentation and continued growth of our social context demands from us a flexible and diverse response, in which the best efforts of others are not to be seen as threats, or as intrusions and incursions into "my patch," or derided as somehow being less than authentically Anglican in their difference; but are to be welcomed as efforts from fellow laborers for the gospel in fields where, as our Lord has said, the harvest is indeed very plentiful, but the laborers few (Luke 10.2).

There are many indicators that the tide is indeed rising, as new congregations reaching new groups of people are declared and fledgling pioneer ministries planned and planted in new population centers throughout the diocese. The fullness of Dr. Freier's legacy in facilitating this, through the legislative functions of the church, his own episcopal leadership, and most of all, his direct support and encouragement, will not be fully known and realized for at least a generation. Yet the seeds of growth are evident. Together we pray that God will give the increase.

---

26. Doug Gay, in his exploration of the ecclesiology of the "emerging church," notes the nimbleness of Anglican churches around the world in responding to the missional situation in creative ways within the confines of their own polity. Gay, *Remixing the Church*, 99–102.

Bibliography

Avis, Paul. *The Anglican Understanding of the Church*. 2nd ed. London: SPCK, 2013.
Barth, Karl. *Church Dogmatics*. Vol. IV. Edited by G. W. Bromiley and T. F. Torrance. Edinburgh: T. & T. Clark, 1961.
Bonhoeffer, Dietrich. *Life Together*. London: SCM, 1954.
Burnham, Andrew. *Heaven and Earth in Little Space: The Re-Enchantment of Liturgy*. Norwich: Canterbury Press, 2010.
Conway, Stephen. "Generous Episcopacy." In *Generous Ecclesiology: Church, World and the Kingdom of God*, edited by Julie Gittoes, Brutus Green, and James Heard, 16–33. London: SCM, 2013.
Cray, Graham. "Focusing Church Life on a Theology of Mission." In *The Future of the Parish System: Shaping the Church of England for the Twenty-First Century*, edited by Stephen Croft, 61–74. London. Church House, 2006.
Frame, Tom. *Anglicans in Australia*. Sydney: University of New South Wales Press, 2007.
Gay, Doug. *Remixing the Church: Toward an Emerging Ecclesiology*. London: SCM, 2011.
Giles, Kevin. *What on Earth is the Church? An Exploration in New Testament Theology*. Melbourne: Dove, 1995.
Giles, Richard. *How to Be an Anglican*. Norwich: Canterbury, 2003.
Hayes, Paul, and Tim Sledge, with John Holbrook, Mark Rylands, and Martin Seeley. *Mission-Shaped Parish: Traditional Church in a Changing Context*. London: Church House, 2009.
Ignatius, "Letter to the Smyrnaeans." *Early Christian Writings*. London: Penguin, 1987.
Jackson, Bob. *Hope for the Church: Contemporary Strategies for Growth*. London: Church House, 2002.
———. *The Road to Growth: Towards a Thriving Church*. London: Church House, 2005.
Kaye, Bruce. *A Church Without Walls: Being Anglican in Australia*. Melbourne: Dove, 1995.
Mosby, Ian. "Afterword: The World and the Church." In *Generous Ecclesiology: Church, World and the Kingdom of God*, edited by Julie Gittoes, Brutus Green, and James Heard, 170–4. London: SCM, 2013.
Nichols, Alan, ed. *Building the Mission-Shaped Church in Australia*. Sydney: General Synod Office, Anglican Church of Australia, 2006.
Percy, Martyn. "Many Rooms in My Father's House: The Changing Identity of the English Parish Church." In *The Future of the Parish System: Shaping the Church of England for the Twenty-First Century*, edited by Stephen Croft, 3–15. London: Church House, 2006.
Pickard, Stephen. "Many Verandahs, Same House? Ecclesiological Challenges for Australian Anglicanism." *Journal of Anglican Studies* 4 (2006) 177–200.
Warren, Robert. *The Healthy Churches Handbook*. London: Church House, 2005.

Indigenous Australians

8

Archbishop Philip Freier and Aboriginal Ministry in the Northern Territory

Joy Sandefur

PHILIP FREIER, ARCHBISHOP OF Melbourne and Primate of the Anglican Church of Australia, brings a range of extraordinary and unusual life experiences to his role. Combined with a personal nature that is humble and adventurous, this makes for an interesting story.

When it was announced that Bishop Freier would become the next Anglican Archbishop of Melbourne, Mr. Chris Natt, member of the Northern Territory parliament, summed up Bishop Freier's time in the Territory in the following words.

> The appointment is recognition of the work done by Bishop Philip Freier and his seven years in the Northern Territory. He will be remembered for a number of things. However, I would just like to highlight a few. His restructuring of Anglicare in the Territory is very significant. It had fallen on tough times and he really made a restructuring difference in Anglicare. He has worked very closely over his seven years with Aboriginal people right around the Territory. He was very much involved in trying to obtain justice for the Stolen Generation. He has overseen the ordination of a significant number of Aboriginal Territorians to the priesthood, both men and women. He has been closely associated with Nungalinya College, which is the theological

college for the training of Aboriginal Christian ministers, as well as his broad commitment to the ordination of women. Six or seven years ago, he was the driving force behind the Council of Churches' opposition to the Territory's mandatory sentencing laws. He was a very loud spokesman on that. He was also the chair of Kormilda College for many years and had a particular interest in Kormilda's Aboriginal students.[1]

Mr. Natt's words of commendation reveal something of the breadth of what Bishop Freier accomplished in the Northern Territory. He worked for the good of all whether in the church or outside the church.

This essay explores and celebrates Bishop Freier's contributions to Aboriginal[2] ministry in the Northern Territory. While Bishop Freier did much to build up the whole diocese, this essay is concerned with his work with the Indigenous churches in Arnhem Land and his desire for them to mature and fully take up their role in the diocese along with the other churches. I start with a discussion of Bishop Freier's experience in and capacity for work among Indigenous communities before examining his support of Aboriginal culture, church, and mission in the Northern Territory.

Formation and Experience within Aboriginal Churches

When Philip Freier became bishop of the Northern Territory in 1999, he arrived from Queensland with experience of the two main types of Anglican church in the Northern Territory: the churches in the towns such as Darwin and Alice Springs and the churches that had emerged from the work of the Church Missionary Society in Arnhem Land. These churches had very different histories but together made up the Diocese of the Northern Territory.

In Queensland, Bishop Freier had worked both with Aboriginal churches that had grown from the work of the Anglican Board of Mission and also with churches that were located in the major towns of the area. After ordination, he was priest in charge of the Anglican church at Kowanyama, an Indigenous community on Cape York Peninsula, and rector at Bundaberg and Banyo. He also lived and worked as a teacher in the Indigenous communities of Thursday Island, Yarrabah, and Kowanyama (formerly Mitchell River Mission). Thus, when he was appointed to the

---

1. Chris Natt, "Congratulations Upon Bishop Philip Freier's Appointment as Melbourne Archbishop," speech during 10th Assembly, Legislative Assembly of the Northern Territory, August 23, 2006.

2. In this essay I am using the word Aboriginal instead of First Nations Peoples, as this is the term used self-referentially in the Northern Territory.

Northern Territory, he had the experience to work on equipping and supporting the Aboriginal churches of Arnhem Land because he understood their cultural context and its challenges to their ministry.

First, Philip already possessed a depth of experience in living and working with Aboriginal people. Philip and Joy Freier had both taught in schools in several Aboriginal communities in North Queensland. They knew the challenges of education and the complexities of life in these communities. Bishop Freier's PhD thesis was a careful study of the history of Mitchell River Mission, now known as Kowanyama, and the interactions between European and local people there. Bishop Freier had a deep respect for Aboriginal languages and had learnt to speak the Kokobera language at Kowanyama. He had also given much thought to the contact history between missions and Aboriginal people and the churches that emerged from the missions in North Queensland. While the Northern Territory and North Queensland are shaped by different histories, there are many similarities.

In his PhD thesis, "Living with the *Munpitch*: The history of Mitchell River Mission, 1905–1967"[3] he writes about the interaction between the Munpitch (Europeans) and Aboriginal people. In particular, he explores the political interplay between Aboriginals, missionaries, senior church officials, and the state government that resulted in a trend towards entrenched pauperization of the people of Mitchell River, even though their labor contributed to the comparative wealth of the mission.[4] He explores the pre-contact history of the area, and he is careful to learn and include how Indigenous people viewed the Whites they encountered. This careful work and research shows that he had thought deeply about the complexities of life for Aboriginal people resulting from the arrival of Europeans.

Second, Aboriginal Christians in North Queensland had a profound influence on Philip's conversion to Anglicanism. Arthur Malcolm, an Indigenous priest and later the first Aboriginal bishop in Australia, had challenged Philip to sort out his spirituality.[5] As a result, Philip had experienced a conversion of identity to become a strong Christian within the Anglican tradition. After his ordination, he returned to Kowanyama as priest in charge of the Anglican church.

While at Kowanyama, Philip had supported Nancy Dick in her journey to ordination as a deacon. The Kowanyama people were very aware that her ordination was ground-breaking for two reasons: first, Nancy would

---

3. Freier, Philip L. "Living with the Munpitch: The History of Mitchell River Mission, 1905–1967." PhD diss., James Cook University, 1999.

4. Freier, "Living with the *Munpitch*," 461.

5. Personal communication from Arthur Malcolm to author, 2006.

be the first local person ordained for their church after eighty years of mission, and second, she would be the first Aboriginal woman in Australia to be ordained in the Anglican Church as deacon.[6] Nancy was ordained on November 29, 1987.[7]

People at Kowanyama were aware that some cultural responsibilities and relationships would make it difficult for Nancy to minister to everyone and gave careful thought to what should happen. Traditional leaders made the decision that Nancy should be released from some of the customary restrictions that would make it difficult for her to relate to people in a way appropriate for her new position as minister of the church, where she needed to be available to all. They decided to release her from avoidance relationships.

> This happened in a ceremonial introduction to kin with whom she could not have contact on account of a recent death and with her *poison cousins*. Men with whom she had been in an avoidance relationship throughout her life.
>
> Even the future possibility of her needing to take on mourning responsibilities was considered: "the people told me there's no need for me to join now, just leave it."[8]

The careful thought of the traditional leaders and others shows that they supported Nancy, a woman, taking on the religious role of a clergyperson in the church and considered how best to enable her to fulfil her new responsibilities in the church.

Thus, when he arrived in the Northern Territory, Bishop Freier already had respect for Indigenous clergy and trusted their ministry. The personal benefits he experienced from their ministry gave Bishop Freier the confidence to ordain Aboriginal men and women.

Third, Bishop Freier respected Aboriginal languages as valid. He has a gift for learning languages, as evidenced by his learning the Kokobera language at Kowanyama. Learning a language fluently gives a person a unique insight into the worldview, religion, relationships, and all that makes up the lives of the people who speak that language. His ability to speak an Aboriginal language meant he arrived in the Northern Territory with a positive view about Aboriginal languages, their use in church and for Bible translation into the languages of Arnhem Land. Ordination services, held in the local church in the community, included as much as possible of the language of the community. Learning a language places you in the position of a learner,

---

6. Freier, "Nancy Dick," 35.
7. Freier, "Nancy Dick," 35.
8. Freier, "Nancy Dick," 35–37.

and as an outsider this is a good position to be in when developing relationships with Aboriginal people. Murray Seiffert tells the following story about when Gundu was ordained at Numbulwar:

> The importance of using local language in liturgy can be illustrated by the following. Bishop Philip was leading an ordination service at Numbulwar. Well into the service a middle-age man walked in and sat on the floor—sand—alongside some others. He was puzzled by this stranger using language. He asked one of the elders: "what language is that?" Not a very flattering question for the conscientious bishop. The elder answered, "Nunggubuyu." "Oh" was the reply, and he settled down, listening intensely to the rest of the proceedings.[9]

Philip and Joy both continue to have strong healthy relationships with the people of Kowanyama. Both were adopted into Aboriginal families at Kowanyama and today still have close ties with those families. Both of them had taught in schools in a number of Aboriginal communities which gave them good insights into the complexities of life for Aboriginal people in those communities.

This meant that when they moved to the Northern Territory, they understood the need for strong, healthy Indigenous churches and sought to build on the work that the Church Missionary Society had done in Arnhem Land. They realized that the Aboriginal clergy and churches needed to continue to mature and develop a stronger and more visible role in the diocese. Strong, healthy, Aboriginal churches needed to have services in their own languages that include preaching, teaching, Bible reading, and liturgy. The churches needed to fully proclaim the word of God. There was an ongoing need to develop local leadership, both lay and ordained. These things will be discussed more fully in the rest of the essay.

Finally, it is important to understand another attribute that Philip brought to his appointment as bishop of the Northern Territory. Philip was an historian. His thesis reveals his skills as an historian. He knew the value of understanding the history of a place before commencing something new.

While the Northern Territory and Queensland have different histories many of the same forces that existed in Queensland were at work in the complex history of the various missions (Anglican and otherwise) in the Northern Territory. As a historian, he was well equipped to learn and understand the history of the context in which the missions, the church officials, and the government of the Northern Territory had interacted with each other.

9. Personal communication from Murray Seiffert to author, 2019.

An understanding of history assists in understanding the broader context in which culture, church, and mission functioned. The churches needed government approval in order to start a mission. The Roper River Mission was established in 1908 as a haven of safety from the massacres.[10] Each mission and organization has its own history and no two are the same. The missions existed with the approval of the government of the day which meant interaction with the government and their policies. Bishop Freier's work as a historian equipped him to understand the history and nature of the interaction of the missions and government. For most of its ninety years in Northern Territory, the work of the Church Missionary Society was necessarily aligned with the policies of the Commonwealth and Northern Territory governments, and many times they were the ones who carried out government policies and programs.[11]

Bishop Freier understood the complexities that played out between the government and missions and how the government had sought to establish their aims through the church missions.[12] This stood him in good stead for his role.

Support of Culture, Church, and Mission

In what follows, I intend first to discuss Philip's support for Aboriginal churches in the Northern Territory in their cultural context and, second, what he did to allow them to continue to grow as healthy churches carrying out gospel ministry in their local situation. This included provision of opportunities for lay and ordained leaders to study and undertake training that equipped them to work out what it meant to live as faithful followers of Jesus in their community. He worked to deepen their understanding that the mission of the church was living, teaching, and proclaiming the gospel. He supported the work of Bible translation into their languages and the use of those Scriptures for learning, teaching, and preaching.

Culture, church, and mission do not function in isolation from each other. An Indigenous church functions in the context of the local Indigenous community and its cultural context. The church's view of how to do mission is shaped by its local context and experience. Culture, church, and mission all interact in a healthy church.

I will use the concepts of culture, church, and mission to discuss the way Bishop Freier sought to support the Aboriginal churches. There will be

---

10. Harris, *We Wish We'd Done More*, 11.
11. Harris, *We Wish We'd Done More*, 215–19.
12. Freier, "Living with the *Munpitch*," 109–11, 128, 160–61.

some unavoidable overlap between them, as they interact with each other in a healthy church. The gospel needs to affirm and challenge local cultures everywhere, including our Western culture. Before proceeding, it is necessary to define these three words.

The use of the word culture in this essay is influenced by what I understand Aboriginal Christians to mean by culture. I have learnt this over many years from listening to them discuss culture and Christianity. For them, culture includes everything. It includes the social rules of how to relate to people and behave, the kinship system, the language of the community, marriage rules, art, ceremonies, stories handed down from the ancestors, definition of land ownership and its management, hunting and gathering. Culture embraces all of life, not just religion and art. I have heard Aboriginal Christians say that because they choose not to participate in traditional ceremonies, it does not mean that they are not Aboriginal. They strongly insist that they are Aboriginal Christians and live in an Aboriginal way.

In this essay, church usually refers to the local body of Christ expressing itself in its Aboriginal context, seeking to live out the gospel and minister to people in a culturally appropriate way. This essay focuses on Anglican churches and sees them as part of the larger context in which they function.

Mission is defined by these churches as living as Christians in their community, proclaiming and teaching the word of God locally, and taking the good news about Jesus to nearby outstations and communities.

Culture

There are many things that can be discussed under culture, as it embraces all of life. I will discuss Bishop Freier's approach to language, relationships, social issues and the challenges that present themselves for Aboriginal Christians living in their society.

Bishop Freier knew from experience how important the acknowledgement and use of language was for the identity of Indigenous people. He did several things to encourage the use of the local language in the activities of the local churches. He acknowledged the local language in each of the Anglican churches in Arnhem Land and learnt to read some Scripture, say a prayer, or use a number of expressions in their language. He also supported its use by having at least the vows of the ordination service, preferably much more, in the local language so that all understood the significance of what was happening.

Bishop Freier supported the use of the local language in all aspects of worship where possible. He encouraged the reading of translated Scriptures where they had them. Early missionaries, confronted by a variety of languages and dialects and lacking in linguistic skills, had not been able to do much in this area,[13] though there were a few people who had contributed, like Len Harris, who worked on some Bible translation into Nunggubuyu.[14] Freier recognized the necessity for churches having Scriptures in their own language if their members were to grow and mature in the faith.

Philip gave strong support to the work of Bible translation by the Summer Institute of Linguistics. He took a personal interest in their work and in the Kriol translation team who over a number of years translated the whole Bible into Kriol. Kriol is the language used in two of the six established Anglican churches in Arnhem Land. They were immensely grateful for his support and interest in their work. He would visit their translation workshops in Darwin, encouraging them with a devotional and his personal interest in their work. To the delight of all who had participated in the translation and experienced his encouragement, Philip returned to the Northern Territory in 2007 to be present at the dedication service of the Kriol Baibul at the Katherine Christian Convention. He also encouraged the translation work in the other languages spoken by the Aboriginal churches in his diocese.

Bishop Freier was aware that many Indigenous people spoke English as a third, fourth, or fifth language, so he encouraged them to use their languages in their churches for preaching, teaching, prayers, singing, and in whatever way they could. As Aboriginal languages had not been encouraged by many people who visited or lived and worked in these remote communities, his encouragement was much appreciated.

Relationships are an important part of Aboriginal society, taking priority over other pressures and responsibilities. Philip and Joy understood this, as both had been adopted into Aboriginal families. If a close relationship dictated that you should stay home from work and attend to a family matter, then that would take priority over work responsibilities and would be attended to first. The kinship system classifies everyone into what is known as a kin group, which in brief defines who you can work with, what relationships must be shown proper respect, and what your responsibilities are to people in various relationships with you. The kinship system also defined your responsibilities for land and ceremonies. Everyone is a manager or a worker in relation to land and ceremony.

An awareness of the significance of relationships and how they work assists in understanding why Aboriginal people choose some people to be in leadership positions. Philip respected these relationships and the way they

---

13. Harris, *We Wish We'd Done More*, 120–27.
14. Harris, *We Wish We'd Done More*, 127–44.

functioned in society. In appointing church leaders, it is important to have leaders from at least the two main halves of the kinship system, known as moieties, so that everyone can be ministered to.

Local Indigenous clergy and lay leaders understand the complexities and importance of relationships and how they come into play in time of crisis or grief. They know who are responsible for decisions, such as when and where a funeral will take place and who will be responsible for managing it.

Philip and Joy, having lived and worked in Indigenous communities for a number of years, recognized the complexities of the social issues, most of which have arisen since the arrival of Europeans and have had a profound effect on local culture and society. These were issues like poverty and a lack of suitable jobs, which result in a lack of resources and money. Alcohol and drug use have resulted in much violence and disruption to family and community life. An increase in the number of suicides and attempted suicides causes much grief and suffering. Poor health and people dying at a young age also take their toll. These pressures on people can explode into arguments and fights, and Christian leaders are often called in to act as peacemakers.

All of these social issues impact on the lives of the lay church leaders and clergy in these communities. Stress from dealing with a constant stream of people with problems places enormous pressure on an Indigenous church and its leaders. The Aboriginal clergy minister in their home communities, so most problems will involve a friend or relative. This results in church leaders being involved in one crisis after another and with little time to recover between the demands placed on them. In time, this takes a toll.

Funerals are another demanding social issue, as an unexpected death can give rise to a number of questions and accusations, such as whether it was caused by a curse or black magic, and if so, who did it? Unexpected deaths are often thought to have a supernatural cause. Most funerals will be for a relative or friend. This all adds an extra layer of complexity for the clergy as they support people alongside the pressure of conducting the funeral. Having a bishop who understood the difficult social context they worked in and its resulting pressures was a great encouragement to the Aboriginal churches, clergy, and lay leaders.

A big challenge for the local churches was in thinking about how to live as Aboriginal Christians. There are things in every culture that the gospel affirms, and things the gospel challenges. Those within Indigenous culture are in the best position to make decisions about what needs to change for them and what is affirmed by the gospel. Whereas some missionaries have worried that the obligations that go with the kinship system are difficult and should be done away with, these churches have kept their kinship system, as it defines social behavior. Christians who decided not to participate in traditional religious ceremonies maintain that this does not take away their Aboriginality and that they are still Aboriginal. They argue that their Aboriginality is defined not only by ceremonies but by the whole of life in their communities. Outsiders sometimes limit Aboriginal culture to ceremonies and art, whereas Indigenous Christians argue that there is much more to being an Aboriginal person. Using Scriptures in their own language assists them in deciding what it means to live as an Aboriginal Christian. Bishop Freier encouraged them to make their own decisions, as they were in the best position to make decisions about what was an appropriate way of life for Christians in their cultural context.

Church

Having sketched some of the cultural situation in which the Anglican churches in Arnhem Land operate, I will now discuss the strategies that Bishop Freier used to strengthen Aboriginal Christians and their churches.

First, Bishop Freier championed ordination of Aboriginal clergy. In this, he continued the work of Bishop Mason, the first bishop of the Northern Territory, and the work of Bishop Wood. In November 1973, Bishop Mason took the courageous step of ordaining Rev. Michael Gumbuli Wurramara as deacon and priest to look after the Ngukurr Parish.[15] This was courageous, because Gumbuli had been trained by local clergy and had not attended a southern theological college. Gumbuli was the first Aboriginal person ordained in the Anglican church of the Northern Territory, though James Noble, one of the Aboriginal missionaries who helped start the Roper River Mission, was the first Aboriginal person in Australia to be ordained deacon.[16] Bishop Clyde Wood also understood the importance for Aboriginal churches to be led by Aboriginal clergy and ordained a number of Indigenous clergy after they had studied at Nungalinya, the training college in Darwin.

When Philip was appointed bishop, there was a need for a new generation of Indigenous clergy, and he set about equipping and preparing men and women for ordination. By this point in time, the General Synod of the Anglican Church and a number of local synods were prepared to ordain women as well as men.

Philip came to the Northern Territory already supporting Indigenous people for ordination, both men and women. He ordained a number of

---

15. Seiffert, *Gumbuli of Ngukurr*, 79. Ngukurr was formerly known as the Roper River Mission.

16. Higgins, *James Noble*, 17, 25–39, 50–51; Harris, *One Blood*, 855.

Indigenous people, but only after careful thought and exploration. This included allowing the local church to decide to support the candidate for ordination, whether male or female. It is not easy to be the minister of the church you are already a part of, and there needed to be careful inquiry into whether the members of the church approved of the choice of person who was to be ordained. A group of local church members were appointed as a discernment group to make a recommendation. Care was also taken to ensure that the candidate for ordination was in good standing in the local community. The process was not rushed. The candidate needed to have completed studies at Nungalinya College (or be close to completion) so that they were qualified to teach and preach. In many cases, the person was already leading and caring for the local church in the absence of an ordained minister. The candidate also needed to speak the local language so that people could understand them. There are four different languages spoken in the six established Anglican churches in Arnhem Land, and that made movement of leaders between them difficult.

As with Nancy Dick at Kowanyama, the ordination service was held in the community so that everyone knew what was happening. When I took the ordination retreat for the ordination of Rev. Yulki Nunggumajbar at Numbulwar, the first Aboriginal woman to be ordained deacon in the Northern Territory, we were careful to do everything in the open so that it was clear no secret business was involved. The service was a joyful occasion, and women were encouraged that they too could take their place as clergy in the church. After the service, during the happy fellowship meeting, I was taken aside and introduced to two women from Umbakumba on Groote Eylandt and informed that they were willing to be ordained to fill the roles of clergy for the church at Umbakumba as no men were available for ordination. In due course, after working through the discernment process described, they were ordained by Bishop Freier.

A second strategy used by Bishop Freier to strengthen the Indigenous churches was to support Nungalinya College, serving as treasurer and supporting and encouraging the principal. In North Queensland, Bishop Freier had supported the work of Wontulp-Bi-Buyu College, a sister college to Nungalinya. Nungalinya was established in 1973 by the Anglican and Uniting churches—later joined by the Catholic church—to provide training for lay church leaders and clergy in a culturally appropriate format. Until it was established, Indigenous candidates were expected to study in southern theological colleges or on Thursday Island. It was too difficult for people to take up this option. The establishment of Nungalinya College meant that training was now available locally and provided in a culturally relevant way. Following the 1980 Elcho Island revival and its widespread effect, people came to Nungalinya to study in increasing numbers. All Aboriginal people are welcome at Nungalinya; currently, they have students from over one hundred different communities.[17] Subjects are taught as intensives, which is a culturally appropriate way of learning—it sits well with people unable to be away from home for a long time.

A third strategy was to encourage the local church to use their language in all areas of the service: preaching, teaching, liturgy, praying, and singing. Bishop Freier also encouraged them to use what Scriptures they had in their language and to continue the translation of Scripture into their language.

A fourth strategy was for Bishop Freier to visit the local churches as much as possible. This was a challenge given their remoteness and the cost of travel, but one that was a priority for him. He also visited their leaders when they were studying at Nungalinya College. As bishop, he appointed diocesan staff who could visit the churches to support them and conduct further training on site.

A fifth strategy was to endeavor to encourage a fuller Indigenous participation in synod and diocesan meetings and gatherings. Where he could, Bishop Freier appointed Aboriginal people to committees and encouraged them to speak up. As such meetings were conducted in English, this posed a challenge to those for whom English is not the first language.

A sixth strategy was to run training workshops when people gathered for events. This has continued, and today it includes the gathering of Aboriginal church leaders around events such as the Katherine Christian Convention, synod and other special events. Diocesan staff also visited the churches and conducted training on site.

A seventh strategy that he used was to call a partners' conference of all the Anglican agencies that were working in the Northern Territory. This was a strategic move to assist the different agencies in understanding what each other was doing and to get them all on the same page. The agencies included the Church Missionary Society, Bush Church Aid, Anglicare, Nungalinya College, Sisters of the Church, Anglican Board of Mission Australia, and others. These conferences have continued.

These seven strategies contributed to the growing confidence of the Aboriginal churches in the Northern Territory.

---

17. Nungalinya college donation appeal letter, June 2019.

Mission

Bishop Freier understood that the Indigenous churches had an idea of mission already. They defined mission as living and teaching the gospel locally and as taking the gospel to outstations and communities near them. They also had some idea of mission on a broader scale in Australia and elsewhere. After all, they had experienced many missionaries coming to them with the gospel. The bishop supported them in mission in several ways.

First, he related to their view that Aboriginal people should indeed be involved in mission. The missionary James Noble had brought them the gospel. James was an Aboriginal man from Yarrabah in North Queensland. It is very likely that James and his wife Angelina spoke the cattle station pidgin that had spread through the area, as both had worked in the cattle industry and were able to communicate with the people who came into the new mission. Christians at Ngukurr maintain that James was the one who communicated the gospel to them.

When three Church Missionary Society missionaries—Huthnance, Sharp, and Joynt, entrusted with starting the Roper River Mission—stopped at Yarrabah on their journey to Roper River, where they planned to start a new mission in the Northern Territory, the Aboriginal church at Yarrabah insisted that some Aboriginal Christians should go with them. James and Angelina Noble were chosen, along with Harold Reid.[18] When there was concern on the part of the three white male missionaries about a woman joining the party, the church voted unanimously to send Angelina with James.[19]

Bishop Freier had lived at Yarrabah, where the story of James Noble was well known. James was the first Aboriginal person to be ordained as a deacon in the Anglican church.[20] This occurred while James and Angelina worked at the Forrest River Mission in the Kimberly region of Western Australia.[21] Philip Freier has worked to promote the story of James Noble; November 25, the day in the lectionary that recognizes him, is the anniversary of his ordination.

Second, Bishop Freier encouraged the Aboriginal churches to raise up people to continue to take the gospel out to other Indigenous communities. The gospel had been brought to them by Aboriginal people, and so it was appropriate that they should take the good news about Jesus to other

---

18. Seiffert *Gumbuli of Ngukurr*, 79
19. Seiffert, *Refuge on the Roper*, 82; Higgins, *James Noble*, 16,19.
20. Seiffert. *Refuge on the Roper*, 79.
21. Sandefur, *Aboriginalisation of the Church*.

Aboriginal people. James Noble was their model. Over the years they have done this by visiting outstations and nearby communities and taking services. James Japanma, Barnabas Roberts, Gumbuli Wurramara, Yulki Nunggumajbar, and William and Marjorie Hall are some of those who have done this. Their resources were not large, but they had the example of James and Angelina to support them. They knew that people who spoke the language of the communities they were going to were best placed to be effective in proclaiming the gospel.

Third, Bishop Freier supported the idea of mission that included living out the gospel as well as talking it. The Aboriginal churches knew that any failure to live out the gospel would be thrown back at them by people in the community. New Christians are watched by church members and people in the community to see if they live up to their new commitment. Aboriginal people are good at observing people and seeing whether they live up to what they claim to be. So, it is important to live the gospel as well as proclaim it. Bishop Freier understood this, and people were not baptized or confirmed in haste. He understood that Aboriginal Christians were keen to share the gospel with members of their own communities. Before people could hear the gospel, they needed to see it lived out.

Fourth, Bishop Freier worked to broaden their horizons. One such action was to find the funds for me to take three female Aboriginal deacons to Cairns for a Mothers' Union conference and then on to Yarrabah for a week. The Mothers' Union conference exposed them to Aboriginal and Torres Strait Islander Christians from the north of Queensland and to learn how these women approached Christian living in their community and carrying out mission. At Yarrabah they spent useful time with Aboriginal clergy and lay Christians, attended services, and were exposed to the way that another Indigenous church carried out mission in their community and further afield.

Bishop Freier's awareness of how the Aboriginal churches approached mission enabled him to encourage the churches to continue to take responsibility for mission, both locally and to neighboring outstations and communities.

Conclusion

Bishop Freier was an excellent appointment to the Diocese of the Northern Territory, in particular for the Aboriginal churches. With his knowledge of Aboriginal culture, church, and mission, he was able to build on the work that others had done. Combined with his deep respect for Aboriginal people and for their culture, this enabled him to build relationships of mutual respect and trust with the clergy, lay leaders, and churches. His ordination of Aboriginal men and women greatly strengthened the churches. Bishop Freier's personal use of and respect for Aboriginal languages encouraged use of the local language and translated Scriptures in all aspects of church services. He accepted and respected these churches, encouraging them to take their rightful place in the life of the diocese. He was especially aware that as Aboriginal Christians, their models were Aboriginal rather than European. He encouraged them to be strong, healthy Aboriginal churches living out and proclaiming the gospel in a culturally appropriate way.

With Bishop Freier's support, the Aboriginal churches became more confident in being church and doing mission in a culturally resonant way. He left the churches with a new generation of clergy who were confident in their role as ministers. There was renewed interest by lay people in attending Nungalinya College to study the Bible and develop ministry skills. The church leaders embraced the opportunities provided by the diocese for further training. People were keen to have more Scriptures translated into their languages.

When Bishop Freier left to be Archbishop of Melbourne, he left behind Aboriginal churches that were more confident of their own ministry. He understood them, and they flourished under his care. These churches continue to respect him and have many fond memories of his time with them.

Bibliography

Freier, Philip L. "Living with the *Munpitch*: The History of Mitchell River Mission, 1905–1967." PhD diss., James Cook University, 1999.

———. "Nancy Dick: The First Aboriginal Woman Deacon in the Anglican Church of Australia." *AJMS* 7:2 (2013) 35–37.

Harris, John. "Language Contact, Pidgins and the Emergence of Kriol in the Northern Territory," PhD diss., University of Queensland, 1984,

———. *One Blood*. Albatross: Sutherland, 1990

———. *We Wish We'd Done More: Ninety Years of CMS and Aboriginal Issues in North Australia*. Adelaide: Openbook, 1998.

Higgins, Geoff. *James Noble of Yarrabah*. Sydney: Mission Publications, 1981.

Sandefur, Joy Lorraine. "The Aboriginalisation of the Church at Ngukurr." PhD diss., LaTrobe University, 1998.

Seiffert, Murray. *Gumbuli of Ngukurr. Aboriginal Elder in Arnhem Land*. Brunswick East: Acorn, 2011.

———. *Refuge on the Roper: The Origins of Roper River Mission Ngukurr*. Brunswick East: Acorn, 2008.

9

"Each in Our Own Language"

The Translation of the Bible into Australian Indigenous Languages

PETER ADAM[1]

"Now I know that Jesus speaks Wubuy."
—MADI MURUNGUN.[2]

"This is what our people need, the Word of God in the language of the people."
—MARATJA DHAMARRANDJI.[3]

---

1. This essay is an expansion of Adam, "People," and my thanks to the editor of the *Reformed Theological Review* for permission to use that material. I am grateful to Aunty Jean Phillips for her continued encouragement to speak and write on Indigenous issues. For help with this essay, thanks to Peter Carolane, Jo Cruickshank, Elizabeth Willis, Joy Sandefur, Ken Rogers, and staff at the Anglican Diocese of Melbourne Archives, the Dalton McCaughey Library, and the Leon Morris Library at Ridley College. I am grateful for all the research of others used in this essay.

2. Lake, *Bible,* 322–23.

3. David Curtis, "Remote and Indigenous Programmes." Article on *Bible Society* website, 2012, https://www.biblesociety.org.au/2012/domestic/indigenous.html.

> "Book for black fellows! Book for black fellows!"
> —WIRADJURI PEOPLE.[4]

> "The Bible, in the vernacular, is a living word yet."
> —MEREDITH LAKE.[5]

> "These books [the Scriptures], therefore, ought to be much in our hands, in our eyes, in our ears, in our mouths, but most of all in our hearts."
> —THOMAS CRANMER.[6]

The Translatable Bible

THE TRANSLATION OF OUR Holy Scriptures is one of the glories of Christianity.[7] It shows that God is the God of all peoples, all cultures, all places, and all languages: "Vernacularisation . . . flows naturally from Christianity's universal vision."[8] It shows that God understands all peoples and their languages and speaks to all peoples in their heart language(s).

It reminds us of Pentecost, when people heard of God's works in their own languages (Acts 2:11). It is a sign of the last days, when all those to whom God has spoken in their own languages are then empowered by the Spirit to speak God's words to others (Acts 2:17, 18). It is also a sign of the future, when we will all sing to the slaughtered and risen Lamb, the Son of God, Jesus Christ:

Bible Society, "Indigenous."

4. Van Toorn, *Writing*, 37.
5. Lake, *Bible*, 75.
6. Cranmer, "Exhortation," 3.
7. By way of contrast, most other religions use, teach, and read their ancient texts in their original languages. I remember seeing small boys in Pakistan learning the Qur'an by heart in Arabic, a language they did not understand.
8. Rademaker, *Found*, 15.

> You are worthy to take the scroll and to open its seals, for you were slaughtered and by your blood you ransomed for God saints from every tribe and language and people and nation; you have made them to be a kingdom and priests serving our God, and they will reign on earth (Rev 5:9, 10).

In addition, if God speaks to us in our own language, then we are more confident to pray, praise, and worship in our own language. For what God speaks, he can surely hear. One of the most powerful features of Cranmer's prayers in the *Book of Common Prayer* is that they use the very words of Scripture.[9] In those prayers, we pray God's words back to him: he teaches us to pray by speaking to us. If God's words to us are effective, informative, and persuasive in any language, then God can certainly hear and understand our prayers in any language.

The translation of the Holy Scriptures into vernacular languages had a mixed history in the church. Within the early Christian Mediterranean world, the Eastern churches had a tradition of translation for liturgy, Christian education, and missionary work. For example, the Copts of Egypt had a translated Bible in the third century. Cyril and Methodius in the 860s began their mission to the Slavs. This was possibly in response to the request "for a teacher to instruct us in the true faith in our own language." They provided literature and preached in Slavonic, translated the liturgy, and trained local clergy. They also translated the psalms and the gospels.[10]

The Western tradition, based in Rome, was slower to use vernacular translations, using the (translated!) Latin Bible, the Vulgate, with all people, whatever their language. (Though Irenaeus had preached in Celtic in Lyon in the second century.[11]) For example, there was no Punic translation in North Africa, which weakened the Punic church.[12] Patrick, though he spoke and preached in Irish, used the Vulgate and trained people in Latin.[13]

Two of the key achievements of the Reformation in England were the translation of the Bible into the vernacular, and the production of a vernacular prayer book. The vernacular Bible enables receiving, faith, understanding, response, reflection, and discussion; it also enables vernacular prayer, worship, mutual ministry, and evangelism.

The translatability of the Bible signified that God came down to speak to everyone. It reflected the incarnation of Christ for the whole human race.

---

9. Adam, *Pure Word*, 51–59.
10. Fletcher, *Barbarian*, 351–64.
11. Sanneh, *Translating*, 67.
12. Sanneh, *Translating*, 67, 68.
13. Fletcher, *Barbarian*, 87, 88.

It had a profound effect on gospel progress, as it had a profound effect on all cultures, languages, and nations into which the Bible was translated. It promoted education in reading and writing, the study of languages, and the idea that great ideas could and should be entrusted to ordinary people, not just the elite. It promoted the democratization of education and learning and knowledge.[14]

Bible translation requires understanding of the Bible, and also understanding of the language and culture of the people who speak the language in view. As Cole observes, "Language for the missionary is the key that unlocks the door of another culture . . . The communication of Christ cross-culturally can only take place effectively in the language in which the recipient thinks and speaks voluntarily."[15]

If God speaks in our language, then he understands our language, and so we can pray from our hearts in our language, and he will understand not just our words, but our hearts. Praying in our own language, in our words, expresses our own identity most easily, both our cultural and personal identity. Sanneh writes, "Translatability is the source of the success of Christianity across cultures . . . The very pluralism that the religion fosters is also the safeguard against monolithic tyranny . . . Christian mission is inadequate until it acquires a vernacular credibility."[16]

Translating the Bible into an Indigenous language looks like an act of colonization. However, as Rademaker tells us, "Translation can be depicted as a kind of conquest or colonization: the taming of one language by another or the successful transfer of meaning from one context into a foreign one. But, of course, translation is more slippery than that."[17] She observes, "Translation of religious texts simultaneously instituted and subverted colonial rule . . . validating local reinterpretations of the texts and establishing local identities."[18]

Translating the Bible empowers communities to read the Bible, reflect on it, and evaluate and critique the cultural baggage of the people who brought the Bible and initiated the translation!

---

14. Woodberry, "Missionary Roots," 244. He points to "Lay vernacular Bible reading" as a key ingredient.
15. Cole, *Mission to Church*, 188.
16. Sanneh, *Translating*, 51, 97.
17. Rademaker, *Found*, 3.
18. Rademaker, *Found*, 9.

Rademaker writes of Australia, "For Christian people, the translation of the Bible placed them on more equal footing with the missionary, as they, too, could be interpreters of the sacred text."[19]

Providing translated Scriptures is a more gracious act than requiring Indigenous peoples to hear the Bible read in English and to pray and worship and sing to God in English. Perhaps the most destructive act was to use pictures and stained-glass windows that portrayed Jesus Christ and his followers as white people. White Bibles, white prayer books, white songs, and white Christs result in white churches and render black people invisible.

Some faithful Bible translators, both missionaries and Indigenous peoples worked hard to translate the Bible into Australian Indigenous languages. This meant finding out the words and structure of each language, producing a written version of the language, and then producing a faithful Bible translation. One byproduct of this was the preservation of many languages that might otherwise have been lost.

Bible translation does not necessarily mean that people have to be able to read or to own a copy of the Bible. Bible translation for an oral language can work without people learning to read. But if the Bible is not translated into your language, then God's words cannot be heard in your language!

Honoring the Heroes: The History of the Bible's Translation into Australian Indigenous Languages

Reynolds celebrates those European Australians who defended in the rights of Indigenous peoples. There are many Christians on his list, including Williams Dawes of the First Fleet; George Augustus Robinson, Chief Protector of Aborigines in the Port Phillip district;[20] John Saunders, Baptist minister in Sydney; Lancelot Threkeld, missionary in New South Wales; Robert Lyon, Louis Guistiani, John Gribble, Ernest Gribble, and Mary Bennet in Western Australia; Ernest Gribble in Queensland; and Charles Duguid in South Australia.[21]

To that list should be added Matthew Hale, Archdeacon of Adelaide, founder of the Poonindie Aboriginal settlement, then first bishop of Perth, and finally bishop of Brisbane.[22] When Matthew Hale met Bishop Short in England, he told him of his desire to work with the Indigenous peoples.

---

19. Rademaker, *Found*, 115.

20. This is his original title; I acknowledge that Indigenous Australians prefer the use of other terms, such as "Aboriginal peoples."

21. Reynolds, *Whispering*, chapters 2–12.

22. See Gourlay, *Good Bishop*.

The bishop replied, "You must come out and be my Archdeacon," and they traveled to Adelaide together.[23]

We should also add the early bishops and clergy of the dioceses of North Queensland, North West Australia, Carpentaria, the Northern Territory, and other outback dioceses around Australia, as also the Bush Brotherhoods, workers with the Australian Board of Missions (ABM), the Church Missionary Society (CMS), and the Bush Church Aid Society (BCA).

However, here we honor those who engaged in the demanding work of translation. The Methodist John Harper was probably the first. He worked on the Wiradjuri language and translated the first chapter of Genesis in 1824.[24] In 1827, Richard Hill encouraged Archdeacon Scott to employ someone to lay down the rudiments of Aboriginal language: "Till this is done, nothing I believe effectual can be achieved."[25]

William and Ann Watson were sent to the Aboriginal mission at Lake Wellington in 1832 by the CMS branch started by Samuel Marsden in Sydney in 1825.[26] William Watson worked on translating the Gospel of John for the Wiradjuri people in NSW in the 1830s and completed a two-thousand-word Wiradju dictionary. He prepared a translation of some of the *Book of Common Prayer* under the direction of Archdeacon Broughton.[27] He recounts reading from the translated Bible, when a number of people "came and sat with me one after another, and paid the greatest attention; they said they understood what I read. When I gave over reading, some of them said: 'Kurrandirung myengoo! Kurrandirung myengoo!—Book for black fellows! Book for black fellows!'"[28]

On April 27, 1835 William Watson led the service, prayed, and preached in Wiradjuri.[29]

Thomas Wilkinson translated parts of Genesis for the Aboriginal Tasmanians exiled to Flinders Island. Governor George Arthur believed that

---

23. Brown, *Short*, 81.
24. Lake, *Bible*, 62.
25. Shaw, *Broughton*, 41.
26. Harris, "Anglicanism," 225. Marsden did not engage in significant ministry to Australia's Indigenous peoples, but did pioneer the mission to New Zealand, with spectacular results; Bridges, "NSW," 180–221, and Yarwood, *Marsden*, 161–80. In the words of Richard Hill, Marsden's colleague, "Why are our poor Aborigines so reluctantly assisted, while New Zealand is so liberally supported?" Yarwood, *Marsden*, 277. However, Marsden did include Indigenous Australians with Māoris in his training college. Seiffert, *Refuge*, 106.
27. Bridges, "NSW," 34.
28. Van Toorn, *Writing*, 37.
29. Bridges, "NSW," 412.

"the Bible is the most effectual mode of introducing civilisation."[30] Yet he described this work of translation as "imprudent!" Arthur "could not understand that the only way to enter the hearts and minds of the Aborigines was through their language."[31]

The Methodist Francis Tuckfield, who came to the Port Philip Settlement in 1838, translated parts of the Bible and taught in the mission school in the local Indigenous language.[32] The Methodist William Thomas, Assistant Protector of Aborigines on the Mornington Peninsula, first led a Sunday service in the Bunurong language in 1840, and made some Bible translations.[33]

The Methodist John Bulmer was an Anglican missionary at Lake Tyers in Victoria. Carolane comments on his use of Indigenous languages in his ministry: "Therefore, in the first decade of the mission, Bulmer conducted his preaching and teaching using a combination of simple English and Brabirrawulung and, if the tribes from New South Wales were visiting, he might use some Ngarago words from the Maneroo region."[34]

Duncan McNab, a Roman Catholic priest, began mission work in Queensland in 1875, with a firm commitment to learn Indigenous language. "I must in the first place rely on the grace of God, and in the second acquire their language and live among them."[35] He recorded some success. "I found that although their dialects are numerous and different, they are intelligible over a great extent of country, and the languages comparatively few . . . I have now in writing 1200 words of the Cabi language . . . and a translation of the Lord's Prayer, the creed, and the commandments."[36]

Lutherans led the way in South Australia.[37] The Lutheran Pastor Schuerman started holding services in the local Indigenous language in Adelaide in 1839.[38] George Taplin in South Australia translated parts of the Bible in Narrinyeri (Ngarrindjeri), and this was published in 1864, the first Indigenous Bible publication.

The most significant project in the nineteenth was at Bethesda, the Lutheran mission at Coopers Creek among the Dieri people. Carl Strehlow

---

30. Lake, *Bible*, 51.
31. N. J. B. Plomley, as quoted in Van Toorn, *Writing*, 100.
32. Piggin and Linder, *Fountain*, 226.
33. Fels, *Protectorate*, 393–7.
34. Carolane, "Bulmer," 137.
35. Arnold, *Mission*, 32.
36. Arnold, *Mission*, 38.
37. Ganter, *Contest*, 183,4.
38. Seiffert, *Refuge*, 63.

and J. G. Reuther translated and published the whole New Testament in 1897.[39]

Presbyterian missionary Bob Love worked with Njimandum, Barungga, and Wonoonmoi in Western Australia to translate the Gospels of Mark and Luke in the 1930s and 40s.[40] The CMS missionary Nell Harris began translation work at Oenpelli in 1933 and published Mark and 1 John.[41] At Roper River and Groote Eylandt, Nell's husband, Len Harris, worked with Grace, Joshua, and Bidigainj, and translated Mark and James into Nungubuyu in the 1940s.[42] At Christmas 1936, Len Harris reported that "we read the Lesson in our Church Services in Gunwinggu for the first time."[43] On Christmas Day, 1940, Nell read a Bible passage in Gunwinggu, and Joseph Garmard translated the sermon into Gunwinggu.[44]

In 1942, the Nunggubuyu leader Madi Murungun came to a great realization after hearing the Bible read in his own language. He used to think that Jesus was only a white man's God but came to understand that Jesus was also the God of black people. "Now I know that Jesus speaks Wubuy."[45] What had changed his mind? The Bible translated into his own language.

There was a later move to increase Bible translation in the 1950s, led by such heroes as Mary Moody, Judith Stokes, Peter Carroll, Earl Hughes, Meryl Rowe, and Julie Waddy in the Northern Territory. This was assisted by cooperation with Wycliffe Bible Translators and SIL (Summer Institute of Linguistics), who arrived in 1961.

In 1972, Donald Shearman, chairman of ABM, recommended a new emphasis on Bible translation and evangelization in vernacular Indigenous languages.[46]

In 2007, the first complete edition of the Bible in an Indigenous language was finally published. This was the *Holi Baibul* in the Kriol language. Wycliffe missionaries John and Joy Sandefur had begun work on the Kriol language and the Kriol Bible in the 1970s.[47] Kriol had developed among Indigenous peoples as a common language, and so this made good sense.

39. Harris, *Blood*, 388.
40. Harris, *Blood*, 837.
41. Harris, *Blood*, 839.
42. Harris, *Blood*, 840.
43. Harris, "Anglicanism," 238. As Harris comments, it took almost 150 years for this to happen!
44. Cole, *Mission to Church*, 126.
45. Lake, *Bible*, 322–23.
46. Freier, "Living with the *Munpitch*," 321, 32.
47. See John Sandefur, "North Australian Kriol and the Kriol 'Holi Baibul,'" in Swain, *Aboriginal*, 41221; and Joy Sandefur, *Aboriginalisation*.

Translation took over twenty-nine years. It was undertaken by a team of native Kriol speakers and finally brought to fruition by Rev. Canon Gumbuli Wurrumara.[48]

Indigenous leader Harry Huddlestone commented on the Kriol Bible, "I always thought I understood English. I read the English Bible every day and I do think I understood it all right. But I suppose I have to sit there and think about it a lot. But when I read the Kriol Bible, I understood it right away."[49]

Inadequacies in Translation

Unfortunately, the history of Bible translation in Australia has not been impressive. "Given the predominance of Evangelical missionaries and missionary societies in the long history of the Christian church in Aboriginal Australia, one of the most surprising and most shameful deficiencies has been the long failure to translate the Bible into the languages of the people."[50]

By way of contrast, at the Baptist center at Serampore in India, William Carey, Joshua Marshman, and William Ward between them translated the Bible into twenty-four different Indian languages and dialects and compiled dictionaries in Marathi, Sanskrit, Bengali, and Punjabi.[51]

Among Indigenous communities, there was a strong connection between their language and their land. "Aboriginal languages both belong to the land and bind their speakers to the land."[52] So the loss of both land and language had a powerful impact on them. Harris writes, "Aboriginal Scriptures and liturgies would have meant more likelihood of a strong and well-equipped Aboriginal Christian community, and missionaries would have gained insight into Aboriginal culture."[53]

As Freier observes, when missionaries underestimated the intelligence of Indigenous peoples, they did not engage in serious teaching and education.[54] He also writes that inability to speak Indigenous languages leads

---

48. Seiffert, *Gumbuli*, 303–6.
49. Harris, *We Wish*, 167.
50. Harris, *Blood*, 829.
51. Hiney, *Missionary Trail*, 223–24.
52. Rademaker, *Found*, 8.
53. Harris, "Anglicanism," 237.
54. Freier, "Mitchell River," 77. And on occasions, this expectation was backed up by excommunication! 78.

to poor communication, poor assessment of intellectual ability, and so no encouragement to Indigenous peoples to engage in evangelism.[55]

Harris comments, "I believe there is a connection between the failure to lay emphasis on Bible translation and the failure to give recognition to Aboriginal leadership."[56]

There were seven reasons for a lack of Bible translation.

The first reason was that of assumed cultural superiority. Europe was assumed to lead the world in culture and civilization, and therefore non-Europeans were inferior, and their culture was inferior as well. Rousseau's notion of the "noble savage" was not popular in Britain. This prejudice was later reinforced by Darwin's ideas, compounded by the rise of the eugenics movement, which taught that inferior stock should not breed. There was little motivation to do the hard work of translating the Bible into obviously inferior languages.

Such an attitude was underpinned by Enlightenment ideas of the superiority of European civilization. Gascoigne has written about the Enlightenment as "the most obvious rival to Christianity in providing an articulate and connected understanding of human beings and their place in the universe."[57] This included an assumption of inevitable progress. In 1814, Governor Macquarie wrote that he worked "to bring these poor Unenlightened People into an important Degree of Civilization."[58] One theory was that uneducated people had black skin, and so civilization would result in the black people in Australia turning white, as had the Europeans![59]

This cultural arrogance was not confined to Australia. Robert Morrison completed his translation of the Bible into Chinese and also produced an English-Chinese dictionary, and a Chinese-English dictionary, in the early nineteenth century. When he offered the dictionaries to the university libraries of Oxford and Cambridge, they refused them on the grounds that they could not see any benefit in acquiring them![60]

The second reason was the sheer number of languages. There were an estimated 500 Australian languages or dialects.[61] This proved a formidable challenge, especially as they were spoken, not written, languages: the translator would need to learn the language, then work with native-language

---

55. Freier, "Mitchell River," 80.
56. Harris, *Blood*, 855.
57. Gascoigne, *Enlightenment*, 1.
58. As cited in Gascoigne, *Enlightenment*, 150.
59. Gascoigne, *Enlightenment*, 149.
60. Hancock, *Morrison*, 117–18.
61. Harris, *We Wish*, 116.

speakers to produce a translation that was true to the original and also effective in communication in a very different culture. Then the people could either learn Bible passages by heart, or the Bible could be published, and people could learn to read it in their language. Indigenous peoples made use of "message sticks" and also communicated by drawings.[62] However, these were not adequate to convey the literary quantity and complexity of the Bible.

The third was that of difficulty in translation. These were not European languages with a familiar linguistic pattern for the translators. They were entirely new and different languages. Most missionaries were not trained linguists and also had other responsibilities that demanded time and energy. Here in Victoria, Edward Parker, a Methodist missionary, was an Assistant Protector of Aborigines. He was committed to translate the Bible, but, as he wrote in 1842, "What can be done with a people whose language knows no such terms as holiness, justice, righteousness, sin, guilt, repentance, redemption, pardon, peace etc., and to whose minds the ideas conveyed by these words are utterly foreign and inexplicable?"[63]

The fourth reason was that so many Indigenous groups were dying out. One early translation team comprised Lancelot Threkeld, a Congregationalist missionary at Lake Macquarie, NSW, and Biraban, an Awabakal man. Actually, Biraban was the translator, because he spoke both Awabakal and English. Threkeld had been commissioned by the London Missionary Society "to acquire such a knowledge of the language of the people . . . to preach to the people in their own tongue, and wonderful works of God."[64] Threkeld's policy was "first obtain the language, then preach the gospel . . . "[65] He and Biraban began the work of translating Luke's Gospel in 1824, and completed it in 1830.[66] However by 1841 the mission had closed, and most of the tribe who spoke that language had died out. Threkeld wrote, "The mission ceased, not from any want of support from the Government, nor from any inclination on my part to retire from the work, but solely from the sad fact that the Aborigines themselves had by then become almost extinct."[67]

---

62. Van Toorn, *Writing*.
63. Attwood, *Country*, 125.
64. Kenny, *Lamb*, 104.
65. Harris, *Blood*, 830.
66. Sutton, *Politics*, 165–67.
67. Harris, *Blood*, 831.

Luke's Gospel in Awabakal was published in 1892 as a historical curiosity.[68] However, as Rademaker observes, Biraban had become an apostle of a translated faith that was both Aboriginal and Christian.[69]

The fifth reason was that so many Indigenous peoples were displaced from their lands that when they found refuge in the government protectorates or reserves, they came with a range of Indigenous languages. When Alf Dyer opened the CMS mission at Oenpelli in 1925, he had eleven Indigenous children who spoke five different languages.[70] There was no common Indigenous language, so it made sense to have English as the common language.

The sixth reason was that missionaries worked from settlements, and the Indigenous peoples were nomadic. As John Dunmore Lang had observed, the best to evangelize the Indigenous peoples was

> to find some zealous missionary who was willing to conform to the Aborigines' wandering habits, who would follow them in a bark canoe as they skimmed across the lakes, who would go hunting with them for possums and bandicoots in the depths of the forest, who would join with them in singing their tribal songs by the evening fire ... Only such a person might secure their confidence and so be able to win them for Christ.[71]

The seventh reason was the strength of government policy, which insisted on the use of English in schools and prohibited the use of Indigenous languages.

As Kidd has written, in Queensland, there was generally inadequate education for Aboriginal children, but there was better provision on church missions. In particular, Presbyterian and Lutheran missions included classes in Aboriginal language, "an important factor in the continuation of Aboriginal culture."[72]

But government policy soon demanded that teaching occur in English. At Piltawodli school in South Australia, for example, the German missionaries taught in the local language from 1839. But the governor closed the school in 1845 and moved the students to the government "Native School," where all instruction was in English.[73] At Cape Bedford, the Lutherans were pressured to abandon teaching in Guugu Yimidhirr. At Arakun in the

68. For more on Threkeld, see Johnston, *Paper War*, 60–103.
69. Rademaker, *Found*, 14.
70. Harris, *Blood*, 839.
71. As quoted in Piggin, *Evangelical*, 47.
72. Kidd, *Black Lives*, 22.
73. Ganter, *Contest*, 181.

1930s, the Presbyterian missionaries were prevented from using the Wik languages in their school.[74] As late as 1950, government policy continued to insist on English. "It cannot be too strongly emphasized that instruction in English will not be confined to formal lessons in language. Every part of the curriculum and almost every lesson should be partly directed towards the acquisition of skill in the use and comprehension of English."[75]

As many missions were in part funded by the government, this forced the missionaries and teachers to implement this policy. It was a policy determined by the aim of assimilation: "The policy of assimilation demands a lingua franca as soon as possible . . . that lingua franca must be English."[76]

It was not until December 1972 that Kim Beazley suggested to the new Prime Minister, Gough Whitlam, that bilingual education would be appropriate. It was announced as policy that night![77] It took many years to implement, but it has been a wonderful development in the education of Indigenous children.

Kim Mahood's essay, "Lost and Found in Translation: Who Can Talk to Country" opens with a quotation from D. H. Laurence's 1923 novel about Australia, *Kangaroo*: "The vast continent is really void of speech . . . this speechless aimless solitariness was in the air. It was natural to the country."[78]

It was characteristic of Europeans, having attempted to silence Indigenous languages, that they then could not hear from Indigenous voices, for they had been rendered inaudible. So also, having dispossessed Indigenous peoples and banished them, they then became invisible. Extermination and assimilation are ways of making people inaudible and invisible.

A translated Bible enables vernacular meditation, prayer, worship, mutual ministry and encouragement, and vernacular evangelism. We can speak to God from our hearts in our heart languages; we can speak to others about God from our hearts in our heart languages.

Anglican Ministry to Indigenous Peoples within Melbourne and Victoria

On Sunday April 24, 1836, the first full services were held in Melbourne. While the liturgy was Anglican, the preacher and only minister present was

74. Lake, *Bible*, 66.

75. Commonwealth Office of Education, "Provisional Syllabus for use in Aboriginal Schools in the Northern Territory," June 1950, as cited in Rademaker, *Found*, 70.

76. L. R. Newby, as cited in Rademaker, *Found*, 70.

77. Rademaker, *Found*, 179.

78. Mahood, "Lost," 29.

a Methodist, Joseph Orton. At the afternoon service, the largest portion in the congregation were Aboriginal people, about fifty in number. The service was in English, but the Aboriginal people showed great interest in the singing![79]

There was great interest in ministry to Indigenous peoples in Melbourne. George Langhorne and then James Smith worked on a settlement by the Yarra (where the Botanic Gardens were later established) from 1835 to 1839. Bishop Charles Perry, who arrived in 1848, had a lively interest in ministry to Indigenous peoples.[80] He was involved in setting up the ABM in Sydney in 1850,[81] which had as one of its stated objectives "training Aboriginal evangelists."[82] He set up the Diocesan Mission Board in Melbourne, 1851, which would focus on Aboriginal peoples and the Chinese in Victoria, as well as Melanesia.[83] In 1854, he set up the Church Missionary Society of Victoria with a similar focus, in the hope that each parish would establish its own Branch Association.[84] Indigenous ministry was done in close association with the Moravians, who were allies, and provided a bench-mark and model for Anglicans.[85]

Charles La Trobe, superintendent and then lieutenant-governor, had a Moravian background, and so was concerned for the welfare and the conversion of Aboriginal peoples.[86] He chaired a committee of religious societies in 1843 to support Indigenous ministry.[87] As a Moravian, his own policy was that conversion should precede civilization. He agreed with the policy of the London Missionary Society, that "no sooner does the Gospel begin to operate upon the mind of the heathen than it leads to the first step of civilization."[88] La Trobe's father, Ignatius, who ran the Moravian training home in Britain, was a staunch supporter of the use of native languages, advising missionaries to live among the people to learn their language.[89] And he also supported the idea that evangelization should precede civilization, contrary to much missionary practice in Australia, which attempted

79. Murray, *Australia*, 132–33.
80. Carolane, "Bulmer," 19–21.
81. Loos, *White Black*, 45, 46.
82. Shaw, *Broughton*, 239.
83. Carolane, "Bulmer," 18.
84. Robin, *Perry*, 174, and Cole, *Church Mission Soc*, 235.
85. Carolane, "Bulmer," 23–31, especially 22.
86. Barnes, *La Trobe*, chapter 14.
87. Barnes, *La Trobe*, 233.
88. Barnes, *La Trobe*, 233.
89. Kenny, *Lamb*, 104.

to civilize first, then evangelize. In his words, "to evangelize is the best way to civilize."[90]

Bishop Perry was in favor of Bible translation when possible. Perry wrote, "The importance of preaching to them in the native tongue, and of translating the Bible and Liturgy, at least in the simple parts, as far as practicable was not to be lost sight of."[91]

One Melbourne Anglican who provided significant leadership in ministry to Indigenous peoples was the Rev. Septimus Chase, who arrived in Melbourne in 1849, served at St. James', then as Vicar of St. Paul's church, and then St. John's Latrobe Street. He was an active member of the committee of the Church of England Mission to the Aborigines of Victoria and provided personal encouragement to many Indigenous peoples and to those who ministered to Indigenous peoples. The *Church of England Messenger* wrote of him, "First, or rather first and last, the neglected native races of the colony found in him their truest protector and best friend. No one we can name has been doing more . . . for the promotion of evangelistic work among the Aborigines and Chinese in Victoria."[92]

Canon Chase's three sons were ordained, and his son Edward Selwyn Chase served at the mission at Yarrabah from 1903 to 1906.

Protector George Robinson and three of the assistant protectors were Methodists. William Thomas, one of the assistants, was later appointed guardian of Aboriginal peoples, and later still, chief government advisor on Aboriginal affairs. He made a serious attempt to understand Indigenous language and customs.[93] As we have seen, he led a service in the Bunurong language in 1840.

There were several missions to Indigenous peoples set up in Victoria. These included the Methodist mission at Buntingdale in 1839; the Anglican missions at Yelta on the Murray (1855), Lake Tyers (1861), Framlingham on the Hopkins River (1864), and Lake Condah near Heywood (1867); and the Moravian missions at Ebenezer (1858) and Ramahyuck on Lake Wellington (1862).[94] Of these, only Lake Tyers and Condah lasted until the twentieth century.

We have already met John Bulmer, a Methodist who served at Yelta and then at Lake Tyers from 1855 to 1913. (He was ordained as an Anglican in 1903.) He learnt Indigenous languages and preached and taught in them.

---

90. Yarwood, *Marsden*, 167.
91. Kenny, *Lamb*, 110.
92. *Church of England Messenger*, "Canon Septimus Chase," August 9, 1895.
93. Barnes, *La Trobe*, 243.
94. Long, *Aboriginal Settlements*, 16.

He developed a great interest in ethnography, to help him to understand the people to whom he ministered. As Carolane explains, "Cross-cultural evangelism required linguistic and cultural translation. Ethnography, therefore, became a major tool for achieving this process and thereby assisted in bridging the gap of cultural difference between the missionary and the missionized."[95] He engaged in expository teaching of the Bible, and trained and used Indigenous teachers and preachers.[96] John and Caroline Bulmer at Yelta and Lake Tyers, and John and Mary Stahle at Lake Condah, served among Indigenous peoples in Victoria for a combined total of 179 years.[97]

There was great encouragement in Victoria with the conversion of Aboriginal man Nathaniel Pepper, through the ministry of Friedrich Spieseke, at the Moravian mission Ebenezer in the Wimmera. Soon after his conversion, Pepper conducted prayer meetings "in the bush"; and evangelized his friends "in his own language."[98] Septimus Chase traveled from Melbourne to baptize him.[99] Carolane comments,

> The genuineness of Pepper's conversion was unquestionable due to the emotional intensity of his response; his immediate desire to give the testimony of his conversion to his tribe in his own language; his ability and willingness to read the New Testament; his eventual work as an assistant missionary under Hagenauer; and his attempts at translating scripture into his own dialect.[100]

One of the most influential events in Melbourne was when Bishop Gilbert White of Carpentaria visited in 1906 to ask CMS to establish a mission at Roper River. The Victorian secretary, the Rev. Arthur Ebbs, responded positively, and the next year CMS agreed to act.[101] Ebbs said that missionaries would need to learn Indigenous languages. "We cannot adequately understand the mind of the black man nor place a right value upon his views until we learn them through his language . . . And is it possible that the British and Foreign Bible Society may yet give them parts of the Bible in their own tongue?"[102]

In 1908, three missionaries left for Roper River, and so began the productive CMS work in what later became the Northern Territory. What

---

95. Carolane, "Bulmer," 136. See chapters 3 and 4.
96. Carolane, "Bulmer," 150, 52.
97. Cole, *Servants*, 79–86.
98. Kenny, *Lamb*, 14, 15.
99. Kenny, *Lamb*, 21.
100. Carolane, "Bulmer," 131. And see Pepper, *Family*.
101. Seiffert, *Refuge*, 52–63, 98, 99.
102. Seiffert, *Refuge*, 65.

principles informed this ministry? In 1911 the Victorian CMS committee resolved, "We are convinced that the Bible, when translated into the languages of the World, is the most potent instrument in our missionary work."[103]

ABM supported ministries at Moore River, Forrest River, Oombulgurri, Moa and Thursday Islands, Pormpuraaw, Kowanyama, Yarrabah, Palm Island, Woorabinda, and Lake Tyers.[104] CMS sent fifty-three missionaries to work with Australian Indigenous peoples in Arnhem Land between 1908 and 1971.[105] Those missions were at Roper River, Emerald River (later moved to Angurugu), Numbulwar, Umbakumba, and Oenpelli, together with a center in Darwin.[106] CMS later helped establish Nungalinya College and sent staff to serve there. BCA, founded in 1919, supported ministry in places such as Kambalda, Geraldton, Mount Magnet, Paraburdoo, Newman, Wickam, South Hedland, Port Hedland, Karratha, Derby, Kununurra, Tennant Creek, Winton, Blackwater, Quilpie, Lightning Ridge, Wilcannia, and Bimbadeen.[107] However, most of these initiatives did not begin until the twentieth century. Both ABM and CMS mostly concentrated their efforts overseas in the nineteenth century.

It is remarkable that in the book *Melbourne Anglicans*, published to mark the sesquicentenary of the Diocese of Melbourne in 1997, that there is no reference to the Indigenous inhabitants of the Port Phillip District, later Victoria, in the nine historical chapters. There is just one brief mention in the final chapter: "This dislocation or buying-off of the original inhabitant was a minor obstacle en route to a Protestant empire of expansionist, civilising, commercialising men and their ladies."[108] There is no mention of the nineteenth-century ministry to Indigenous peoples. There is no mention of any Indigenous Anglicans, and no mention of the precious ministry of members of the diocese among Indigenous peoples in Victoria and throughout Australia through ABM, CMS, and BCA. A remarkable example of invisibility!

Fortunately, the arrival of Archbishop Freier in 2006 has resulted in a higher profile for Indigenous matters in the diocese, including the adoption of a Reconciliation Action Plan and the presence of more ordained Indigenous peoples.

103. Seiffert, *Refuge*, 137.
104. Loos, *White Black*, viii.
105. Cole, *Church Mission Soc*, 325–44.
106. Cole, *Church Mission Soc*, 168–206, and Cole, *Mission to Church*.
107. Breward, *History*, 116.
108. James Minchin in Porter, *Melbourne*, 203.

So, in terms of Melbourne and Victoria, there was some local work done in the nineteenth century and a wider commitment across Australia in the twentieth century through CMS, ABM, and BCA. Notable contributions more recently have been in Bible translation and the founding of Nungalinya College in Darwin.

What of Anglicans across Australia?

Archdeacon (later Bishop) Broughton wrote in 1829 that "because of her advantageous position in the colony, the Church of England should strive to be the Mother of Missionaries to the native population."[109]

However, it must be admitted that Anglicans have not always lived up to that ideal. Other denominations such as the Methodists, Moravians, Lutherans, and Presbyterians often took the initiative, and Anglicans lagged behind.

Bishop Hale found great difficulty in gaining support for Indigenous ministry in Perth and Brisbane.[110] Though Bishop Parry had invited John Gribble to Perth to work among Indigenous peoples, when Gribble was attacked by wealthy farmers, the governor, and the press, the bishop failed to support him, probably because he was trying to raise money to build the cathedral and could not afford to offend wealthy people.[111] Gribble's son was told, "Your father was sacrificed to build the Cathedral . . . we were raising money for it at the time."[112]

Bishop White of Carpentaria, speaking in Melbourne in 1901, pointed out that the Lutherans had begun a mission in Carpentaria in 1886, and the Moravians had opened one on behalf of the Presbyterians in 1891, but the Anglicans were still to act. He compared the energy of the German church with the inactivity of the English church, and challenged Anglicans to "imitate the Germans."[113] Similarly, Bishop Frodsham of North Queensland, speaking in Melbourne in 1906, admitted, "We have certainly done very little to preach the gospel to the people we have dispossessed."[114]

We see signs of the weakness of the Anglican contribution in the lack of Aboriginal people being ordained. James Noble was deaconed in 1925, because John Gribble requested it, but he was never priested. The

---

109. Bridges, "NSW," 272.
110. Gourlay, *Hale*, 37–56, 67–104.
111. Harris, "Anglicanism," 229–30.
112. Reynolds, *Whispering*, 128.
113. Freier, "Living with the *Munpitch*," 107.
114. Harris, "Anglicanism," 233.

next Indigenous ordinations took place in 1975! Two Torres Strait Island men were deaconed in 1919 and priested in 1925. This may well have been because of the culture of evangelization and training done by the London Missionary Society, before they handed over their mission to the Anglicans in 1915.[115] In 1953, CMS missionaries put forward four men for ordination, but the bishop of Carpentaria required them to spend six years in a distant theological college. They decided not to go ahead.[116]

Remarkably, the Indigenous peoples who lived in Tasmania are nearly invisible in Stephens's history of the Diocese of Tasmania.[117] In his discussion of the founding of the church, there is no mention of the Indigenous inhabitants, as there is no mention of the Black War or the Black Line, nor of the attempt to remove all Indigenous peoples from the main island and send them to the Flinders Island mission at Wybalenna. He describes the history of the diocese as "not always a pretty tale,"[118] but there is no mention of injustice to Indigenous peoples as an aspect of the ugliness. Furthermore, he mentions the ministry of Marcus Brownrig of St. John's Launceston, and of Bishop Montgomery, to the Indigenous peoples living on Flinders Island, but describes it as a ministry to "half-castes." [119] Montgomery used that expression, but it is a remarkably offensive word to use in 1991 without comment, implying as it does an ideology of caste.

It is a relief to turn to Hilliard's history of the Anglican Church in South Australia.[120] Here are numerous references to Indigenous peoples, though not as the previous owners of the land. He mentions the settlement at Poonindie set up by Archdeacon Mathew (sometimes Matthew) Hale, later bishop of Perth and then of Brisbane. This lasted from 1850 to 1894, when it was sold off.[121] BCA society ran Koonibba Aboriginal mission.[122] St. Francis House in Semaphore, set up by ABM, provided accommodation for part-Aboriginal young people from 1947 to 1960.[123] In 1981, the committee called Anglicans Supporting Aborigines was formed, and a lay chaplain

---

115. Harris, "Anglicanism," 234, 45.
116. Harris, *Blood*, 857.
117. Stephens, *Tasmania*.
118. Stephens, *Tasmania*, 1.
119. Stephens, *Tasmania*, 119–20. For information on Montgomery's ministry to Indigenous peoples see Withycombe, *Montgomery*, 67–87.
120. Hilliard, *South Australia*.
121. Hilliard, *South Australia*, 37. See also Brown, *Short*, 84–91.
122. Hilliard, *South Australia*, 104.
123. Hilliard, *South Australia*, 115, 17.

was appointed to minister to them.[124] More recently, an Aboriginal man, Chris McLeod, has been appointed an assistant bishop to minister among Indigenous peoples.[125]

However, neither of these histories acknowledge that the Crown land granted for churches and church housing was formerly Indigenous land, nor that it is stolen land. Some recognition of this unfortunate truth is called for. In the words of Reynolds,

> When the British formally annexed eastern Australia on 7 February 1788, they claimed sovereignty and, what was more exceptional, ownership of all the property as well. In one extraordinary proclamation, the Crown expropriated the land of perhaps half a million people over the eastern half [of] a continent. Once done, it remained undone for more than 200 years, to be partially remedied in the High Court's Mabo judgment of 1992. This was in inescapable birth stain that coloured everything else that followed.[126]

The "Crown grants" of land to the churches were grants of stolen land. In the words of Jeremy Bentham in 1803, "This flaw is an incurable one."[127] Blindness to this grave reality leads to blindness to Indigenous peoples and deafness to their voices.

Our government has apologized for the "stolen generation." We have not yet apologized for stolen land, stolen livelihoods, fractured families, lost languages, crushed culture, lost lifestyles, demolished social structures, or for damaged or obliterated animals, plants, birds, and fish.

Lessons from New Zealand

It is instructive to compare missionary work in Australia with New Zealand, which was much more successful. Marsden preached the first sermon in New Zealand on Christmas Day, 1814, accompanied by three missionaries who stayed to continue the ministry. Despite many setbacks and failures, by the time Bishop Selwyn arrived in 1842, he was able to state that he found the whole Māori race had been converted to Christianity![128] The combined

---

124. Hilliard, *South Australia*, 156.

125. Diocese of Adelaide website, "Bishop Chris," https://adelaideanglicans.com/bishop-chris.

126. Reynolds, *Whispering*, x. The western part of Australia was similarly annexed and appropriated in 1827.

127. As quoted in Reynolds, *Whispering*, x.

128. Yates, *Conversion*, 15–17, 116.

effects of the ministries of CMS, the Methodists, and the Roman Catholics had produced a remarkable result. How had this happened? One advantage of New Zealand was that all the Māori spoke the same language, even though their tribes were often at war with each other. But there were two striking features of the mission in New Zealand.

The first was the translation, teaching, publication, and circulation of the Bible. The New Testament was completed by 1837, and the whole Bible by 1857. The *Book of Common Prayer* had been translated by 1827. So the Māori could hear the Bible and read the Bible in their own language, pray in their own language, and teach the Bible to others in their own language. Newman claims this was the first Bible translation in the Southern hemisphere.[129] So many Bibles were published that it was reckoned that there was one Bible for every two Māori![130] One man walked 250 miles to buy a copy of the New Testament. "One thing only do I desire . . . the Word of God."[131]

The second was that as a result of this biblical literacy, the Māori were able to be taught and trained as preachers and evangelists. One Methodist mission had seventeen Indigenous assistants.[132] Henry Williams commented on the Māori's proficiency in leading in prayer, "having a greater command of language."[133] William Williams took an evangelist with him to Wangai, and then left him in charge of the mission.[134] In the South Island, the Methodist James Watkin trained twenty-six Indigenous preachers, while in the North Island, Joseph Mathews of CMS offered two or three hours of instruction to Indigenous preachers before they preached their sermons.[135] The Roman Catholics made good use of lay Māori catechists.[136] William Williams commented, "the Word has only been preached by Native Teachers."[137] Remarkably, their evangelistic enthusiasm even led to them traveling to convert hostile tribes.[138] Bishop Selwyn reckoned that the influence of Māori teachers and preachers often exceeded that of their tribal chiefs.[139]

129. Newman, *Bible and Treaty*, 313.
130. Yates, *Conversion*, 127.
131. Newman, *Bible and Treaty*, 110.
132. Yates, *Conversion*, 62.
133. Yates, *Conversion*, 77.
134. Yates, *Conversion*, 77, 78.
135. Yates, *Conversion*, 112.
136. Yates, *Conversion*, 109, 10.
137. Yates, *Conversion*, 101.
138. Yates, *Conversion*, 124.
139. Yates, *Conversion*, 109. Unfortunately, Bishop Selywn was reluctant to ordain

Conclusion

It is a privilege to contribute to this presentation to Archbishop Freier. I praise God for his commitment to the Indigenous peoples of Australia in his work as a teacher at Thursday Island, Kowanyama, and Yarrabah, and as an advisory teacher in Aboriginal education in the Queensland Education Department. He researched and wrote his PhD on the history of the Mitchell River Mission, served as bishop of the Northern Territory, and continues to advocate for Indigenous peoples.

Harris celebrates the ministry of early Indigenous Australians in using the Bible to evangelize their peoples.[140] He names Thomas Bennelong, James Mgunaitponi (Unaipon), David Unaipon, James Wanganeen, William Kropinyeri, Moses Uraiakuraia, James Noble, James Djipanyma, and Garbala Minimere (Barnabas). To these names we should add that of Nathanial Pepper. In the words of Michael Gumbuli, "They were the example to us, Old James and Old Barnabas . . . they really were the missionaries themselves. So were Old Elizabeth and the other old Christian ladies. They showed us the way."[141]

In this essay, I have tried to show that the Bible should be the chief instrument of Christian mission. When the Bible is translated and taught, then people are able to meditate, pray, praise, and worship in their own language. When people are trained to use the Bible in ministry and evangelism, then they will be confident to speak of Christ to others. This viewpoint reflects the Anglicanism of the ordination services in the *Book of Common Prayer*, in which the instrument of ministry handed to those being ordained is the translated Bible.[142]

These ideas merely express the teaching of Scripture:

> But as for you, continue in what you have learned and firmly believed, knowing from whom you learned it, and how from childhood you have known the sacred writings that are able to instruct you for salvation through faith in Christ Jesus. All scripture is inspired by God and is useful for teaching, for reproof, for correction, and for training in righteousness, so that everyone who belongs to God may be proficient, equipped for every good work.

Māori. It was eleven years before he ordained a deacon and twenty-four years before he ordained a priest. Newman, *Bible and Treaty*, 273, 319.

140. Harris, *Aboriginal Evangelists*, 9–20.
141. Harris, *Aboriginal Evangelists*, 20.
142. Adam, *Pure Word*, 48–51.

You then, my child, be strong in the grace that is in Christ Jesus; and what you have heard from me through many witnesses entrust to faithful people who will be able to teach others as well.

Do your best to present yourself to God as one approved by him, a worker who has no need to be ashamed, rightly explaining the word of truth.[143]

---

143. 2 Timothy 3:14–17, 2:1, 2, 15.

Bibliography

Adam, Peter, "People from Every Language: Australia's Indigenous Peoples and God's Gospel Plan." *Vox Reformata* 83 (2018) 5–24.

———. *The "Very Pure Word of God": The Book of Common Prayer as a Model of Biblical Liturgy*. London: Latimer, 2012.

Arnold, John. *Mission Impossible*. South Brisbane: Matthew Hale, 2013.

Attwood, Bain. *The Good Country: The Djadja Wurrung, the Settlers, and the Protectorate*. Clayton: Monash University Publishing, 2017.

Barnes, John. *La Trobe: Traveller, Writer, Governor*. Braddon: Halstead, 2017.

Breward, Ian. *A History of the Australian Churches*. St. Leonards: Allen and Unwin, 1993.

Bridges, Barry J. "The Church of England and the Aborigines of New South Wales." PhD diss., University of New South Wales, 1978.

Brown, Judith M. *Augustus Short, D. D. Bishop of Adelaide*. Walkerville: Hodge, 1973.

Carolane, Peter. "Instinct for Mission: John Bulmer, Missionary to the Aborigines of Victoria, 1855–1913." PhD diss., University of Melbourne, 2009.

Cole, Keith. *A History of the Church Missionary Society of Australia*. Melbourne: Church Missionary Society Trust, 1971.

———. *From Mission to Church: The CMS Mission to the Aborigines of Arnhem Land 1908–1985*. Bendigo: Keith Cole Publications, 1985.

Cole, E. K. *Servants for Jesus' Sake: Long-Serving Victorian CMS Missionaries*, Bendigo: Keith Cole Publications, 1993.

Cranmer, Thomas. "A Fruitful Exhortation to the Reading and Knowledge of Holy Scripture." In *Certain Sermons or Homilies appointed to be read in churches in the time of Queen Elizabeth of famous memory*, edited by John Griffiths, 1–10, London: SPCK, 1864.

Fels, Marie Hansen. *"I Succeeded Once": The Aboriginal Protectorate on the Mornington Peninsula 1839–40*. Canberra: Australian National University Press, 2011.

Fletcher, Richard. *The Barbarian Conversion: From Paganism to Christianity*. Berkeley: University of California Press, 1999.

Freier, Philip L. "The Anglican Church of Australia and Indigenous Australians: The Case of the Mitchell River Mission." *Journal of Anglican Studies* 1:2 (2003) 62–80.

———. "Living with the *Munpitch*: the history of Mitchell River Mission 1905–1967." PhD diss., James Cook University, 1999.

Ganter, Regina. *The Contest for Aboriginal Souls: European Missionary Agendas in Australia*. Acton: Australian National University Press and Aboriginal History Inc., 2018.

Gascoigne, John. *The Enlightenment and the Origins of European Australia*. Cambridge: Cambridge University Press, 2005.

Goodman, Charles. *The Church in Victoria during the Episcopate of the Right Reverend Charles Perry, First Bishop of Melbourne, etc*. Melbourne: Melville, Mullen and Slade, 1892.

Gourlay, Michael. *The Good Bishop: The Story of Mathew Hale*. Brisbane: Mathew Hale Public Library, 2015.

Hancock, Christopher. *Robert Morrison and the Birth of Chinese Protestantism*. London, T. & T. Clark Theology, 2008.

Harris, John. *A New Story in an Old Land: The First Aboriginal Evangelists.* Heidelberg: Bush Church Aid, 2015.

———. "Anglicanism and Indigenous Peoples." In *Anglicanism in Australia*, edited by Bruce Kaye, 223–46. Carlton South: Melbourne University Press, 1998.

———. *One Blood: 200 Years of Aboriginal Encounter with Christianity.* Sutherland: Albatross, 1990.

———. *We Wish We'd Done More: Ninety Years of CMS and Aboriginal Issues in North Australia.* Revised Edition, Adelaide: Openbook, 1998.

Hilliard, David. *Godliness and Good Order: A History of the Anglican Church in South Australia.* Netley: Wakefield, 1986.

Hiney, Tim. *On the Missionary Trail.* New York: Atlantic Monthly, 2000.

Johnston, Anna. *The Paper War: Morality, Print Culture, and Power in Colonial New South Wales.* Crawley: University of Western Australia, 2011.

Kenny, Robert. *The Lamb Enters the Dreaming: Nathanael Pepper and the Ruptured World.* Melbourne: Scribe, 2007.

Kidd, Rosalind. *Black Lives Government Lies.* Redcliffe: Dr. Ros Kidd, 2002.

———. *The Way We Civilise.* St. Lucia: University of Queensland Press, 1997.

Kyme, Brian, and Carroll Jan. *Grit and Grace: The Story of the Anglican Board of Missions—Australia.* Mirabooka and Beechboro: John Septimus Roe Anglican School, 2013.

Lake, Meredith. *The Bible in Australia: A Cultural History.* Sydney: NewSouth, 2018.

Long, J. P. M. *Aboriginal Settlements: A Survey of Institutional Communities in Eastern Australia,* Canberra: Australian National University Press, 1970.

Loos, Noel. *White Christ Black Cross: The Emergence of a Black Church.* Canberra: Aboriginal Studies, 2007.

Mahood, Kim. "Lost and Found in Translation: Who Can Speak to Country?" *Griffith Review* 63 (2018) 29–46.

Naden, Kathryn, and Michelle Wigton, Francine Riches, and Monica Short. *A Celebration of God's Faithfulness: AEF History, etc.* Highpoint City: AEF, 2017.

Newman, Keith. *Bible and Treaty: Missionaries among the Māori—A new perspective.* Rosedale: Penguin, 2010.

Murray, Iain H. *Australian Christian Life from 1788: An Introduction and an Anthology,* Edinburgh: Banner of Truth, 1988.

Pepper, Phillip, with Tess De Araugo. *You Are What You Make Yourself to Be: The Story of a Victorian Aboriginal Family 1842–1980.* South Yarra: Hyland, 1989.

Piggin, Stuart. *Evangelical Christianity in Australia: Spirit, Word and World.* Melbourne: Oxford University Press, 1996.

Piggin, Stuart, and Robert D. Linder. *The Fountain of Public Prosperity: Evangelical Christians in Australian History 1740–1914.* Clayton: Monash University Publishing, 2018.

Porter, Brian, ed. *Melbourne Anglicans: The Diocese of Melbourne 1847–1997.* Melbourne: Mitre Books, 1997.

Rademaker, Laura. *Found in Translation: Many Meanings on a North Australian Mission.* Honolulu: University of Hawai'i Press, 2018.

Reynolds, Henry, ed. *Aborigines and Settlers.* Stanmore: Cassell, 1972.

———. *This Whispering in Our Hearts.* Revised edition. Sydney: NewSouth, 2018.

Robin, A. de Q. *Charles Perry, Bishop of Melbourne: The Challenges of a Colonial Episcopate, 1847–1876.* Nedlands: University of Western Australia Press, 1967.

Sandefur, Joy. "The Aboriginalisation of the Church at Ngukurr." PhD diss., La Trobe University, 1998.

Sanneh, Lamin. *Translating the Message: The Missionary Impact on Culture*. Maryknoll: Orbis, 1989.

Seiffert, Murray. *Gumbuli of Ngukurr: Aboriginal Elder in Arnhem Land*. Brunswick East: Acorn, 2011.

———. *Refuge on the Roper: The Origins of Roper River Mission Ngukurr*. Brunswick East: Acorn, 2008.

Shaw, G. P. *Patriarch and Patriot: William Grant Broughton 1788-1853*. Carlton: Melbourne University Press, 1978.

Stephens, Geoffrey. *The Anglican Church in Tasmania: A Diocesan History to Mark the Sesquicentary, 1992*. Hobart: The Trustees of the Diocese, 1991.

Sutton, Peter. *The Politics of Suffering: Indigenous Australian and the End of the Liberal Consensus*. Carlton: Melbourne University Press, 2009.

Swain, Tony, and Deborah Bird Rose. *Aboriginal Australians and Christian Missions*. Adelaide: Australian Association for the Study of Religions, 1988.

Van Toorn, Penny. *Writing Never Arrives Naked: Early Aboriginal Cultures of Writing in Australia*. Canberra: Aboriginal Studies, 2006.

Withycombe, Robert. *Montgomery of Tasmania: Henry and Maud Montgomery in Australasia*. Brunswick East: Acorn, 2009.

Woodberry, Robert D. "The Missionary Roots of Liberal Democracy." *American Political Science Review*, 102:2 (2012) 244-74.

Yarwood, A. T. *Samuel Marsden: The Great Survivor*. Carlton: Melbourne University Press, 1977.

Yates, Timothy. *The Conversion of the Māori*. Grand Rapids, MI: Eerdmans, 2013.

10

James and Angelina Noble

Pioneer Australian Anglican Missionaries

Wei Han Kuan

JAMES AND ANGELINA NOBLE were Aboriginal Christian missionaries and leaders from the earliest part of the twentieth century. They were strong in the grace that is in Jesus Christ. They took what they heard from white missionaries who served them and entrusted it to others, especially to other Indigenous Australians. Their lives were full of evidence of suffering as soldiers of Christ.

Their story deserves to be better known by all Australians. Philip and Joy Freier know this story well from their years in North Queensland and in the Northern Territory. The Nobles feature in Philip's doctoral dissertation on the history of the Mitchell River Mission—Kowanyama—where the Freiers lived for seven years.[1] During their seven years in the NT the Freiers witnessed first-hand the Nobles' legacy at Ngukurr. This is a story close to the Freiers' hearts and a priority for so much of their lives and ministries, and I am honored to have been invited to contribute this essay to this *Festschrift*.

---

1. Freier, "Living with the *Munpitch*."

Early Years

James Noble is most commonly introduced as Australia's first ordained Aboriginal minister, deaconed at St. George's Anglican Cathedral, Perth, on September 13, 1925.[2] A photograph confirms the many descriptions of him as a striking man: six feet tall, athletic, handsome, with an intelligent and noble bearing.[3]

James was of full Aboriginal descent, born in 1876 near Normanton, a town in the Gulf Country region of northwest Queensland.[4] As a teenager, he began working as a drover, moving cattle stock between the Doyle family properties of Riversleigh on the Gregory River in Queensland and Invermien near Scone in New South Wales. Alec Doyle recounted his memory of Noble asking his father, James Doyle, to be allowed to stay at Invermien and be educated.[5] James Doyle agreed, and Noble was taken under the family's wing. He was given employment during the day, and James Doyle organized for him to be educated by staff from the nearby Scone Grammar School.

James Noble's intelligence and sense of humor is apparent in this Alec Doyle recollection:

> Another thing I remember is an incident which the then Bishop, Bishop Stanton, told with great gusto as a joke against himself. During a visit to Scone, the Bishop stayed at Invermien, and went for a walk in the garden before breakfast. Seeing a black boy raking the garden path he went over to have a word with him, and, to open the conversation, said, "That fella Mr. Doyle: how long he bin sit down alonga Invermien?" He was somewhat shattered by Noble's reply, "My Lord, Mr. Doyle has resided at Invermien for the past thirteen years."[6]

The Doyles were observant Christians, and together with the Doyle children Noble attended Sunday School classes at St. Luke's Scone. The name James Noble is entered into the parish's baptismal register on July 1, 1895. This is the earliest written record of his Christian name. Was he named after his patron, James Doyle?

---

2. Higgins, *James Noble of Yarrabah*, 1. This volume was self-published and is now almost impossible to access, with only six library copies in Australia. Higgins interviewed descendants and family members who were first-hand eyewitnesses, recording in detail recollections that are nowhere else to be found.

3. Gribble, *Problem of the Australian Aboriginal*, frontispiece.

4. James's birth year is ascertained from the information supplied at his subsequent baptism and from the wedding register at Yarrabah.

5. Higgins, *James Noble of Yarrabah*, 1–5.

6. Higgins, *James Noble of Yarrabah*, 3.

Formal baptismal records only tell part of the story. Here is James's own account of his conversion:

> Before I became a Christian . . . I was a bush native. My mother and father died in the bush. I first saw white people when I went to a station in the Leichhardt country and at that time I was only a boy. I stayed there for a long time and the station owner took me to his home at Scone, NSW. All that time I had been droving. I learned to read at the Grammar School at Scone. I reached the fourth class at school, and up to that time I had heard a lot about prayers, religion and churches. Then a missionary came along and lectured on missions . . . He was the Rev. Mr. Boyce. That was when I heard the real things that influenced me. I felt I wanted to do some good. I wanted to go to New Guinea, where Mr. Boyce came from, but I was not permitted to do that, owing to the prevalence, of disease there.
>
> I was at Townsville for three or four years and afterwards at Yarrabah, where Mr. Gribble was stationed, and I stayed there with him. I was not a missionary at that time, but was wishing that some day I would be.[7]

In recalling his conversion, what stood out for Noble were the missionary origins and missionary impulse of his Christian faith.[8]

Within a few seasons, the much cooler climate of NSW began to have a deleterious effect on the young Noble's health. He was sent to live with Canon Alfred Edwards, Rector of Hughenden in North Queensland. Edwards had studied at Moore College and been ordained in Sydney for the Diocese of North Queensland in 1880. He had been immediately posted as a missionary to Herbert River. He was honored for his service in the north when he was appointed an honorary canon of North Queensland in 1887. It seems that he was selected as just the right kind of mentor for the young mission-minded man.[9] Unfortunately, Edwards died on February 12, 1898, not long after Noble's arrival.

This was a potentially disastrous development for Noble. His athletic prowess attracted the attention of racing promoters, who saw a money-making opportunity. This account was recorded later:

---

7. "'Hoblah Jim.' First Native Clergyman. Rev. James Noble and His Mentor." *Daily News* (Perth, WA), September 17, 1925.

8. One subsequent postcolonial commentator has attempted to reinterpret his experience as that of a black man finding success by becoming a European, thus subjugating most—but not all—of his Indigenous culture and experience. See Mukuka, *Call Me a Black Man*.

9. Cable Clerical Index, 766.

> Mr. Gribble told of an early experience in the career of his dusky friend when he was asked to fall victim to the wiles of well known sporting celebrities who were profoundly impressed by his ability on the running track ... However "James" was not persuaded to discard his mission ambitions.
>
> When the interviewer ventured the suggestion that he must have been very smart on the track to attract such much notice, "James," who was standing close at hand popped his head around the door and smilingly acknowledged that that was so. "One hundred and fifty yards in fourteen seconds," he admitted.[10]

That is fast by any standard. At this time, Christopher Barlow, bishop of North Queensland, "took considerable interest in Noble."[11] Barlow's churchmanship has been described as initially Evangelical, but moving to a more moderate liberalism with a focus on spirituality in worship and the personal faith of the clergy.[12] These were his earlier years, and Barlow considered Noble in danger of drifting. So he asked the missionary at Yarrabah to take him on. Thus, James Noble arrived at Yarrabah some time in 1898.[13] It was there that James Noble began his long association with Christian ministry, mission work, and his mentor, Ernest Gribble. It was also at Yarrabah that James Noble met his future wife, Angelina.

Angelina Noble's early history ought to fill the contemporary Australian reader's heart with great sadness, anger, and a steely determination to right the wrongs of our past. She was born in an Aboriginal community near Dalby, Northern Queensland, around 1879, but kidnapped as a young girl by a white man, a traveling horse trader.[14] She was, in outback slang, a "stockman's boy": an Aboriginal girl with hair cut short and dressed as boy, forced to accompany the man through his travels and function as his concubine. Renamed "Tommy," her sexual slavery came to an end when the local police around Cairns freed her. She was immediately sent to the

---

10. "'Hoblah Jim.'"

11. Harris, *One Blood*, 518.

12. Thorn and Vockler, "Barlow, Christopher George."

13. Higgins wrongly dates Noble's arrival to "about 1896," which is too soon, as the reason for Noble's move was Canon Edwards's death in early 1898.

14. Jan Kociumbas claims that Angelina was part-Aboriginal: Kociumbas, "Noble, Angelina." An article in the Port Pirie paper mentions in passing that James was married to "Angelina, a half-caste" ("James Noble," *Recorder*, Port Pirie, SA: March 26, 1925). Higgins, who had access to family members at Yarrabah, makes no mention of this, and remarks that she was born near Winton (*James Noble of Yarrabah*, 16).

mission at Yarrabah. Higgins records the memory of Ernestine Yeatman, "an old Yarrabah identity":

> She [Angelina] came over here in a stockman's suit, cowboy hat and everything; riding boots. When the police brought her down from the jailhouse in Cairns they thought she was a young man. She never showed that she was a girl till they found out when they were doing their toilet, you know. They found she was a woman. They got a surprise.[15]

Yeatman also reported that "Angelina was very young when she married James Noble." A photograph of the couple with Horace Reid, reproduced by Higgins, seems to confirm that assessment.[16]

James Noble's first wife had been Margaret "Maggie" Frew. They were married by 1900.[17] When compared to the written records, the chronology and details of the next two years seem to have been confused in the memories collected by Higgins, whose details are subsequently followed by later writers.[18] The trauma of these early years could have easily confused the memory of second-hand witnesses as they recollected to Higgins some seventy years later.

James and Maggie had a daughter, Blanche Margaret, who only lived ten months, from July 1901 to May 1902.[19] Maggie was described as "a nice

---

15. Higgins, *James Noble of Yarrabah*, 16.

16. Photograph is at Higgins, *James Noble of Yarrabah*, 18. See also Register of Baptisms, Yarrabah Bellenden Kerr Aboriginal Mission, 1891–1927, AIATSIS MS3234. Transcript available online at http://www.cifhs.com/qldrecords/locyarrabah.html. Records show that an "Angelina" was baptized at Yarrabah in July 1902: unknown parents, no family name, age presumed as "about 21 years old." It seems reasonable to assume that this is Angelina Noble's record and that she would have arrived in Yarrabah earlier that year. If this is correct, then Angelina was either a very young-looking twenty-one-year-old or her probable age was revised upward, probably to endorse her capacity to enter into marriage.

17. The Register of Baptisms indicate that she was born around 1880, the date of her baptism was May 24, 1900; married "Jimmie Noble"; and records her death in April 1902.

18. There are good reasons for giving priority to the contemporary written records. They are less likely to have been clouded by the passage of time; and there are no obvious social or political reasons for the records to have been amended or falsified at the time.

19. Higgins (*James Noble of Yarrabah*, 15) identifies the child as James Hilton, an identification followed by subsequent writers. This does not agree with the Register of Baptisms, which identifies the child as Blanche Margaret; James Hilton is identified in the Register as the first child of Angelina and James. Higgins also describes Maggie as passing away a short time after her baby's birth.

gentle girl, but very delicate," and she died in April 1902, a month before her child's death.

Soon after in that year, James and Lizzie Moore, the first matron of the Yarrabah hospital, were engaged. Sadly, Lizzie died just before the set wedding date in July 1902.[20] She had contracted a fatal disease from one of her patients.

James and Angelina Noble were married on 15 October 1902.[21] A son, James Hilton, was born on 17 August 1903, but died that year.

The few years between 1898 and 1903 were clearly tumultuous ones for James and Angelina. On his side there had been ill-health, a move from NSW to Queensland, possible spiritual wandering, death of a mentor he barely got to know, a new life at Yarrabah, and the deaths of a wife, a fiancée, and two children. On her side there had been a torrid experience of kidnapping, slavery, and abuse, ended by her rescue and arrival at Yarrabah in early 1902. She was baptized on July 25, 1902, married less than two months after, then soon pregnant, giving birth but losing James Hilton only after a few months.

James and Angelina were therefore no strangers to suffering in these early years. Suffering, however, did not embitter them. Christian faith transformed their experience of suffering into enduring missionary service in the name of Jesus Christ.

Yarrabah Mission

The Yarrabah Bellenden Kerr Mission had been founded by the Rev. John Gribble in 1892, only six years before John Noble's arrival.[22] Gribble was a missionary and fierce advocate for Aboriginal peoples. He dared to take on the colonial establishment of the day and paid a high personal price for it.[23] In John Harris's assessment, John Gribble was driven by his sense of the absolute necessity of personal salvation found in Christ, his outrage at the injustices against Aboriginal people, and the failure of the Christian community to bring them the knowledge of Jesus Christ. Yarrabah was the last in a line of missions founded by Gribble as a place of refuge, protection,

20. See handwritten notes appended to the Register of Baptisms: " . . . zie Moore confirmed in Brisbane, died sunday [sic] 20. 7.1902."

21. See Yarrabah Marriages, 1901–1916, a transcript of a photocopy of a Register of Marriages, 1901–1916 (original lost), http://www.cifhs.com/qldrecords/YarrabahMarriages1901_1916.html.

22. See Gribble's ADB entry ("Gribble, John Brown").

23. John Harris provides an excellent overview of Gribble's ministry. See Harris, *One Blood*, 407–27.

and instruction, but he died in 1893 before the mission could be fully established. That work was left to his son Ernest Gribble.

Ernest Gribble took up his father's work and traveled extensively through the region to encourage people to come to Yarrabah to receive refuge, medical help, and training in practical skills. Harris describes how Gribble found very many children in the surrounding fringe camps, "orphaned, starving and diseased," very young addicts of opium and alcohol, and very young girls having been abused by Europeans and Chinese and Filipino traders. In Harris's view, it was Gribble's passion to rescue these that led to rapid early growth at Yarrabah.[24]

Gribble's philosophy was to "place as much as trust as possible in the most able of the people."[25] He delighted to list the roles occupied by Aboriginal people at Yarrabah: organists, music teachers, dispensary matron, motor mechanic, engineer in charge of the mission's launch boat, an ex-prisoner now "drummer in the brass band, Mission dentist, extracting and filling teeth, and . . . sacristan and server at the Church," printers at the mission press.

Aboriginal people had leading roles in the Yarrabah hospital and on several farms growing vegetables, fruit, cotton, dairy cows, and pigs. The mission also had an operating fire brigade that carried out weekly training, and a rifle corps. It was not all work and no fun: there were also a sailing club, sports teams, and a subsequently famous brass band.[26] Yarrabah's Court of Justice met weekly to deal with "complaints and misbehaviour." Menmuny, or King John, an early convert and recognized elder, played a leading role as its president. In spiritual matters, Aboriginal men like Alick Bybee were free to take the initiative to organize and preach at informal services for Aboriginal people camped on the fringes of the mission compound.[27]

By the time James and Angelina Noble were married at Yarrabah in 1902, it had become home to perhaps a hundred people. James moved quickly into leadership and was noted as an able preacher and teacher of the faith. He held a lay reader's license and was Yarrabah's synod representative. In 1905, there were no less than nine outstations. The largest of these at Bukki Creek was under James's direction, with Angelina playing a vital role alongside. Their early years of marriage at Yarrabah were years of training and development for what was to come.

---

24. Harris, *One Blood*, 502–3.
25. Gribble, *Forty Years*, 117–18.
26. Gribble, *Forty Years*, 122.
27. Higgins, *James Noble of Yarrabah*, chapter 2. Also, Harris, *One Blood*, 506.

The Mitchell River Expedition

James and Angelina's potential for missionary work was recognized as early as 1904, when they were selected to accompany Gribble to Mitchell River on the western side of North Queensland to explore starting a similar work there. It was probably at this point that James Noble first considered himself "a missionary" in fulfilment of his early ambitions.

A mission at Mitchell River had been envisaged for some time by the bishop of Carpentaria, Gilbert White.[28] In 1904, a full-scale missionary expedition involving Gribble, three white men, and six Yarrabah Aboriginal missionaries, including the Nobles, was undertaken.

The presence of the Aboriginal men certainly assisted, but Angelina's contribution was perhaps the more significant for building trust among the locals. Philip Freier writes of her contribution to the expedition:

> The presence of Angelina Noble had opened up for the missionaries a whole new domain of interaction and confidence with the women and children. Whilst bush Aborigines had seen Aboriginal men as native police, stockmen or general retainers to whites, it is most unlikely that they would have encountered an Aboriginal woman travelling freely with her husband in a party of whites. The main experience of Aboriginal women with whites was that of rape or abduction into concubinage, with those Aboriginal women on the station precincts mostly detained against their will. Coming as she had through these experiences herself, Angelina would have been well placed to understand the apprehensions of the Aboriginal women and their fears for the safety of their own children in the presence of whites.[29]

Angelina's gender and linguistic and relational gifts were the keys to her ability to win trust from the locals. She got to know them well enough to be able to explain the story of an English-speaking Aboriginal woman living among their tribe: this woman had been abducted, lived among the whites where she had learnt the language, and then escaped to return to her tribe with a child who had been fathered by a white man.[30]

The party returned to Yarrabah, having laid the foundations for a new mission, later known as Kowanyama.

---

28. Freier, "Living with the *Munpitch*," 106. See chapter 4 for an account of the various expeditions that relate to the founding of the Mitchell River Mission, Kowanyama.
29. Freier, "Living with the *Munpitch*," 133–34.
30. Freier, "Living with the *Munpitch*," 133. See also Gribble, *A Despised Race*, 63.

Roper River Mission

Four years later, James and Angelina Noble's missionary focus and desire led to them volunteering to join three white missionaries from the Victorian Church Missionary Association on a founding expedition to the Roper River.[31] The CMA was a progenitor of the present-day Church Missionary Society. It had been in charge of the Aboriginal work at Lake Condah and Lake Tyers, in Victoria, since the mid-1800s. In 1906, news reached the south of the injustices and desperate situation for Aboriginal people in Arnhem Land. Pastoral lease holders, most notably the massive London-based Eastern and African Cold Storage Company, were determined to exterminate Aboriginal people on their leases in order to secure their interests, and they employed gangs of men to hunt and shoot on sight all Aboriginal inhabitants.[32]

Despite being in a parlous financial state, the Victorian CMA determined that God was calling them north. The collective determination of that generation of Christians is still stirring reading today.[33] An exploratory visit to Roper River was made by Bishop White and the CMA's general secretary, Rev. Arthur Ebbs, in 1907. The necessary funds were raised by 1908, and George Huthnance, Reg Joynt, and Charles Sharpe were sent. Practical as well as spiritual qualifications were needed. Huthnance, a farmer and teacher, was ordained specifically for the role, Joynt was a teacher, and Sharp a stockman.[34]

They visited the successful mission at Yarrabah en route, and close to the end of their fortnight's stay, called for volunteers to join them. The Nobles and Horace Reid stepped forward. Horace was reputedly Yarrabah's best builder and had obtained the highest marks in the Queensland Anglican Church's Sunday School examinations.[35] The group's leader, Huthnance, was initially reluctant to take a woman on the hazardous and demanding enterprise. A secret community ballot was held, and the unanimous verdict was that the highly valued and accomplished Angelina should go. One boy

---

31. See Seiffert, *Refuge on the Roper*, chapter 3.
32. Harris, *One Blood*, 696.
33. Harris, *One Blood*, 693–703. Also, Berthon et al., *We Are Aboriginal*.
34. Despite the CMA being headquartered at St. Paul's Cathedral in Melbourne, Huthnance was deaconed by the Evangelical bishop of Bendigo, John Langley, in January 1908. Joynt was also later deaconed by Bendigo in September 1918 for Carpentaria and the work at Roper River. See Cable Clerical Index. Then Archbishop of Melbourne, Henry Lowther Clarke, known to be antagonistic towards Evangelicals and their endeavors centered around the CMA and Ridley College, remained aloof.
35. Murray Seiffert, *Gumbuli of Ngukurr*, 79.

apparently wrote, "Please send Angelina because she can do work among the women men could not do."[36]

Higgins extracted this report of the event from the Yarrabah newspaper, dated August 21, 1908:[37]

> All Yarrabah is much stirred at the going of James, Angelina, and Horace to the Roper River Mission. Their loss is a great one to our mission, but the satisfaction that we are really helping on another mission to the Aborigines more than makes up for the loss.
>
> James and Angelina are a splendid couple, and the sorrow at their going was very sincere, especially at Bukki Creek where James had long been lay reader . . .
>
> We had some grand services before they left. On the Wednesday night . . . we had a dismissal service. Dadda (Gribble) spoke to us about home at Yarrabah; and asked them to never forget it, but to come back when they had done their duty . . . but if God did not wish them to return to their home at Yarrabah, then there was still another and better home where we might be reunited when we have done our work for God . . .
>
> James spoke for a little while, saying he would like to say a lot, but could not. He spoke of his love for Yarrabah and the longing that some of them had to help many more of their brothers and sisters. He knew that God had called him to leave his beautiful home—the happiest life he had ever had—to go and help those blacks who were wild, wild as he himself had been for many years. He would never forget us, but go away to obey our Lord Jesus Christ who had left his own most beautiful home to come and help us live on earth . . .
>
> We were all sorry to part, but neither we nor they would have had them turn back. We love them too well for that. They will earn a brighter crown because they have taken up the cross of self denial to follow our dear Saviour, Jesus Christ. We cannot help feeling proud at Yarrabah.

James Noble was at last realizing the missionary ambitions first sown in him at his conversion under Rev. Boyce of New Guinea. The Yarrabah missionaries' perspective was eternal, knowing that they may never return home but that an eternal lodging and reunification with loved ones in Christ

---

36. Higgins (*James Noble of Yarrabah*, 19) contains this anecdote, but with a slightly different form of words than a report of the incident in "James Noble," *Recorder*, Port Pirie, SA: March 26, 1925.

37. Higgins, *James Noble of Yarrabah*, 19–20 from Yarrabah's *Aboriginal News*, August 21, 1908.

awaited them. They looked to the Lord Jesus as their exemplar: just at Christ had left his beautiful home in order to serve them, they would leave theirs to serve their "wild" black brothers and sisters.

The work at Roper River got off to a flying start as the local Aboriginals realized that the mission was a refuge from the hunting gangs and white violence against them. White and Ebbs's previous visits and the presence of the three black Yarrabah missionaries—including a woman—accelerated acceptance and trust. Gajiyuma, a respected elder who had met White and Ebbs earlier, led the way in gathering people from various clans at Roper River for refuge. Harris records the words of Barnabas Roberts, an Alawa man, who was a young boy at the time: "If the missionaries hadn't come, my tribe would have been all shot down."[38]

Refuge was an important motivator and theme. However, equally as significant was the coming of the gospel. Gajiyuma died in peace at Roper River within a year of the mission's founding with these final words, recorded by Reg Joynt, on his lips, "Jesus been talking alonga me. Him been tell me no more be frightened to die. Me no more frightened fella."[39]

For reasons of persistent ill-health, the Nobles were to depart and return to Yarrabah by June 1910—serving less than two full years at Roper River. That same year, Horace Reid moved to Katherine. Despite the relative brevity of their time there, the Yarrabah missionaries were remembered for years and generations afterwards as the ones who brought the gospel to Ngukurr, as the Roper River community is now known. James Noble exercised a preaching and teaching ministry of a kind that meant that his name, in particular, was associated with the coming of the gospel.[40]

Forrest River

By 1908, Ernest Gribble had served at Yarrabah for eighteen years. He was exhausted and suffered a breakdown. Hospitalized in Brisbane, he never fully recovered and resigned in May 1910 to become Rector of Gosford, NSW. Neither he nor his friends the Nobles ever gave up their missionary spirit and identity. Upon his return to Yarrabah, James Noble wrote to Gribble asking that if he were ever to start another mission, "to send for him at once."[41]

---

38. Harris, *One Blood*, 704.
39. Harris, *One Blood*, 705.
40. Harris, *One Blood*, 707; Seiffert, *Gumbuli of Ngukurr*, 79.
41. Higgins, *James Noble of Yarrabah*, 26.

James did not have to wait long. In 1913, an urgent plea for help came from the bishop of North West Australia, Gerald Trower. The Forrest River Mission in the Kimberleys was in danger of collapse. Just as at Roper River, pastoralists were clearing the land of Aboriginal people. However, at Forrest River, the Aboriginal inhabitants were more willing to counter violence with violence. Trower recognized the danger and reached out to the day's pre-eminent missionary to the Aboriginal peoples, who had made such a success of Yarrabah. Gribble was quick to take on the new challenge, and just as quick to enlist the help of his trusted friends and capable missionaries, James and Angelina Noble. They arrived from Yarrabah in April 1914.

Gribble wrote to the Secretary of the Australian Board of Mission (ABM) calling for one other missionary. ABM's *Review* of June 1914 called for that volunteer and carried this statement with regard to the conditions of service at its Forrest River Mission:

> The Mission has for its object the conversion to Christianity of the Aborigines of the North West, and their advancement in civilisation by means of education and by instructing them in such kinds of work as are suited to the climate of their country . . .
>
> The Bishop is unable to offer any inducement in the way of salary. It is necessary that those who join the Mission should do so with the single desire to live for, and willingness, if it be so, to die in their work because it is Christ's.[42]

The risks were real, and conditions typically difficult. Gribble arrived and acted in his typical authoritarian style, but unlike the previous missionaries he showed real kindness in tending to the sick and injured rather than constructing walls and putting up barbed wire around the camp. Importantly, just as at Yarrabah, Gribble was willing to trust the locals.

Once the Nobles arrived, the team began to accelerate their work of giving practical as well as spiritual instruction. Within the first year, a large number attended weekly services, where James led and preached regularly. A school was opened, and locals learnt to trust their children to the mission school, leaving them there for lessons when the rest of their context was unsafe for children.

Angelina played a key part in this. Four children were born to the Nobles at Forrest River, and as a black woman with children there, she was someone the local women could trust. Angelina's linguistic gifts were also critical, especially as James was weak in this area. According to the Nobles' daughter, Love Kiuna, who was born at Forrest River, her father never really picked up the local language and was limited to his native language from

---

42. ABM *Review*, June 1914. Extracted at Higgins, *James Noble of Yarrabah*, 26–31.

Normanton. By contrast, Angelina spoke "five languages over there" as well as "the language from Darwin."[43] Angelina translated for James, Gribble, and public authorities. Her linguistic capacity would have been matched by the cultural insight that comes from learning a new tongue. She was the only woman worker at Forrest River for at least six years. She was in charge of the school dormitory, health care, all the baking, and the teaching of cooking and laundry skills.[44] It was no wonder at all that Gribble had the highest esteem for her as a missionary.[45]

Progress in the first eleven years was rapid, with many conversions and baptisms. James Noble declared:[46]

> Too often I hear people say you can't teach the black man. When I hear a man say that, I ask, "Well what am I?" God is strong, and the missionary does good things in His name. Eleven years ago they were all heathen people at Forrest River. Then Mr. Gribble came and devoted his life to the Master. He came to try and save the black people, and God has blessed his work. Instead of the wild bush and nothing else at Forrest River, there is now a cross standing.
>
> Once upon a time black people ate black people. All people like meat, and black people like it, too, but Mr. Gribble came and the good news spread. "No more cannibalism." They put all that away. God is strong.

In early 1925, Gribble and James Noble embarked on what would become a successful nine-month missionary deputation tour throughout Australia, telling the story of the Forrest River Mission and calling for more support. The tour began in Perth and included Kalgoorlie, Collie, Bunbury, Adelaide, Port Pirie, Melbourne, Geelong, Sydney, Newcastle, and Brisbane.[47]

The Missionary Exhibition in Bedford Hall, Perth, was the typical format. It was opened by the archbishop on the Tuesday evening, March 10, 1925, and ran for three days. Curios from China, New Guinea, and Forrest River were on show and on sale. James Noble spoke three times each

---

43. Higgins, *James Noble of Yarrabah*, 41–42.
44. Higgins, *James Noble of Yarrabah*, 39–45.
45. Gribble, *Forty Years*, 180.
46. "Abo. Ordained," *The News* (Hobart, Tas.) September 16, 1925.
47. See "James Noble's Visit to Narrogin," *Great Southern Leader* (Pingelly, WA), February 20, 1925. Searching for "James Noble missionary" on https://trove.nla.gov.au results in very many newspaper reports of the tour from the various locations across that year.

day.⁴⁸ As the tour progressed, it became apparent that James's heartfelt and impassioned presentations were a powerful drawcard. In Adelaide, James had such an effect on the locals that a social gathering was organized in his honor. The *Glenelg Guardian* reported that

> Mr. James Noble, the aboriginal preacher... has won the hearts of everyone and has made many friends during the time he has been in the parish. The social committee felt that they could not let him leave for his home without showing him in some way their feelings of love and respect. Quite a large number of parishioners were present at the Kiosk Hall on Friday night, and Mr. Noble was given a rousing reception.⁴⁹

In Newcastle it was reported that "Mr. James Noble, who has become exceedingly popular among the exhibition audiences, spoke in an earnest, sincere way on the good effects upon those of his countrymen in the passing from Heathenism to Christianity."⁵⁰

It was also in Newcastle that Gribble reported on having more than two hundred children in the mission school, 1,500 cattle, 1,000 horses and donkeys, five hundred sheep, and other stock. James had the opportunity to publicly acknowledge and give credit to Angelina. He declared that much of the success of the mission was due to Angelina and her facility with languages—having learnt the local Forrest River dialect within the first six months and subsequently gaining the other languages used locally also. James also revealed that he hoped to one day visit England; however, he declared in his next breath, "My creed is a simple one, I go where I can preach."⁵¹

Higgins reports that in Melbourne, as James came on to the platform before a large gathering, the entire audience, including the bishops and other speakers on the platform, rose "as one man in homage... to the Aboriginal with the spiritual face."⁵²

The tour culminated in James Noble's ordination as a deacon at St. George's Cathedral, Perth, that September.⁵³ He had been studying for or-

---

48. "Missionary Exhibition," *South Western Times* (Bunbury, WA), March 10, 1925.
49. "Brighton News," *Glenelg Guardian* (Glenelg, SA), June 18, 1925.
50. "Missionary Exhibition," *Newcastle Morning Herald and Miners' Advocate* (Newcastle, NSW), June 29, 1925.
51. "Among the Blacks," *The Newcastle Sun* (Newcastle, NSW), June 29, 1925.
52. Higgins, James Noble of Yarrabah, 46–47.
53. "Native Deacon: Tribesman in Holy Orders," *The Telegraph* (Brisbane, Qld) September 16, 1925. The article noted that James had just completed a twelve-month tour of Australian cities and was now en route back to Forrest River. It also noted that, "Mr. Noble's success among the natives has been greatly aided by his wife Angelina, who speaks six native languages. They have six children"—the eldest of whom, Ruth Roper,

dination for a number of months, possibly encouraged by Bishop Trower, almost certainly by the ABM and Gribble. Reporting on the ordination, the ABM *Review* printed the following:

> James Noble's life has been one of Christian service for the benefit of his race, and the steps taken in ordaining him was [sic] not hastily taken. In every way he has proved himself worthy of the office to which he has now been appointed in the Church, and will, we hope, be the first of a long line of native clergy as in other churches in ancient and modern times.[54]

It seemed that James and Angelina's missionary work at Forrest River was poised for fresh growth and new possibilities. But it was not to be. Their sufferings were not yet complete.

Forrest River Massacres

In July 1922, a group of police on the hunt for cattle killers entered the Marndoc Aboriginal Reserve in which the mission was located and massacred a large number of Aboriginal people. Locals reported to Gribble that "the country all stink from the dead fellows." The safety of the Reserve had been violated; Gribble wrote to the authorities, urging an inquiry but to no avail. Worse, the southern part of the Reserve was handed over to two returned servicemen, Overheu and Hay, for settlement. They had already lost their licenses to hire Aboriginal people because of excessive cruelty, and the course of the next few years was set. Further murders and violence followed over the next four years, culminating in Australia's second-last large-scale massacre of Indigenous peoples, just a few months after James's ordination.

In May 1926 there was a confrontation between Aboriginal people and the settlers.[55] Hay confronted an elder, Lumbulumbia, flogged him, and broke his spears. The old man then killed Hay with a broken spear. Retaliation to this act was brutal and disproportionate. Wyndham police organized a party of thirteen, who rode through the area, "capturing, chaining and finally killing every Aborigine they could find."[56]

Gribble had initially assisted the police, believing that the authorities had the right to arrest and bring Hay's killer to justice, but also wanting to

---

at age eighteen, was in charge of the mission school's dormitory.

54. "Ordination of James Noble" *ABM Review*, November 12, 1925.

55. Higgins incorrectly dates these events to 1925 in *James Noble of Yarrabah*, chapter 8.

56. Harris, *One Blood*, 512. See 511–14.

find out for himself what they were doing, and he prevented at least one massacre. Once he got the police off the Reserve via the mission's launch boat, he dispatched James Noble, an expert tracker, to investigate.

Harris extracts this passage from the Forrest River Mission journal of June 21, 1926, which led to the subsequent Royal Commission:

> Noble returned this evening, having found the spot on the Upper Forrest where the police shot and burned their native prisoners. He brought back a parcel of charred remains. The natives were shot on stones in the bed of the river. Blood is still all around.[57]

At least thirty of those killed were known to the missionaries. Local Aboriginal people claim that there were hundreds of victims; the men were shot, and women and children were clubbed to death in several locations. The exact figure will never be known, as investigations were delayed by the unwillingness of the government, church, politicians, and locals in Wyndham to heed Gribble's pleas for an immediate investigation.

Commissioner Woods only began his work in 1927, with most of the evidence having been washed away by the wet season of 1926. Still, twelve victims were able to be identified. The Wyndham police were found to have acted in self-defense and were transferred out of the region. The entire white Wyndham community shunned Gribble and the mission, which therefore began to struggle to operate. Gribble was to leave soon after in 1928, sacked by the ABM, with the local Aboriginal people weeping at his departure. The Nobles followed in 1932.[58]

Epilogue and Conclusion

Gribble had moved back to Queensland to serve at Palm Island. He wrote to ask the Nobles to join him there, but for unknown reasons they were not allowed to reside on the island. Instead, they lived on nearby Esk Island and ministered across both. James's health was failing, and within a year the family relocated back to Yarrabah; James had indicated he wanted to die at home.

The picture of his final years at Yarrabah are of an Aboriginal man returning to his cultural roots and loves: fishing, hunting, teaching younger

---

57. Harris, *One Blood*, 513.

58. The Forrest River Mission struggled on and was eventually closed in 1969. Aboriginal people were determined to resettle it as Oombulgurri in the early 70s, receiving multiple injections of government assistance. It struggled with dysfunction and abuse, closing in 2011. It seems that the blood of the slain cries out from the ground there.

men how to make shields, boomerangs, stone tomahawks, spears from stingray stings. He maintained Christian ministry in visiting the sick and leading services, but he was also growing senile.[59] James Noble died in a Cairns hospital on November 25, 1941, and is buried at Yarrabah.

Angelina was the "old lady," a term of respect and honor: the one who administered discipline to the younger children, the matriarch of the Noble clan. She outlived James by twenty-three years, dying at Yarrabah on October 19, 1964. She is buried with him. Her life and ministry are remembered and honored today in the recently founded Angelina Noble Centre.[60]

Gribble was a complex man and no absolute saint. However, his policy of seeking to empower Aboriginal people enabled James and Angelina Noble's lives and ministries. They followed their mentor in their willingness to leave their home culture, live among the people they sought to serve, learn new languages and practices, teach and preach the gospel of Christ, give their people practical help and practical skills, and love and build up the church wherever they lived.

As missionaries, James and Angelina played a part in the founding of Kowanyama and Ngukurr, the Mitchell and Roper River Missions. Remembering with fondness that black people brought them the gospel is part of the Ngukurr story, a theme later mirrored in the Ugandan Festo Kivengere's brief tour of the region in 1959. A Gunbalanya Aboriginal man reflected on Festo's ministry with words that would have applied just as well to James Noble:

> We are so glad that our brother in Christ has come here. He speaks of the same Jesus we know, he speaks of the sure love of God which we know. He tells us those things which the [white] missionaries have told us for years, but now we can see clearly that Jesus Christ is also the Saviour of black men.[61]

James and Angelina's ministry at Forrest River gave the Christians of the nation hope that something positive was being done for the dispossessed Aboriginal peoples of the land. That dream was shattered, and too little is known of what later happened to those who had become Christians at the mission and survived the atrocities of that time.

The Nobles are still remembered and honored at Yarrabah, which remains a center of Aboriginal Christian life, especially in the north. Bishop Arthur Malcolm—the first Aboriginal Anglican bishop, consecrated in

---

59. Higgins, *James Noble of Yarrabah*, 61.

60. See https://www.actheology.edu.au/research/angelina-noble-centre.

61. Shilton, *Speaking Out*, 90. Shilton was one of the organizers of Kivengere's tour of the north, accompanied him, and took notes on the tour.

1985—is a descendent who acknowledges his debt to James for paving the way.[62] He ought not be alone in giving thanks to God for the Nobles.

Praying for, finding, training and equipping, enabling, giving opportunities in ministry leadership, persisting in encouragement of Aboriginal leaders of today and the future, and sending Australian Aboriginal and Torres Strait Islander men and women as missionaries of the gospel of Christ to the peoples of the world—these are some of the priorities for action that emerge from reflecting on the James and Angelina Noble story. May many others follow where they have led the way.

ABORIGINAL AND TORRES STRAIT ISLANDER PEOPLE ARE WARNED THAT THESE IMAGES MAY CONTAIN IMAGES OF PEOPLE WHO ARE NOW DECEASED.

Rev. James Noble, his wife Angelina (left) and their family at Forrest River Mission, 1925[63]

---

62. Higgins, *James Noble of Yarrabah*, foreword by Arthur Malcolm. See also Morton, *Arthur Malcolm*.

63. State Library of Western Australia image number 4383B/125. Sourced from the collections of the State Library of Western Australia and reproduced with the permission of the Library Board of Western Australia.

Bibliography

Berthon, Peter, et al., eds. *We Are Aboriginal: Our 100 years: from Arnhem Land's First Mission to Ngukurr Today*. Ngukurr: St. Matthew's Anglican Church, 2008.

Cable, Kenneth, Noel Pollard, and Leonie Cable. *The Cable Clerical Index of Clergy Who Served in the Anglican Church of Australia from 26 January 1788 through to Those Ordained or Serving by 31 December 1961*. Unpublished MS. Sydney: Moore College, various dates.

Freier, Philip L. "Living with the *Munpitch*: The History of Mitchell River Mission, 1905–1967." PhD diss., James Cook University, 1999.

Gribble, Ernest. *Forty Years with the Aborigines*. Sydney: Angus & Robertson, 1930.

———. *The Problem of the Australian Aboriginal*. Sydney: Angus & Robertson, 1932.

"Gribble, John Brown (1847–1893)." In *Australian Dictionary of Biography*. National Centre of Biography. Canberra, ACT: Australian National University, c.2006. http://adb.anu.edu.au/biography/gribble-john-brown-3668.

Harris, John. *One Blood: 200 Years of Aboriginal Encounter with Christianity: A Story of Hope*. 2nd ed. Sydney: Albatross, 1994.

Higgins, Geoff. *James Noble of Yarrabah*. Lawson, NSW: Mission Publications of Australia, 1981.

Kociumbas, Jan. "Noble, Angelina (1879—1964)." In *Australian Dictionary of Biography*. National Centre of Biography. Canberra, ACT: Australian National University, c.2006. http://adb.anu.edu.au/biography/noble-angelina-8533/text13641.

Morton, Clive. *Arthur Malcolm AO: Australia's First Indigenous Bishop*. Brisbane: Harry Edwin Clive Morton, 2005.

Mukuka, George Sombe. *Call Me a Black Man, for That Is What I Am: Missionary Activity in Australia 1920–1990: James Noble and the "Aboriginalization" of the Australian Clergy*. Baltimore: PublishAmerica, 2013.

Seiffert, Murray. *Gumbuli of Ngukurr*. Brunswick East: Acorn, 2011.

———. *Refuge on the Roper: The Origins of the Roper River Mission Ngukurr*. Brunswick East: Acorn, 2008.

Shilton, Lance. *Speaking Out: A Life in Urban Mission*. Sydney: Centre for the Study of Australian Christianity, 1997.

Thorn, Barbara, and John Charles Vockler. "Barlow, Christopher George (1858–1915)." In *Australian Dictionary of Biography*. National Centre of Biography. Canberra, ACT: Australian National University, c.2006. http://adb.anu.edu.au/biography/barlow-christopher-george-5133.

Women

11

No Longer Male and Female

Women's Leadership and the New Testament in Australian Anglicanism

DOROTHY A. LEE AND MURIEL PORTER[1]

IT GIVES US GREAT pleasure, as one ordained and one lay woman, to write this essay on the situation of women in leadership in the Anglican Church of Australia in a book dedicated to Archbishop Philip Freier. Over many years, as both Primate and Archbishop, Dr. Freier has been a friend to women across the church, encouraging their discipleship and leadership and supporting them in the difficulties many face in the church. In his own diocese he has ordained many women as deacons and priests and consecrated two women as bishops, and he currently has two women assistant bishops. He has taken seriously issues such as domestic violence against women and has promoted the ministry of Indigenous women across the church. As recipients of his pastoral care and encouragement for our ministries, we express

---

1. This essay is dedicated to the memory of The Rt Rev. Barbara Darling (1947–2015), who was consecrated bishop by Archbishop Philip Freier in May 2008. See Porter, "Second Female Bishop."

here our gratitude for his unflagging support for women's ministry, whether lay or ordained.

This essay begins with an overview of the current situation in the Anglican Church in Australia in relation to women's leadership, followed by an outline of how the current situation emerged in response to fresh understandings of the biblical witness. From there it re-examines the biblical witness, with a particular focus on the New Testament. We draw on recent scholarship to support our contention that the Bible itself encourages women coequally with men in their contribution, at every level, to the life of the church and the proclamation of the gospel in the world. We conclude by stressing the need to "read, mark, learn, and inwardly digest" the teaching of sacred Scripture on the ministries of the church and those gifted to share them.

The Current Situation

The Anglican Church of Australia has had women priests since 1992. When the Australian General Synod finally passed legislation that year, allowing women to be priests in dioceses that adopted the legislation, informal discussion turned to when the move would be accepted across the country. Many confidently expected that even the Diocese of Sydney, the leader of the opposition to women clergy, would inevitably fall into line. It might take ten years or so, it was thought, but by the twenty-first century, women clergy would be the new normal across the Australian Anglican Church.

The expectation was naïve. Almost three decades later, Sydney has, if anything, increased its opposition. Not only are women still not ordained as priests in that diocese, but the numbers of women deacons there remain persistently low. In 2015, the latest available statistic, women deacons constituted just 6 percent of the total number of clergy in the diocese, only double what it had been in 1991.[2] By contrast, in 2015 women clergy in the other metropolitan dioceses—Adelaide, Brisbane, Melbourne, and Perth—ranged from 26 percent (Adelaide) to 34 percent (Brisbane) of the total clergy number, between three and four times the level it had been in 1991.[3]

Another key opposing diocese has, however, moved significantly. In 1992, no-one was predicting that the Diocese of Ballarat, a deeply

---

2. Reilly, "A Little Compendium," 26. Without Colin Reilly's diligent research, tracking the numbers of women clergy in the Australian Anglican Church would be extremely difficult, as there has not been a national directory since 2015. This is soon to be rectified by Broughton Publishing, under the editorial leadership of Mr. Reilly.

3. Reilly, "A Little Compendium," 26.

conservative Anglo-Catholic opponent of women priests, would change its mind. Until just over a decade ago, Ballarat Diocese was as fierce an opponent of women in ordained ministry as Sydney Diocese; its bishops had been leading outspoken opponents in all the General Synod debates over the years. It had taken twenty-two years, but in 2008, three women were ordained deacon there. There was no suggestion then that the diocese would move to ordain women priests. However, when a strong supporter of women priests, bishop of Willochra, Garry Weatherill, was elected bishop of Ballarat in 2011, change came quite quickly. Bishop Weatherill instigated a consultative process that saw the diocesan synod support the General Synod legislation for women priests by substantial majorities in 2013. Two women priests were ordained a short time later.

This move reduced the number of dioceses where women are not ordained priest to four—Sydney, Armidale,[4] North West Australia, and The Murray. All have ordained women as deacons however, with The Murray—the last diocese against women in any ordained ministry—coming on board in 2017. Two women deacons were ordained there that year, following the passing of legislation by the diocesan synod the previous year.

Because dioceses have autonomy under the Australian Anglican Church's constitution, women priests and bishops from other dioceses are not fully recognized in these four dioceses; their clerical status is not recognized beyond that of deacon. This is extremely painful for the women concerned, who see this as an unacceptable denial of their orders. It also introduces a stark division into the ordained ministry Australia wide.

This divide has also influenced outbreaks of opposition in dioceses that affirm women clergy, with some evidence of what might be termed a backlash. Anecdotal evidence has suggested a pulling back in parts of dioceses that have ordained women to all three orders. In particular, women from the Evangelical stream have reportedly felt less affirmed in their vocation to priestly ministry in some places where the doctrine of male headship is upheld. In some parishes led by conservative Evangelical clergy, lay women have found their leadership roles circumscribed as well. The situation for women in leadership in Australian Anglicanism today is not as rosy as the 1992 breakthrough seemed to predict.

Nevertheless, despite this persistent opposition, there is still much to celebrate. Across the country at the time of writing, there were 656 women clergy in active ministry, comprising a quarter of the active clergy. They

---

4. Although Armidale Diocese is always designated as one of the four Australian dioceses opposed to women as priests, it has actually ordained two women priests after briefly adopting the General Synod legislation, Julie McKay in 1996 and Rebecca Eastman in 2003.

are serving as parish priests, chaplains, cathedral deans (four), precentors and canons, archdeacons (twenty-two), and bishops (five out of forty-nine). And also an archbishop: Kay Goldsworthy AO was installed as Archbishop of Perth in 2018.[5]

Six Australian cathedrals have appointed women as deans—Adelaide, Bathurst, Bendigo, Gippsland, Newcastle, and Port Pirie—although just one of them, Adelaide, is a major city cathedral. Bendigo, the first cathedral to appoint a woman dean (Peta Sherlock, Dean 2006–2011), last year appointed its second woman dean (Elizabeth Dyke).[6] At the time of writing, there are currently women deans in four cathedrals—Bendigo, Sale (Gippsland), Newcastle, and Port Pirie (Willochra).

By now, more than ten years after the first consecrations, we might have expected a higher number of women appointed as bishop along with a more even spread across the dioceses. But in the eleven years since the first women were consecrated (Kay Goldsworthy, Perth, and Barbara Darling, Melbourne, both in May 2008), only another seven women have become bishops. Of the nine women consecrated in Australia, one, Barbara Darling, has since died, and two—Sarah Macneil and Alison Taylor—have retired. Of the six still active, only Archbishop Goldsworthy is a diocesan bishop. Both Gippsland and Grafton dioceses, where women were diocesan bishops (Kay Goldsworthy, bishop of Gippsland 2015–2018; Sarah Macneil, bishop of Grafton 2014–2018) have since appointed male bishops to replace them, and none of the other dioceses that have elected diocesan bishops since 2008 have selected women. The six women bishops still in active ministry are based in just four dioceses: Adelaide has one (Assistant Bishop Denise Ferguson), Perth has two (Archbishop Kay Goldsworthy and Assistant Bishop Kate Wilmot), Melbourne has two (Assistant Bishops Genieve Blackwell and Kate Prowd), and Newcastle has one (Assistant Bishop Sonia Roulston).

The number of women bishops is not likely to increase in the near future, because there is an age problem. The first women bishops, Kay Goldsworthy and Barbara Darling, were also among the first women ordained. The large group of women ordained priest in those first large-scale ordinations in 1992–1993 had been patiently waiting, in a variety of non-ordained ministries, for the opportunity to have their priestly vocations honored. Necessarily, they were older than their male counterparts. But the trend for women to be ordained at an older age than men—the average is some ten years older—has continued.[7] This means they have not had sufficient

---

5. Reilly, "Active Clergy Gender Summary."
6. Reilly, "Active Clergy Gender Summary."
7. Reilly, "Clergy Gender and the Stained-Glass Ceiling."

priestly experience to be considered for the episcopate until they are too close to retirement.

It is unfortunate that there is no organization with a comprehensive watching brief on women's experience in ordained ministry in the Australian Anglican Church. The General Synod disbanded its Women's Commission, which had begun working on such a brief, in 2010. Unlike its sister organization in the Church of England—formerly MOW, now reconstituted as WATCH[8]—the Movement for the Ordination of Women in Australia is now a small organization with limited reach.

WATCH in England also upholds the role of lay women. It states that "women contribute to the life and work of their churches in myriad ways. We support, respect and encourage laywomen, and want to ensure their status and place in the church is undiminished while that of ordained women rises."[9] Lay women in Australia receive no such recognition, let alone support; they have been largely forgotten.

Gender equality in national and diocesan church institutions would enable a greater focus on lay women, and for more than a decade there has been a concerted push for gender equality in church governance. To date, it has not had great success. The most recent General Synod, held in 2017, noted its disappointment that a 2007 resolution calling for equal representation of women on General Synod bodies had not been implemented. Only three of the General Synod's twenty-seven bodies had achieved that result in 2017. It reissued its call, asking the Standing Committee to recommit to 50 percent equal representation of women by December 2019 "wherever legislatively and practically possible." It asked dioceses to commit to the same target and called for regular reporting of the situation.

The 2017 General Synod itself fell short of the target, with women comprising only a third of the total clergy and lay members. But at least that figure is significantly higher than was the case in 1995—the first General Synod following the legislation for women priests. At that General Synod, women comprised just 18 percent of the total, with women clergy only about 3 percent.

---

8. Women and the Church (WATCH), a lively ongoing women's movement in England, was founded in 1996. It describes itself as "a national organisation working actively for gender justice, equality and inclusion in the Church of England." One of its objectives is "the monitoring of the current deployment of women in ministry." See Women and the Church, "About WATCH." It compiles and publishes up-to-date statistics of the situation for women clergy and ordinands in the Church of England: see WATCH, "Report."

9. Women and the Church, "About WATCH."

The Standing Committee elected by the 2017 General Synod came close to the equal representation target, with women comprising 44 percent of its elected members. Lay women in particular were winners in that election, with six of the nine elected lay positions going to women. Just two of the nine elected clergy positions went to women clergy, however.

The Standing Committee success rate has not been replicated across the General Synod's key bodies, its seven commissions. While two—Church Law and Public Affairs—are headed by lay women, neither of those commissions has an equal number of women. The only one that does meet the target—in fact, just exceeds it—is the Safe Ministry Commission, where five of the nine members are female. The Commissions with the smallest number of female members are Doctrine and Ecumenical Relations (two each: one ordained, one lay). It is hard to see how all the commissions will meet the 2017 target in the near future, because the political demands to appoint senior male personnel from the major dioceses—particularly theologians and lawyers—are hard to resist. Presumably the Standing Committee and the commissions will fall back on the "wherever legislatively and practically possible" line as their excuse.

Melbourne Diocese has responded radically to the call for gender equality in church governance. From 2019, its key governance body (other than synod), the Diocesan Council, is required by diocesan legislation to have women constitute 50 percent of both the elected clergy and the elected lay members. No "wherever legislatively and practically possible" opt-out clause here! Given there will be only twelve elected members in the reconstituted body, this is a significant move. The 2018 diocesan synod that passed the legislation mandating this change also called on "vicars and parish leaders across the Diocese to seek opportunities to facilitate equal representation of women on Parish Councils and as Churchwardens . . ."[10] It will be interesting to see if the change to the Diocesan Council membership will be reflected across the diocese, and how quickly that change might come about.

The Women's Ordination Story

The Broader Context

The issue of women's ordination arose in the Anglican Church of Australia when it was becoming a significant movement in the Anglican Communion

---

10. Articulated during the "order of business and legislation" at Melbourne Synod, 2018.

worldwide in the early 1970s. It had first been mooted in the mid-nineteenth century by pioneer American feminists who were as much concerned for women's roles in the church as for female suffrage, but the concern was not seriously taken up by mainstream churches until after the First World War. It was strongly resisted, mainly because church leaders insisted on a divinely-instituted "female inferiority." The bishops of the Anglican Communion, meeting at the 1920 Lambeth Conference, said that while women would one day share a spiritual equality with men in the spiritual world that was to come, in the "present world of action . . . man has a priority." Marriage and motherhood summed up women's God-given vocation, they said.[11]

The notion that women have spiritual equality with men in this world was not easily suppressed, however, even if it took hold in the mainstream churches only in fits and starts in the twentieth century. By the late 1960s, it was gaining significant ground at last. In Australia, the Methodist Church ordained its first women clergy in 1969, followed by the Presbyterian Church in 1974. The smaller Congregational Church had had women ministers since the 1920s. The Uniting Church, formed from all three churches in 1977, began its life with a strong contingent of women clergy.

The first woman priest in the Anglican Communion was ordained in the Diocese of Hong Kong in 1944.[12] At that time, Li Tim Oi, technically a deaconess (though she was effectively functioning as a deacon), was leading the Anglican parish in Macao, a church packed with war refugees. Male priests visited to celebrate the sacraments, but in time this became impossible as the Japanese occupation intensified. Rather than leave the parishioners without sacramental ministry, the far-sighted Bishop R. O. Hall of Hong Kong decided to ordain her as a priest. Recognizing in her the charism of priesthood, he decided it was better to break church order by ordaining her than leave people without sacraments in what was clearly a time of critical pastoral emergency. As he later explained to the Archbishop of Canterbury, her gender was a secondary consideration in terms of her obvious leadership gifts and the needs of her flock.

The ordination was clandestine, with both Bishop Hall and Li Tim Oi undertaking dangerous journeys across enemy lines to meet in the mainland city of Zhaoqing. Once word leaked out, her ordination was roundly condemned, and for many years she was forced to lay aside her orders. As the Cultural Revolution took hold in China, she was totally forgotten by the Anglican world, emerging years later to return quietly to priestly ministry

---

11. See Porter, *Women in the Church*, and Porter, "The Christian Origins of Feminism."

12. See Harrison, *Much Beloved Daughter*.

once women priests had gained wider acceptance. Her diocese, Hong Kong, initiated the next stage as well, ordaining two more women priests in 1971 after the 1968 Lambeth Bishops' Conference had reopened the question and the newly-formed Anglican Consultative Council had given its approval. Later in the 1970s, women were ordained in the United States (1974) Canada (1976) and New Zealand (1977).

Australia

In 1977, the Australian Anglican Church decided by General Synod resolution that theological objections did not constitute a barrier to the ordination of women. This resolution followed the recommendation of a report on the ministry of women prepared by the General Synod Commission on Doctrine. All but one of the twelve members of the Commission—which included a stellar array of bishops and theologians—agreed with the recommendation that theologically there was nothing to stop women being ordained. The twelfth member, Sydney theologian Broughton Knox, argued against women's ordination on the grounds of male headship, the same grounds on which it is still opposed in Sydney Diocese.

The 1977 General Synod resolution, passed by an overall majority of 60 percent, recommended that the church "take the appropriate steps when practicable" to enable women to be ordained. The ideal clearly was for the door to be opened to women in all three orders at the same time, but that was not to be. Those "appropriate steps" would prove to be the sticking point, and the second two in particular—women as priests and bishops—would be extremely difficult to achieve. They ended up being separated by fifteen years. The 1977 majority, while welcome, was not sufficient. If General Synod legislation for women clergy were required, a minimum of two-thirds majorities in each of the three houses of General Synod—clergy, laity, and bishops—would be necessary. Then those same majorities would need to be repeated at a subsequent General Synod meeting.

Many had hoped that legislation would not be needed, not just to avoid the synodical demands but as a matter of principle, given that there is no specific legislation for the ordination of male clergy in the Australian church's constitution. Decisions of the Appellate Tribunal, the Anglican Church of Australia's highest legal body, in 1980 and 1985 had suggested that legislation might not be necessary.[13]

Nevertheless, legislation was pursued, largely to put the matter beyond doubt and as a means of ensuring sufficient support for change, but just

13. Appellate Tribunal, "Marriage of Divorced Persons," and "Admission of Women."

one in a succession of attempts passed readily—the 1985 canon for women deacons, which received more than 75 percent of votes in each house of the General Synod. At that same General Synod, although the overall vote in favor was almost 70 percent, a canon for women priests failed by just a few votes in the House of Clergy. Subsequent attempts failed in 1987 and 1989 until finally, in November 1992, General Synod passed the Law of the Church of England Clarification Canon, permitting women to be priests.

Between 1987 and 1992, several diocesan-based attempts had been made to break the impasse, just one of which, in the Diocese of Perth, succeeded. Thus, the first Australian ordination of women priests happened in Perth in March 1992, under local authorization; that event became the single most important factor in ensuring the ultimate success of the 1992 General Synod canon. That canon is currently church law in all Australian dioceses except Armidale, North West Australia, Sydney, and The Murray, all of which have nevertheless adopted legislation permitting women deacons.

Once women were ordained as priests, pressure began to mount to allow them to become bishops. General Synod legislative attempts in 2001 and 2004, although they reached strong overall majority support of more than 60 percent, failed to reach the stringent requirements of the constitution. But was legislation actually necessary, given the minimum canonical requirements for becoming a bishop are satisfied if the person is at least thirty years of age, has been baptized, and is a priest?[14] In 2005, twenty-eight members of General Synod submitted this question to the Appellate Tribunal. The tribunal ruled in their favor in September 2007, opening the door to the first consecration of women bishops. Kay Goldsworthy was consecrated in Perth on May 22, 2008, closely followed by Archbishop Freier's consecration of Barbara Darling in Melbourne on May 31.

The New Testament and Women's Ministry

Those who continue to oppose women's authority in the church, along with those who are part of the backlash against women's ordination and lay leadership, claim to derive their teaching from the Bible and also—though to a lesser extent—the tradition of the church. Focus is mostly on a number of passages in the Pauline corpus that seem to condemn women to silent submission under male authority, in the structure of the home as well as in

---

14. Clause 74 (1) of the Constitution of the Anglican Church of Australia states: "'Canonical fitness' means, as regards a person, that: the person has attained at least 30 years of age; (b) the person has been baptised; and (c) the person is in priests' orders."

the structures of the Christian community. The argument is bolstered by the belief that women in the early church never held authority in relation to men. In their view, patriarchy—the rule of men over women—is part of the divine intent for the stability and flourishing of human life.

What this perspective fails to take into account is that interpretation of the biblical witness is shaped by the context of the interpreter. Those who oppose women's leadership do not perceive their own bias in their reading of the text, though they are often quick enough to point it out in those who disagree with them. Yet awareness of context is critical in biblical interpretation: not just because we need to make allowances for our own perspective but also because our own perspective can give us new insights into the biblical text that previous generations may not have had.

We also need to be wary of finding "proof texts" to argue a case from the Bible while disregarding the weight of biblical theology, a method of reading that takes seriously the whole canon of Scripture. The Evangelicals who opposed slavery in the British Empire and in America in the nineteenth century, for example, based their convictions not so much on individual texts but on the impulse of the gospel for freedom and the biblical respect for the dignity of every human being as created in the image of God.[15] Other Christians argued from solitary texts, taken out of context, that the Bible permitted slavery.

In more recent years, considerable work has been done in reading and rereading the biblical texts from new perspectives and with additional knowledge, driven by belief in the ongoing, inspiring work of the Holy Spirit. Some of this work has come from the Evangelical wing of Anglicanism, particularly on texts from within the Pauline corpus, and it has proved of benefit to the whole church.[16] The continuing opposition to women's equality in leadership comes largely from those who are ill-acquainted with this growing body of material that spans the breadth of the Christian church. Beginning with the Gospels, in canonical order, it reveals the extraordinary place given to women as disciples and leaders within the New Testament world.

This new reading of the Bible takes into account the context of the biblical world, which itself illuminates the remarkable nature of what the New Testament teaches from within its own worldview. The Greco-Roman and Jewish worlds were patriarchal and had a clear bias towards men,

15. See for example Harwood, "British Evangelical Abolitionism."

16. See for example *Christians for Biblical Equality* which argues that "the Bible, properly interpreted, teaches the fundamental equality of men and women of all ethnic groups, all economic classes, and all age groups." CBE International, "Mission Statement."

particularly in public life. Authority and rule were considered male prerogatives, and men were thought to have the needful qualities for leadership, such as reason, initiative, daring, self-promotion, and courage. Women were regarded as better suited to domestic duties and had the requisite virtues of modesty, self-effacement, and submissiveness. The majority of women were politically and socially powerless and subject to suppression and abuse, while a minority were able to negotiate their world and make very real, if infrequent, contributions to public life.

Those who today continue to refuse women's ordination and require wifely obedience within the home inhabit a similar world. Yet this adherence is concealed under the label of "complementarianism,"[17] which avows the equality of women with men and makes no overt objection to women in public life. Such a worldview shows considerably less consistency than the ancient world of Aristotle, where women's "natural" qualities, including their inability to reason, gave a type of justification for this patriarchal perspective. A more honest and consistent approach today would be to say that women lack leadership qualities, are less rational and more emotional than men, and that their abilities simply do not equip them for public life or leadership of any kind. In that case, they should equally oppose women in politics, in teaching of any kind, and any other trade or profession that might give them authority over men. The logic of this view, while consistent, exposes its absurdity.

Over against the ancient (and modern) world, Jesus himself had an extraordinary way of relating to women, unusual in his day and in many parts of ours:[18] he neither put them down nor patronized them but related to them, in all their needs and gifts, with the utmost seriousness.[19] His vision of the kingdom or reign of God gave rise to a community of equal persons gathered around him, women as well as men, many of whom left their homes and possessions to follow him. The Gospels in different ways attest to the remarkable freedom Jesus had in relating to women as persons, as disciples, as leaders.[20]

In the Synoptic Gospels, for example, women are followers of Jesus who stay with him on his journey to the cross, even when the apostles have deserted him (Mark 15:40-41). In a passage often overlooked yet of critical importance, Luke tells us that these women have been among Jesus' disciples during his ministry in Galilee and are recipients of his healing (Luke

---

17. Further on this, see Giles, *What the Bible Actually Teaches on Women*, 1-34.
18. Giles, *What the Bible Actually Teaches on Women*, 76-93.
19. Sayers, "The Human-Not-Quite-Human," 121-2.
20. See especially Bauckham, *Gospel Women*.

8:2). On that basis they have becomes his disciples, journeying with him throughout his ministry. Indeed, they make possible his ministry by funding it from their own resources (Luke 8:3). Just as the apostles give up their possessions to follow Jesus, so the holy women redirect their possessions to funding Jesus' ministry and the large circle of disciples who share it, in accord with Jesus' teaching on discipleship (Luke 14:33). It is probable, too, that the Galilean women are among the seventy disciples who are sent out on mission in pairs (Luke 10:12, 17–20).[21]

The Synoptic Gospels include among Jesus' followers the twelve apostles, of whom the innermost group is Peter, James, and John, but they also present an inner group of women who have a special relationship to Jesus. Luke, for example, names Mary Magdalene as the chief among these disciples. She is portrayed neither as a prostitute nor as an anointer of Jesus but is rather a disciple who supports Jesus' ministry and becomes the witness to the resurrection. "Magdalene" meaning "strong tower," is most likely a nickname given her by Jesus and not simply a name indicating her town of origin in Galilee (Magdala).[22]

There are other women named too, most of whose names are unfamiliar to Christians today. Joanna, for example, is another prominent disciple who comes from a wealthy and influential background, being a member of the royal court of Herod Antipas, who has clearly left the comfort and luxury of her home to travel with Jesus and the Galilean peasants who surround him; she too is a witness of the resurrection (Luke 24:10). Another woman is Susanna, an otherwise unknown disciple (Luke 8:3). The Synoptics all mention another Mary as witness to Jesus' death and resurrection (e.g., Matt 27:56; 28:1), and Mark speaks of Salome who may also be the mother of the apostles James and John (Mark 15:40, 16:1; Matt 20:20–21, 27:56).

The Gospel of John tends to focus on Jesus' meeting with a number of individual women who come to faith in him, sometimes through doubt and struggle. At the beginning of his ministry, the mother of Jesus declares her trust in his word (John 2:5); at the end of that ministry, Jesus gives her and the beloved disciple to one another, signaling the birth of the Christian community (John 19:25–26). The Samaritan woman discovers that Jesus, as the giver of the Spirit, is the source of living water, quenching her deepest thirst for life (John 4:7–26). She acts in an apostolic way in bringing the villagers to faith in him (John 4:39).[23]

---

21. Karris, "Women and Discipleship in Luke," 1–20.
22. ABC, "Jesus' Female Disciples—The New Evidence."
23. Lee, *Flesh and Glory*, 71–77.

In John's portrayal of the Easter message, Martha and Mary encounter Jesus as the resurrection and the life and confess their faith in him through word (Martha's confession, "you are the Christ," John 11:27) and through action (Mary's anointing of Jesus as an acknowledgement of his costly sacrifice in raising her brother, John 12:3-8).[24] Finally, Mary Magdalene, as the "apostle of the apostles," is the primary witness to the resurrection in this Gospel, the first to recognize the risen Christ, and the first to be given the commission to proclaim him to others (John 20:16-18).[25]

In the popular imagination, the apostle Paul is often viewed, in contrast to Jesus, as a misogynist. Yet this is far from true.[26] Paul had a significant number of female colleagues who worked with him in ministry and mission. At the end of his Epistle to the Romans, for instance, he names nine women coworkers, including Prisca (Priscilla), a theologian and teacher, Phoebe, a deacon in the church in Corinth,[27] and Junia, an apostle (Rom 16:3-16).[28] Other letters mention a number of other women, also coworkers with him in his calling as an apostle. Paul had no problems working with women in leadership, either in mission or in ministry.

Even more important is Paul's core statement on the meaning of Christian baptism and its radical implications for the life of the church: "For you are all children of God through faith in Christ Jesus. For as many of you as were baptized into Christ have put on Christ. There is no longer Jew or Greek, there is no longer slave or free, there is no longer male and female; for you are all one in Christ Jesus" (Gal 3:26-28; own translation). A new humanity is formed in belonging to Christ through baptism, a new status as children of God. In baptism we enter into communion with Christ who, in his risen life, transcends all human distinctions, whether of race, class, or gender.[29]

Thus, though a Jewish male, Christ through the resurrection embraces all human beings, gathering them into his divine identity through baptism. The death and resurrection of Christ make possible transformation of life as opposed to the old order of sin, domination, and death. The original equality of men and women before the fall is now restored in Christ (Gen 1:26-2; compare Gen 3:16). Women need no longer be subservient to men but can

24. Lee, *Flesh and Glory*, 197-211.

25. Lee, *Flesh and Glory*, 212-32.

26. Giles, *What the Bible Actually Teaches on Women*, 94-129; Keener, "Was Paul For or Against Women in Ministry?"

27. See especially Gooder, *Phoebe*.

28. Bauckham, *Gospel Women*. 109-202, who associates the apostle Junia with the disciple Joanna.

29. Byrne, *Paul and the Christian Woman*, 1-14.

take their full place in the Christian community, as in the home: created in the divine image, they are now remade in the image of Christ.

The rest of the Pauline corpus should be set within the context of this key passage in Galatians. Texts that seem to support male headship at home and the silence of women in church need to be read anew in that light. Not all the texts, moreover, say what people have assumed in the past. First Corinthians 11:2–16, for example, despite its difficulties, makes it clear that women are able to participate fully in worship: they bring the highest gift of all, prophecy, and have their own authority to speak in the assembly (1 Cor 11:10).[30] Other texts might reflect the context of early communities, a context that we can only guess.

Take, for example, 1 Timothy 2:11–15, which seems to silence women and place them firmly beneath male authority. Some argue that the text is not written by Paul but reflects a later situation where the church, faced with the Roman empire, has to tone down the radical edge of the gospel (such as women's authority to lead and teach). Others argue that it is written by Paul and that a careful study questions the traditional translation. Thus, the text refers not to women in general but to "a woman" (singular), and it might be a specific person or married couple that the text has in mind; it may in other words refer to a situation now lost to us.[31] Furthermore, it is quietness that is called for on the woman's part, not silence. The text does not say explicitly that the woman should submit to her husband but that she should simply "submit." This could well mean the kind of submission every Christian should cultivate in listening to the word of God. Finally, the word usually translated "have authority" actually means to "bully," "coerce," or "dominate," and the whole clause means something like: "to teach so as to coerce or dominate a man (husband?).

This reading would then cohere with the letter's concern for those who support false teaching. It could refer either to several women or to one woman who is teaching erroneous views, and in a contentious way, here instructed to cultivate a quiet and receptive openness to the word of God, the same openness required of men.[32] This need not exclude women from leadership or from having teaching authority; indeed, Ephesus is the place where Priscilla instructs Apollos in true doctrine (Acts 18:24–26).

Another example is a literary form called "household codes," found in the Pauline corpus (e.g., Col 3:18–4:11; Eph 5:22–6:9; 1 Pet 2:13–3:7), which contain instructions for the Christian home based on Hellenistic

---

30. Hooker, "Authority on Her Head"; Payne, "Wild Hair," 10–11.
31. Mowczko, "Interpretation of 1 Timothy 2:12."
32. Belleville, "Exegetical Fallacies."

philosophy.[33] These texts reflect a setting where Christians are struggling to survive in the hostile world of empire. Though they may seem less radical than other texts, such as Galatians 3:26–28, they are attempting to protect Christians in danger zones and to tone down those aspects of the gospel that are, in their context, too radical to be lived out in full. Thus, they appear to support the institution of slavery and slave-ownership, the docile obedience of children to their parents, the submission of wives to their husbands, and even the compliance of citizens to the Roman emperor.

At the same time, the household codes soften these structures with godly virtues that should, with Galatians 3 and the Gospels' witness kept firmly in mind, eventually undermine them.[34] We do not copy the patterns of the household codes, which represent Christian attempts to keep the peace, but rather follow the radical edge of the gospel of freedom and equality. This gospel liberates women, slaves, children, and citizens from compliance to authoritarian conformity. The working out of the true gospel of freedom calls for mutual submission and self-giving love for all Christians within both the structures of the church and that of the family.[35]

From this brief discussion, it is apparent that there is no theological obstacle to women's leadership and authority from the New Testament texts. Nor is there requirement that women should obey their husbands—unless that demand is accompanied by the concomitant claim that women in society more widely should not hold positions of leadership and authority. Within the Anglican Church, we need to become more biblically literate and much more aware of the exegetical and interpretative work currently being undertaken by men as well as women, who love and value the Scriptures and believe in their liberating impetus. In Australia, we need to encourage women's leadership alongside that of men, both in lay and ordained positions, including membership of committees. Diversity is a gospel value that can lead to more imaginative and expansive forms of mission, ministry, and evangelization for the church in ever-new contexts.

---

33. Lu, "Woman's Role."

34. Females were married very young in the ancient world, often in their early teens, to males who were perhaps twice their age. Husbands were better educated than their wives, with greater life experience and knowledge. For a young married woman (a girl, by our standards) to obey her older and more mature husband in the world of the Roman empire makes some sense, unlike today where wives are of similar age, life experience, and education as their husbands.

35. Fee, "Cultural Context of Ephesians 5:18–19."

Conclusion

This essay has argued that the Anglican Church in Australia, in its majority took a courageous decision to ordain women to the three-fold order of deacons, priests, and bishops. It did so not to conform to the values of the world and pursue progressive "left-wing" agendas, but precisely in order to live and act more faithfully in accordance with the biblical witness. The New Testament makes it plain that women, coequally with men, are drawn into ministry by virtue of their baptism into Christ. Women's identity in Christ gives the grounds for their capacity to be leaders in the church, whether as lay or ordained women. There is no gender barrier in the New Testament, any more than there is a barrier based on race, culture, or class. Jesus is indeed the Savior of the world (John 4:42).

At the same time, our history and our current situation show that much work still lies ahead of us. The inflexibility of dioceses who cling to the patriarchal ordering of church and home are closed to new insights from Scripture and theology. There is also the backlash to be taken into account, including in dioceses that are most hospitable to women's ministry. There are still very few women serving as bishops and many committees that lack equal and fair representation, particularly at the level of General Synod.

Our calling—whether as women or men, as lay or ordained—is to take hold of what we have been given by divine grace, and to summon the church (as well as the world) to hear anew the good news of the gospel. This alone has the capacity to transform human lives—and, eventually, the whole of creation—under the beneficent reign of God. The gospel invites each one of us to play our part, unimpeded by gender, in the mission of Christ's church. Only by doing so will we achieve the Pauline baptismal vision of a community where we are all one in Christ; where there is "no longer Jew or Greek . . . no longer slave or free . . . no longer male and female."

Bibliography

Appellate Tribunal. "Admission of Women to Holy Orders re Prayer Book Usage 1985." General Synod of the Anglican Church of Australia.

———. "Marriage of Divorced Persons and Admission of Women to Holy Orders 1980." General Synod of the Anglican Church of Australia.

Australian Broadcasting Commission. "Jesus' Female Disciples—The New Evidence: Part 1." With Helen Bond and Joan Taylor. *Compass Summer Series*. ABC Religion and Ethics. Broadcast July 7, 2018. Published February 28, 2019. https://www.abc.net.au/religion/watch/compass/jesus-female-disciples—-the-new-evidence—-part-1/10857492.

———. "Jesus' Female Disciples—The New Evidence: Part 2." With Helen Bond and Joan Taylor. *Compass Summer Series*. ABC Religion and Ethics. Broadcast July 14, 2018. Published March 11, 2019. https://www.abc.net.au/religion/watch/compass/jesus-female-disciples—-the-new-evidence—-part-2/10214404.

Bauckham, Richard. *Gospel Women. Studies of the Named Women in the Gospels*. Grand Rapids, MI: Eerdmans, 2002.

Belleville, Linda L. "Exegetical Fallacies in Interpreting 1 Timothy 2:11–15." *Priscilla Papers* 17 (2003). Accessed July 24, 2019. https://www.cbeinternational.org/resources/article/priscilla-papers/exegetical-fallacies-interpreting-1-timothy-211–15.

Byrne, Brendan. *Paul and the Christian Woman*. Homebush, NSW: St. Paul Publications, 1988.

CBE International. "Mission Statement." *CBE International* website. Accessed July 24, 2019. https://www.cbeinternational.org/content/cbes-mission.

Fee, Gordon D. "The Cultural Context of Ephesians 5:18–19." *Priscilla Papers* 16 (2002). Accessed July 24, 2019. https://www.cbeinternational.org/resources/article/priscilla-papers/cultural-context-ephesians-518–69.

Giles, Kevin. *What the Bible Actually Teaches on Women*. Eugene, OR: Cascade Books, 2018.

Gooder, Paula. *Phoebe: A Story (with Notes). Pauline Christianity in Narrative Form*. London: Hodder & Stoughton, 2018.

Harrison, Ted. *Much Beloved Daughter*. London: Darton, Longman & Todd, 1985.

Harwood, Thomas F. "British Evangelical Abolitionism and American Churches in the 1830's." *Journal of Southern History* 28 (1962). Accessed July 24, 2019. https://www.jstor.org/stable/2205310?read-now=1&seq=20#metadata_info_tab_contents.

Hooker, Morna D. "Authority on Her Head: An Examination of 1 Cor 11:10." *New Testament Studies* 10 (1963) 410–16.

Karris, Robert J. "Women and Discipleship in Luke." *Catholic Biblical Quarterly* 56 (1994) 1–20.

Keener, Craig S. "Was Paul For or Against Women in Ministry?" *Enrichment Journal* (2001).

Lee, Dorothy A. *Flesh and Glory. Symbolism, Gender and Theology in the Gospel of John*. New York: Herder & Herder, 2002.

Lu, Shi-Min, "Woman's Role in New Testament Household Codes: Transforming First Century Roman Culture." *Priscilla Papers* 30 (2016). Accessed July 24, 2019. https://www.cbeinternational.org/resources/article/priscilla-papers/woman's-role-new-testament-household-codes.

Mowczko, Marg. "An Interpretation of 1 Timothy 2:12 that Joins the Dots of 2:11–15." Blog post. Published August 30, 2017. Accessed July 24, 2019. https://margmowczko.com/interpretation-of-1-timothy-212/.

Payne, Philip B. "Wild Hair and Gender Equality in 1 Corinthians 11:2–26." *Priscilla Papers* 20 (2006) 9–18.

Porter, Muriel. "Second Female Bishop Barbara Darling Broke Ground in Anglican Church." *Sydney Morning Herald*, February 26, 2015. Accessed July 24, 2019. https://www.smh.com.au/national/second-female-bishop-barbara-darling-broke-ground-in-anglican-church-20150226-13p9lg.html.

———. "The Christian Origins of Feminism." *St. Mark's Review*, 149 (1992) 59–65.

———. *Women in the Church: The Great Ordination Debate in Australia*. Melbourne: Penguin, 1989.

Reilly, Colin, "A Little Compendium of Australian Anglican Diocesan Statistics: Numbers from the Ecclesia Anglicana Australis Database." The Bishop Perry Institute for Ministry and Mission 2017 newsletter. Accessed July 24, 2019. https://bishopperryinstitute.org.au/newsletter/.

———. *Active Clergy Gender Summary, 2019*. Melbourne: unpublished research 2019.

———. *Clergy Gender and the Stained-Glass Ceiling, 2019*. Melbourne: unpublished research, 2019.

Sayers, Dorothy L. "The Human-Not-Quite-Human." In *Unpopular Opinions*, 116–27. London: Victor Gollancz, 1946.

Women and the Church. "About WATCH." *Women and the Church* website. Accessed July 24, 2019. https://womenandthechurch.org/about-watch/.

———. "A Report on the Developments in Women's Ministry in 2018." *Women and the Church* website. Published February 26, 2019. Accessed July 24, 2019. https://womenandthechurch.org/resources/a-report-on-the-developments-in-womens-ministry-in-2018/

12

Our Father in Heaven, or Is It Our Mother in Heaven?

Kevin Giles

I AM DELIGHTED AND honored to be invited to contribute an essay to this *Festschrift* in celebration of Archbishop Philip Freier. Dr. Freier has led the Diocese of Melbourne since his instalment in December 2006, and the Australian Anglican Church since he was elected as the Primate in September 2014. As I am a convinced Evangelical egalitarian, I thank God for Dr. Freier's strong support of women in church leadership. He has supported the ordination of women since the debate began, has helped as a bishop to find them parish appointments, and—very significantly—has appointed them as assistant bishops in Melbourne, first Barbara Darling (consecrated 2008), then Genieve Blackwell (installed 2015) and Kate Prowd (consecrated 2018).

For the last forty years, the traditional way of speaking and thinking of God as a man—as "he"—has been under fire in our cultural setting. There is a reason for this. Today, the prevailing view is that men and women are of the same dignity, ability, and leadership potential, and most Christians now believe this is what the Bible teaches in principle. Thus, for many, thinking of God as literally male and not female is objectionable. As a consequence, many churches encourage the use of inclusive language when addressing God in prayer or speaking of God, and some churches encourage worshipers to pray, "Our Mother in heaven . . . "

Such changes have met with a hostile response from many Evangelicals, especially those who designate themselves complementarians. They argue that the Bible speaks of God in male terms, and specifically and frequently as "Father." On this basis, they assert that "patriarchy"[1] is what the Bible teaches,[2] and that we cannot and should not reject what is revealed in Scripture.

The importance of this debate is seen in its consequences. Those who encourage the use of inclusive language for God begin with the premise that God equally values men and women and thus delights to see women in leadership in the world and the church. In contrast, those who insist that God should be seen and spoken of in male terms almost invariably want men to be in charge wherever possible. The radical Roman Catholic theologian, Mary Daly, some years ago, accurately captured the logic of arguments supporting the idea that God is male not female when she said, "If God is male, then male is God."[3]

In centuries past, most Christians implicitly assumed God was male; but almost universally across the ages, theologians have been of another opinion. They have agreed that God is neither male nor female. He is Spirit (John 4:24). Athanasius, Augustine, and Aquinas all argued against speaking or thinking of God as a man/male. This closed the debate for theologians until very recently. The liberation of women has not just reopened the question; it has put it high on the theological agenda. English Evangelical theologian Alister McGrath makes the question "Is God Male?" the very first issue he addresses in his exploration of the doctrine of God.[4]

---

1. This term literally means, "the rule of the Father"; in practice it almost invariably speaks of the ultimate authority of the oldest male in an extended family. Patriarchy was the norm until modern times. It is not intrinsically evil or necessarily inimical to the welfare of women. Part of the responsibility of the patriarch was to ensure the safety and wellbeing of the women set under him and to arrange their marriages. It reflects a world where women could not support themselves and were set under a man all of their life. The problem is that it implies that women are like children who need looking after and that they must do as they are told. What is more, in a fallen world, all too often patriarchy leads to the marginalization and abuse of women. In most matters, the Bible reflects the world of its writers; they took this for granted, and this included patriarchy. This taken-for-granted world of the biblical writers cannot be understood as prescriptive revelation. If it were, we would need to embrace every aspect of the life assumed by the biblical writers.

2. This is the basic thesis of the Köstenbergers' book, *God's Design for Man and Woman: A Biblical-Theological Survey*. See also Moore, "After Patriarchy, What?"

3. Daly, *Beyond God the Father*, 19.

4. McGrath, *Christian Theology*, 205–7.

The Three Options

Broadly speaking, there are three options for understanding the gender of God:

1. The Bible depicts God in male terms, and we must accept this. God is literally male, not female.
2. The Bible predominantly depicts God in male terms, but this must be changed. No longer can we accept that God is male and not female. It is perfectly acceptable to pray, "Our Mother in heaven."
3. The Bible predominantly uses male language of God yet not exclusively and male language used of God should not be taken literally.

Let me now elaborate on these three alternatives.

1. *The Bible tells us God is male, and we should submit to the authority of Scripture*

Although Christian theologians in the past have agreed that the God revealed in Scripture is not literally a male, the implicit and almost universal belief has been that God represents the male in his ruling responsibilities in the world. Thus, the Bible reflects patriarchy from cover to cover. In post-1970s conservative Evangelical theology, this traditional way of thinking about God has been reformulated in trinitarian form and made the basis for the permanent subordination of women. Those who make this argument today euphemistically designate themselves "complementarians." They argue that when the Bible uses the names "Father" and "Son" of the first two persons of the Trinity, these words are to be taken literally. The Father is a real father, and the Son is a real son. Neither name is metaphorical. Just as the Father, as a father, is "head over" the Son, so the Son, as a son, must obey his father. This divine hierarchical ordering, complementarians add, prescribes the hierarchical ordering of the sexes.

Until very recently, this line of reasoning was endorsed by all complementarian theologians. For example, Wayne Grudem, the *de facto* leader of the complementarian movement, says that Paul is unambiguous on this matter, quoting 1 Corinthians 11:3 as proof:

> Paul makes the parallel explicit when he says, "I want you to understand that the head of every man is Christ, the head of woman is her husband, and the head of Christ is God." Here is a distinction in authority . . . . Just as God the Father has authority

> over the Son, though the two are equal in deity, so in marriage, the husband has authority over his wife, though they are equal in personhood. In this case, the man's role is like that of God the Father, and the woman's role is parallel to that of God to the Son.[5]

And,

> The Father and the Son relate to one another as a father and a son relate to one another in a human family; the Father directs and has authority over the Son, and the son obeys and is responsive to the directions of the father. The Holy Spirit is obedient to the directives of both the Father and the Son.[6]

Pushing the human analogy even further, he adds:

> The gift of children within a marriage, coming from both the father and the mother, and subject to the authority of the father and the mother, is analogous to the relationship of the Holy Spirit to the Father and the Son in the Trinity.[7]

This literal identification of God as male was enthusiastically endorsed by all Evangelical complementarians until 2016, when a small number of them broke rank, arguing this that this language was idolatrous. God was being depicted literally in human terms.[8] Responding specifically to these quotes, the complementarian Reformed theologian Todd Pruit wrote that this

> parallel between the Father and the Son to a husband and wife is worse than troubling. And, as we can see from the passage cited above, it leads to the inevitable comparison of the Holy Spirit to the child of the divine husband (Father) and wife (Son) These parallels have far more in common with pagan mythology than biblical theology.[9]

What we learn from Dr. Grudem is that the minute we take words used of God literally, we depict God in human terms. This is idolatry. For this reason, theologians in past times have agreed that language about God should not be understood literally or, more technically, "univocally." Human

---

5. Grudem, *Systematic Theology*, 459–60.
6. Grudem, *Systematic Theology*, 249.
7. Grudem, *Systematic Theology*, 257.
8. I tell the story of the "civil war" that followed among complementarians in my book, *The Rise and Fall of the Complementarian Doctrine of the Trinity*.
9. Pruitt, "A Mythological Godhead."

language used of God is metaphorical or, again to use the technical term, "analogical."[10] An analogy is one kind of metaphor. Analogical language conveys truth, but what that truth is must be established. For Evangelical Christians, the content of words used of God should be found by appeal to Scripture, not by appeal to fallen human relationships. Thus, to say God is love is certainly true, but we cannot define divine love in human terms or in terms of fallen human relationships. What God's love involves is revealed in Scripture. It is here that it is given content. In the Bible, God's love is most profoundly revealed in his giving of his only Son in death for our salvation.

It is the same with the human terms "Father" and "Son" when used of God. They certainly convey truth about God, but our human understanding of these terms does not give them content, as Grudem and most complementarians insist. In the Bible, the Father-Son relationship speaks of mutual love, intimacy, and oneness, not of the subordination of the Son. The title "the Son" identifies Jesus Christ as the messianic Son of the King of Kings. As the eternal Son of the eternal King, he rules for ever and ever (2 Sam 7:2–4; Isa 9:7; Luke 1:33; 2 Pet 1:11; Rev 7:10–12, 11:15; Eph 1:20). What is more, to argue by way of human analogy that the Son of God is eternally subordinated in authority to the Father is a denial of the primary Christian confession, "Jesus is Lord."

What we see in Scripture is that God is nether male nor female. He transcends human gender differentiation. The doyen of Evangelical theologians, Millard Erickson, is particularly critical of those who depict God the Father in patriarchal terms. He argues that those who do this seek to impose their own values by selectively quoting from Scripture and by absolutizing the cultural world of the Bible:

> God is not bound by gender and sex; he transcends both. It is quite possible that the patriarchal depiction of God that we find in much Christian theology is an illicit development of the masculine motifs in isolation from other qualities and from the biblical contexts in which they were originally given.[11]

For those who speak constantly of "the authority of Scripture," this answer to the complex and deep question of whether God is male and not female is very appealing. The Bible depicts God in male terms, and we must accept this. God is literally male, not female. The problem is that we end up with a God who seems to be man writ large. God is understood in terms of human life.

---

10. A very fine academic discussion of the nature of human language used of God is found in Soskice, *Metaphor in Religious Language*.

11. Erickson, *God in Three Persons*.

2. The Bible does depict God as male and not female, but we can do better today

In contrast, many contemporary Christians have come to the conclusion that, in today's world, we can no longer accept that God is male. Among those who opt for this answer, there are many different opinions, and to be fair to any one of them would not be possible in this short essay. Most who take what might be called the radical solution to the question under discussion argue that the only way forward is to reject or re-word what is given in the Bible. We should no longer speak of God as the Father or as male, or of the Trinity as Father, Son, and Spirit.

One much-quoted example of this approach is seen in the book by the Roman Catholic theologian Elizabeth Johnson, *She Who Is: The Mystery of God in Feminist Theological Discourse.*[12] Johnson's work is important because she openly argues that, in today's world, women should understand God in feminine terms. God is a "she," not a "he." She argues that all human language used of God, including the language of the Bible, is "symbolic." By this she means it is beyond human understanding. Its content is "utterly incomprehensible."[13] In a patriarchal society, people gave content to the Bible's "symbolic" language from within their cultural experience, where men were preeminent. It follows that we are free to give content in terms of our cultural experience, specifically in light of women's experience. Making women's experience the "lens" through which language used of God is understood is essential for women to flourish, she argues. She finds a path forward in the way the Bible speaks of God as Wisdom personified. In the Hebrew and Greek Old Testament, *Hokmah/Sophia* (wisdom) is a grammatical feminine noun.[14] Johnson thus renames the three persons of the Trinity "Mother-*Sophia*, Jesus-*Sophia* and Spirit-*Sophia*, one living God—SHE WHO IS."[15] This last title is her rendering in feminine language of God's self-revelation to Moses in the story of the burning bush (Exod 3:14).

The logic of this argument should be carefully noted. Johnson is arguing that in patriarchal times men created God in their own image; today, women are free to create God in *their* own image. In other words, what we believe about God is up to us to decide. Any thought that God has revealed himself in Scripture is lost.

---

12. Johnson, *She Who Is*.

13. Johnson, *She Who Is*, 10.

14. This argument lacks logical force. Languages that assign gender to nouns do not make grammatical gender prescriptive of natural gender.

15. Johnson, *She Who Is*, 15.

Yet there are very significant problems with renaming God. Our name identifies us; and to rename God gives him another identity. He becomes another God. If we rename God in terms taken from our culture, or from our experience as a man or a woman, we change how God is self-identified in Scripture. We create God as we would like him to be.

Now to the Trinity: there have been many attempts to rename the Trinity in non-male language besides those suggested by Elizabeth Johnson. For example, "Source, Word, and Spirit"; "Creator, Redeemer, and Sanctifier"; "Parent, Child, and Paraclete"; "Mother, Daughter, and Spirit"; and "Mother, Lover, and Friend." They are all problematic. Replacing the titles Father, Son, and Spirit with Creator, Redeemer, and Sanctifier or other similar gender-neutral terms eliminates the imagery of personal relationship and love. Replacing them with Mother, Daughter, and Child or similar non-male designations simply changes one sex for another.

I am unconvinced by this solution to the problem. The Bible speaks of God predominantly using male terms. The language certainly raises many questions in our contemporary egalitarian culture, but to rename God is overkill. It completely discounts what is given in Scripture, giving us the freedom to create God in our own image. I argue, and I would have much support, that the God we worship as Christians has revealed himself and his character. We have not created him in our own image writ large. We are not free, therefore, to rename God as we please or to give him a sex change.

3. *The Bible depicts God predominantly in male terms but not exclusively or literally as a male*

I now outline my own position. This involves a number of interlocking arguments.

First, we should believe that God is not literally either male or female. He is "Spirit" (John 4:24). For this reason, God can make man and woman in his image and likeness (Gen 1:27)—not only man. Indeed, we should believe that God is more unlike than like any man. He does not have a father and mother or a wife, he does not procreate by sexual union, he does not have a body that can identify him as male or female, and he does not grow old and die. Thus, the titles Father and Son should not be taken literally. The Father is like a human father in some limited ways and not like a human father in very profound ways.

Second, we cannot simply rename God. In the New Testament, God is called "Father" some 254 times. We cannot exclude this name. A better approach is to study how the Bible uses this title and other titles used of God.

On doing this, we immediately see that the Bible is at pains to exclude all sexual and gender overtones when speaking of God generically or in trinitarian terms as the Father, the Son, and the Spirit. He is rather consistently depicted as a God who loves deeply, cares profoundly, feels intensely, and stoops to serve. Today, these are often called "feminine" qualities. We ought not be surprised that there are many examples in the Bible of God the Father and of God the Son being likened to a woman or spoken of in feminine imagery. I am about to explain why.

Third, we may concede that in a patriarchal culture, male names for God did predominate, and that in our culture, more balance is needed. In the Bible, besides the title Father, God is addressed as the Almighty, the King, and the Lord, but also as a rock, a fortress, a shepherd, a light, a friend, and a potter, among other names. What is more, God is often described in motherly terms. He is said to comfort and nurture "her" children (Hos 11:3–14; Deut 32:18; Isa 42:14, 49:15, 66:13). There are also about a dozen verses where God is said to gather his children under his wing like a mother bird (Ps 91:4; Luke 13:34; Matt 23:37 and more). All these titles and descriptions of God should be used today and highlighted in our culture.

Finally, we are not limited to using the titles or descriptions of God found in Scripture. There is no problem with addressing God in terms not explicitly given in the Bible, so long as they do negate or contradict clear biblical teaching or totally replace biblical ones. For example, a prayer could begin with God of Abraham and Sarah, or God of Joseph and Mary, or God of Aquila and Priscilla, or in any of innumerable ways.

Here, I would like to qualify that I do not think we are absolutely forbidden from calling God "Mother," likening him to a mother, or speaking of him in feminine ways (though I am not suggesting, for example, that we can transpose the title "Father" for "Mother" in the Lord's Prayer). Indeed, John Calvin allows that God may be addressed as "Mother." In commentating on Isaiah 46:3, the great Reformer says: "It is the intention of the Prophet to show . . . the Jews . . . that God, has manifested himself to be both their Father and their Mother," because he "will always assist them."[16]

Regarding the Trinity, there is also nothing wrong with speaking from time to time of the Creator, Redeemer, and Sanctifier, or one of several other gender-neutral triads. However, triads like Father, Mother, and Child, or Spirit-*Sophia*, Jesus-*Sophia* and Mother-*Sophia*, which completely redefine the Trinity, seem to me to be very problematic.

---

16. Calvin, *Commentary on Isaiah*, 3:436–37.

The Maleness of Jesus

Some feminists have also raised the issue of the maleness of Jesus—and not without reason. Complementarians characteristically argue that Jesus' maleness proves that God has given precedence to men. For example, Andreas and Margaret Köstenberger, much-published and militant Evangelical complementarians, say that the fact that Jesus was a man, not a woman, is of profound theological significance. It *implies* male headship.[17] This inference or deduction is not endorsed by orthodox theologians writing on Christology. Paradoxically, the Köstenbergers acknowledge this last point in wording that stands counter to their thesis: "It was Jesus' humanity, not his maleness, that was essential for our salvation . . . "[18] What the Köstenbergers and other complementarians have done in making this argument is ignore how Scripture identifies Jesus. In Scripture, the title "Son" (of God) is a lofty honorific title. In the case of Jesus, it identifies him as the long-awaited messianic Son of the King of Kings, who is destined to rule forever and ever in all might, majesty, and authority, not as the subordinate and submissive Son who must obey the one set over him.

To be the incarnate Son of God, Jesus had to be a man or a woman. We may presume that the Son could have become incarnate as either man or woman, as both sexes are made in God's image and likeness. However, for reasons not revealed, he was incarnate as a man. This fact does not imply that God prefers men.

The word "incarnation," we should note, literally means "in-fleshed" (see John 1:14). Human flesh can be either male or female. Thus, we may rightly also speak of the eternal Son becoming "human." Nevertheless, despite the appeal of this non-sexist language, it is more accurate to speak of him becoming "man," for this is what he did. He became a man and not a woman.

What can be said in answer to this sexual particularity?

One possible answer is that it was necessary for God to become a man in order to be the counterpart of the man, Adam. Commentators of Romans 5:12–21 invariably tell us that Paul is depicting the first Adam as representative "man," disobedient to God, and Christ as representative "man," obedient to God. However, if women are saved by Christ the second Adam, which they are, then Adam and Christ in this theological juxtaposition are representative humankind in sin and grace respectively. It follows that it is not Christ's maleness that is theologically significant but his humanness.

---

17. Köstenberger and Köstenberger, *God's Design*, 82–83.
18. Köstenberger, *God's Design*, 83.

Another intriguing suggestion as to why God revealed himself in the man Jesus of Nazareth is that if the Son of God was to demonstrate the powerful renunciating power for the salvation of others, then he had to be a man. Self-chosen humiliation and renunciation imply giving up what you have. In the incarnation, the all-powerful God lays aside all his privileges, becomes a servant, and dies on the cross for men and women (Phil 2:4–11). A woman could not demonstrate the renunciation of power for the salvation of others, because she represents the powerless and the humbled in the world.

Yet another oft-made suggestion is that the Son had to be male to be the revelation of the Father. In biblical times, a son represented his father, and Jesus is called the Father's "only Son" (John 1:18). A daughter did not represent her father; when married, she became part of another family.

Other reasons have been put forward as to why God became incarnate as a man and not a woman, but all suggestions are conjecture. God has not revealed his mind on this matter.

When we turn to the Gospels, we note that, in the incarnate Son, sexual identity and gender are not an issue. Jesus was a man and not a woman, but the Gospels never suggest that he had romantic attachments, let alone that he married. He related as well to women as to men and valued them in the same way. He saw them alike in sin and alike in need of salvation. He stood in opposition to the characteristic sins of men that drive them to want to set themselves over others, especially women. He extolled the virtues of humility, forgiveness, gentleness, self-sacrifice, and practical love. Men and women across the centuries have sensed that they can relate to this man like no other. They have rightly understood that the Son of God took "the form of a slave, being born in human likeness" (Phil 2:7) and died on the cross, not to oppress them but to set them free.

Finally, I point out that if God had become incarnate as a woman, we would be asking why it was as a woman and not as a man.

Conclusion

There are no easy answers to the profound and pressing contemporary question: is God male and not female? Nevertheless, I have argued, that there are some things we ought not do and some things we ought to do when speaking of God in our new egalitarian cultural context. In developing my case, I have presupposed that the Bible is our primary source for our knowledge of God as he has most fully revealed himself in Jesus Christ. On this basis, I have argued that we should not think or speak of God as man and not woman in any literal sense. God is not a man or a woman writ large. He transcends gender. The human binary distinction of male or female cannot be applied to him. He is God Almighty, who has created the universe and made man and woman in his image and likeness. Positively, on this basis I have argued that we should not speak of or address God solely in male terms. The God revealed in Scripture is a "motherly father." He loves us, cares for us, and graciously guides us into safe pastures. We must therefore speak of God in our cultural context in inclusive ways.

What is so appealing in this answer for us contemporary Christians is that it honors both men and women; neither sex is given preference. That this is the right answer is suggested in the first chapter of our Bibles. At the apex of his creative work, God says, "Let us make humankind in our own image, according to our likeness, and let them have dominion . . . " (Gen 1:26). Man and woman alike are made in God's image and likeness, and to both is given the mandate to rule over God's world. In this text, God is the creator of this world and man and woman; he rules over them, and side by side they rule over his creation. He creates them; they do not create him.

Bibliography

Calvin, John. *Commentary on the Book of the Prophet Isaiah*. Volume 3. Translated by William Pringle. Grand Rapids, MI: Eerdmans, 1948.

Daly, Mary *Beyond God the Father*. London: The Women's Press, 1985.

Erickson, Millard. *God in Three Persons: A Contemporary Interpretation of the Trinity*. Grand Rapids: Baker, 1995.

Giles, Kevin. *The Rise and Fall of the Complementarian Doctrine of the Trinity*. Eugene, OR: Cascade, 2017.

Grudem, Wayne. *Systematic Theology: An Introduction to Biblical Doctrine*. Downers Grove, IL: InterVarsity, 1994.

Johnson, Elizabeth. *She Who Is: The Mystery of God in Feminist Theological Discourse*. New York: Herder and Herder, 1992.

Köstenberger, Andreas, and Margaret Köstenberger. *God's Design for Man and Woman: A Biblical-Theological Survey*. Wheaton, IL: Crossway, 2014.

McGrath, Alister. *Christian Theology, an Introduction*. Oxford: Blackwell, 1990.

Moore, Russell. "After Patriarchy, What?" *JETS* 49/3 (2004) 569–76.

Pruitt, Todd. "A Mythological Godhead." Blog post on *Mortification of Spin*. July 9, 2016. Accessed July 19, 2019. http://www.alliancenet.org/mos/1517/a-mythological-godhead#.WRkDoO6GOUk.

Soskice, Janet Martin. *Metaphor in Religious Language*. Oxford: Clarendon, 1985.

The Church in the World

13

At the Third Altar

The Vocation of the Church in the World

Stephen Pickard[1]

"Where Your Treasure Is..."

THE STORY OF LAURENCE of Rome (Latin: *Laurentius*, 225–258 AD) is well known and rightly celebrated.[2] Laurence was one of the seven deacons of Ancient Rome under Pope Sixtus II. When Sixtus became pope in 257, he ordained Laurence as a deacon, and though still young he was appointed first among the seven deacons who served in the patriarchal church. Laurence was therefore called "archdeacon in Rome." It was a position of great trust that included the care of the treasury and riches of the church and the distribution of alms among the poor. At that time, the Roman au-

---

1. This essay is a revision of an address originally given at the National Anglicare Conference in Canberra in 2015.

2. Feast Day 10 August; a lesser festival under the title "Laurence, deacon, martyr, 258.", observed in many Anglican Provinces. The Melbourne based society, Brotherhood of St. Laurence, bears his name.

thorities had established a rule that all Christians who had been denounced must be executed and their goods confiscated by the Imperial Treasury. At the beginning of August 258, Emperor Valerian issued an edict that all bishops, priests, and deacons should immediately be put to death. Pope Sixtus was captured at the cemetery of St. Callixtus while celebrating the liturgy and executed forthwith.

After the death of Pope Sixtus, the prefect of Rome demanded that the person responsible for the church's treasures, Deacon Laurence, turn over the riches of the church. Tradition has it that Laurence asked for three days to gather together the wealth. He worked swiftly to distribute as much church property as possible to the poor so as to prevent it being seized by the prefect. On the third day, at the head of a small delegation, he presented himself to the prefect. When Laurence was ordered to give up the treasures of the church, he presented the poor, the crippled, the blind, and the suffering, naming these as the true treasures of the church. One account records him declaring to the prefect, "The church is truly rich; far richer than your emperor." The consequence of this act of defiance was that Laurence, the last of the seven deacons, suffered a martyr's death.

Who are the treasures of the church? "Truly I tell you, whatever you did for one of the least of these brothers and sisters of mine, you did for me." (Matt 25:40). It is quite clear whom Jesus regarded as the treasures of his society: the least. We may be permitted to extrapolate: it includes those forgotten, ignored, looked down upon, those who are passed by on the other side of the road, those 60 million people today wandering the face of the earth looking for a home. Those fleeing in boats, dying in trucks, caught in crossfire—the poorest and most forlorn.

The words of Jesus remain arresting: "For where your treasure is, there your heart will be also" (Matt 6:21). The Brotherhood of St. Laurence is a concrete example of how the gospel gives answer to these haunting words of Jesus. These same words of Jesus remind the church of its commitment to the poor and marginalized; to those forgotten and disempowered by government policies that disenfranchise the poor and exacerbate inequalities. In the spirit of St. Laurence, this society is acutely aware of where the true treasures of the people of God are to be found. Basic to Christian faith is an affirmation that all human beings are created in the image of God; none is superior to others, and all are worthy of recognition and respect. To bear the image of the Maker is to bear the image of the One who treasures all people irrespective of race, creed, color, language, or religion.

The spirit that inspired courage and faithfulness in St. Laurence is the Eternal Spirit of the Father of Lights, incarnate in the life of Jesus. This Spirit of Holiness is not prepared to sacrifice the poor and disadvantaged to the gods of power at the altar of greed. In truth, the altar of greed occupies a prominent place in our present-day Australia. This altar is built upon the maxim, "I consume, therefore I am." Greed has an insatiable appetite. It is a voracious altar, and it consumes so many. The litmus test is simple: the level of inequalities between the "haves" and the "have nots" is increasing. And alas, we of the "haves" are, without even thinking, complicit in this new consumer religion, which consumes the lives of the "have nots." Perhaps the greatest challenge for governments of nations is to encourage the design and implementation of social structures and policies that are generative of a just redistribution of resources for the sake of the common good.

This ethical and moral imperative is articulated in the third and fourth Marks of Mission of the Anglican Communion:

3. To respond to human need by loving service

4. To transform unjust structures of society, to challenge violence of every kind and pursue peace and reconciliation.

In this essay, I want to consider the wealth and treasures of the church within the greater economy: not the monetized economy of state and corporate life, but the economy of God's love. Where do the treasures gathered by St. Laurence fit within God's new economy, and what might that mean for how the poor are regarded within society? I want to address the matter of what St. John Chrysostom calls the "altar of the poor"—an altar very different from the altar of greed upon which the poor are too quickly placed. In doing so, I am mindful of the work and advocacy of our Primate, Archbishop Philip, regarding those considered the least of society. In particular, I think of his work among the First Peoples of this country and more recently his advocacy for the plight of refugees and asylum seekers.

St. Chrysostom, Advocate for the Poor

I want to turn to the fourth century preacher and writer St. John Chrysostom, Archbishop of Constantinople (modern day Istanbul) 347–407 AD.[3] Constantinople was one of the great cities of the ancient world. Chrysostom was known for his eloquence in preaching and public speaking. He was a fierce denouncer of wealth, envy, greed, and abuse of authority by both ecclesiastical and political leaders. He had a saying: "As a moth gnaws a garment, so doth envy consume a man."

---

3. See for example, Stephens, *St. John Chrysostom*.

This "prophet of charity" gained a reputation as the "golden mouth" of the ancient world. In an age that did not have sophisticated means of communication—few books, no email, internet, podcasts, twitter, or TED talks; where aural communication was the staple diet—Chrysostom was an orator and preacher of the highest caliber. He could hold his hearers with conviction, argument, and oratory.[4] Chrysostom was, above all, an advocate for the poor and a constant thorn in the side of the wealthy. His seven sermons on Lazarus and the rich man, on the theme of wealth and poverty, are justly famous in the early church.[5]

The Orthodox Church priest and theologian Fr. Florovsky writes that Chrysostom "simply could not evade social problems without detaching Christianity from life, but social problems were for him emphatically religious and ethical problems."[6] He was concerned with the renewal of society and the healing of social ills. He was preaching and practicing charity, founding hospitals and orphanages, helping the poor and destitute. He wanted to recover the spirit of practical love. He wanted more activity and commitment among Christians to follow the way of Jesus into the world. Chrysostom was always against compromise, appeasement, and adjustment. No doubt he would not have made a good politician in today's world—those who chop and change their principles or simply bully others to get their way, driven by self-interest but dressing it up as care for the common good.

At a recent ecumenical roundtable at the *Australian Centre for Christianity and Culture* in Canberra, the guest speaker, Bishop Geevarghese Mor Coorilos,[7] referred to the three bankruptcies of the contemporary church: first, the ethical and moral bankruptcy of a church infected as it is by monetized host cultures and seemingly unable to attend to its real treasures; second, an intellectual bankruptcy that entailed a failure to reason together and instead was driven by ideological forces, and third, a prophetic bankruptcy that led to a loss of voice and advocacy for the needy. His presentation had echoes of Chrysostom's concern for a prophetic, integral, and practical Christianity.

---

4. Barack Obama is a fine modern example, e.g., his oration at the funeral of the nine people murdered in the Charlottesville Church, Virginia, USA. Obama spoke, paused for what seemed an eternity, then spoke, then of course broke into song.

5. Roth, *St. John Chrysostom*.

6. Florovsky, *St. John Chrysostom*.

7. The Rt Rev. Dr. Coorilos is Metropolitan of the Diocese of Niranam Diocese of Malankara Jacobite Syriac Orthodox Church. He is also Moderator of the World Council of Churches Communion on World Mission and Evangelism; Metropolitan of Niranam Diocese of Malankara Jacobite Syriac Orthodox Church; President of Kerala Council of Churches.

For Chrysostom, that meant connecting faith with helping those he saw lying and scrounging on the streets and in the lanes of Constantinople. Not surprisingly, one of Chrysostom's constant and favorite subjects was that of wealth and misery. He was not primarily a social reformer, even if he had his own plans for Christian society. He was concerned with the ways of Christians in the world—with their duties, with their vocation. In his sermons, we find, first of all, a penetrating analysis of the social situation. Chrysostom found too much injustice, coldness, indifference, self-interest, suffering, and sorrow in the society of his day. It was all about the acquisitive spirit of life. This acquisitive spirit breeds inequality, and therefore inequality and injustice. He was upset and angered by the fruitless luxury of life. He regarded wealth as a standing temptation. Wealth, he argued, seduces the rich, though wealth itself has no value; it was a guise under which the real faces of human beings were concealed. Those who held possessions came to cherish them and were deceived; they came to value and rely on them. All possessions, not only the large ones, were dangerous, insofar as people became accustomed to relying upon what was, by its very nature, passing and unreal. How would we moderns survive this preaching? He was a tough nut, precisely because he cared for the poor.

The Altar of the Poor

In one of Chrysostom's sermons on poverty, based on the Apostle Paul's first letter to the church at Corinth (1 Corinthians 9), Chrysostom is concerned to connect the church and its central act of worship, the Eucharist, with the poor of the world. His point was simple enough: what's the point of breaking bread week in, week out, sharing a common cup to remember the One whose life was given for others, if this has no connection to what is happening in the world to those in need? This is an age-old issue and a very real contemporary issue. Chrysostom addresses the issue head on. He desires a practical Christianity, but he also desires a principled practice. He wants to engage the head and heart of the body of Christ. Chrysostom has a heart for the poor. So, his theology is not playing with words but a robust defense of his love for the poor. And he needs to make his case because of the apathy, ignorance and prejudice of the wealthy of the great city of Constantinople.

In so doing, Chrysostom appeals to the image of the altar.[8]

The first altar is the altar of Christ's cross and resurrection. The stone that was rolled away from the tomb becomes the new stone of the altar of Christ. This new altar is prefigured in the Old Testament—the altar of the

---

8. Chrysostom, "Homily 20."

temple, upon which the sacrifices were offered. With the coming of Christ, the stone altar of Old Testament sacrifice is radicalized. Christ becomes the new altar. Through Christ's sacrifice, he forms from the stone altar of ancient times a new, living body. Christ's life of loving service and sacrifice comes to finality in the cross. It is the basis of our life. We owe everything to the altar of the cross, and it gives our life meaning and purpose.

However, the cross of Christ has no independent existence. Rather, the altar of the cross is "refracted, as it were, into two closely connected altars":[9] (1) the stone altar made up of the ecclesial body of Christ (which is the second altar), and (2) a special part of that body, the poor (which constitutes the third altar). Chrysostom states in his homily the stone altar "is made of Christ's members themselves, and the body of the Lord becomes your altar." In other words, the altar of the cross expresses itself practically in two altars that are established in the world.

The church gathers to remember the life of Jesus by breaking bread as a symbol of his life given and by drinking from the common cup as a symbol of the life poured out for others. This is an altar of thanksgiving (as the Greek word "Eucharist" signifies). This is the sacrament of salvation and healing. It constitutes the second altar, for it flows from the first altar of the cross of Christ.

However, according to Chrysostom, what makes this second altar of the body of Christ more "awesome" than the altar of the Old Testament is not simply Christ, but the poor. This is the third altar. The stone altar becomes holy because Christ's body touches it; but that body is especially holy and sacred because of the presence of the poor of that body.[10]

Chrysostom was critical of the church of his day because on the one hand, it honored the stone altar "because it receives Christ's body," but on the other hand, that same church treated with contempt "those who are themselves the body of Christ . . . as they die." He was referring to the poor. The poor, he said, "are the most sacred part of the altar 'made' by the Eucharist." He states, "You can see that altar [of the poor] everywhere, lying in the lanes and market places." He observes that while the priest invokes the Spirit at the Eucharist, the people of God invoke that same Spirit "not by speech but by deeds because nothing so kindles and sustains the fire of the Spirit as this oil [of sacrifice at the altar of the poor] poured out in abundance."

9. See Tillard, *Flesh of the Church, Flesh of Christ*, 69.
10. Chrysostom would have joined with those of more recent years who refer to the Church's "preference for the poor." The late former bishop of Liverpool and former English cricketer, David Sheppard, wrote a book and preached about the church's "bias to the poor"—a modern day Chrysostom perhaps? In Australia, the late Dr. John Roffey was in the same mold.

So then, for Chrysostom there are three altars; they are all related, and each has a place in the kingdom of God. Moreover, without the third altar of the poor, the cross and the Eucharist are diminished. Or, from a different point of view, the Eucharist that celebrates Christ's life and sacrifice is not complete until the church as the body of Christ offers its sacrifice on the altar of the poor. Here is the final altar that shines a light upon the Eucharist and Christ's life.

Following Chrysostom, we might state that the altar upon which the Eucharist is celebrated is simply stone, and those who gather at this altar remain stony-hearted if they are not connected to a third altar, the altar of the poor. How can the church remember Jesus, who gave his life that the world might live, if that same church forgets the world that is in need and the world that Christ came to save? The altar of the sacrament has to express itself at the altar of the poor. In this way, the poor become a sacrament of Christ's broken body.

Presiding at the Third Altar

The identity and mission of the church will be strong, loving, wise, and fruitful if it is orientated towards the third altar. The core mission of the church is only core as it encompasses the life of the poor.

But the poor is code for all those who are left out or lack something essential to their wellbeing. It encompasses those on the margins; those neglected, despised, forgotten, ill-treated, abused; those regarded of no account socially, economically, politically, and spiritually.

What this also means is that as the church invests deeply in its core mission and seeks the altar of the poor in the world, it illuminates, enhances, and completes the identity and mission of the church that gathers at the Eucharist. The body of Christ formed from the cross of Christ—the body that gathers at the altar of Christ—always in truth includes the altar of the poor. Following Chrysostom, it is the poor who make the Eucharist real. Every consecration of the bread and wine at the Eucharistic altar is simultaneously a consecration of the ecclesial body to a life of sacrifice at the altar of the poor. From this point of view, it matters little whether it is high church or low church, conservative or liberal, charismatic or contemplative, Roman Catholic, Orthodox, Pentecostal, or Protestant; everything depends on whether it is *true* church. And the litmus test of the church's truthful remembering of Jesus will be its sacrifice at the altar of the poor.

This is at heart a story of the Eucharistic life of the church of Jesus Christ, continued in the world for which Christ died and rose again. And the spiritual nourishment that comes from remembering a life given orientates, focuses, and energizes work at the third altar. Working at the third altar can be exhausting: people get burnt out, lose energy, even despair at times. The body count at the third altar seems to mount. More often, they are overwhelmed by the policies and practices of the state and the powers of global corporations that squeeze the life-blood from the least. We need to be reconnected to the other two altars. An integrative and practical Christian practice includes an appropriate element of transcendence, reminding us that we don't live and work in our strength; there is a resource, a source of renewable energy to be found as people gather to remember the living God in their midst. Even our best work at the third altar can become another form of self-love unless it is given back to the Lord for blessing and renewal.

Chrysostom wanted to alert and motivate the comfortable and the wealthy to get involved and find real religion. He also wanted to remind those whose who understood this—who already saw the poor and labored hard—that their work was not ultimately owned by them, that they were following in the footsteps of one who referred everything back to God.

The Identity of the Poor

In Peter Brown's, *Through the Eye of a Needle*, a remarkable book on wealth and the emergence of Christianity in the West in the fourth and fifth centuries, the author states that "it is the redefinition of the Christian poor (derived from the Old Testament) that did most to secure the eventual triumph of Christianity in the cities in the course of the fifth century."[11] But what in particular was it in this redefinition that was so transformative and led to the expansion of the church? In his carefully argued and documented book, Brown shows that the fundamental change was one of perception. "The adoption of a view that saw the poor not only as beggars but also as persons in search of justice and protection reflected mounting pressure within the Christian communities themselves to engage in forms of social action that had wider effects than mere charity to the destitute."[12]

Brown refers to the two tracks that developed in relation to the image of the poor. On the one hand, the "wretched poor" and destitute of Christian teaching were identified as the "needy and useless" that the church felt a responsibility for. On the other hand, the poor came to understand themselves after the manner of ancient Israel (i.e., requiring justice) and more like the *plebs* of Rome. The implication of this understanding was

11. Brown, *Through the Eye of a Needle*, 80.
12. Brown, *Through the Eye of a Needle*, 80.

that the poor were vulnerable persons, not beggars; they belonged at the core of society, not at the margins. Brown notes that the adoption of language from the Hebrew Scriptures concerning the poor "gave to the average inhabitant of late Roman cities a new purchase on the powerful" and also "provided them with new advocates in the persons of Christian bishops and clergymen."[13] In this context, the bishops became "the modern avatars of the prophets of ancient Israel." This development of the fifth century was an important element in the expansion and place of Christianity in the West. As the "lesser townsfolk" of the cities (the poor and needy; the *plebs*) identified with the poor of Israel, they "did not present themselves as 'others'—as beggars—but as 'brothers.'"[14] The famous bishop of Milan, Ambrose, had articulated—as early as the 380s—this new relationship between the bishop and the urban communities. All were citizens and worthy of care and attention, whether they were the urban rich, middle, or lower classes comprising the plebs. All were brothers and sisters in the Lord. This inclusivist approach to mission had a transformative effect on society and on the credibility and attractiveness of the Christian God. Ultimately, it had a major impact on the expansion of the church.

It was Chrysostom's view that if one lost sight of the treasures of the church then one also lost sight of the reason for the church's existence. This is the altar upon which the people of God are called to labor. Chrysostom captured it well when he appealed to the image of the bee: "The bee is more honored than other animals, not because she labors, but because she labors for others." Laboring at the third altar for others is where we find the true treasures of our common humanity. At this altar, we offer a sacrifice of praise and give ourselves as a way of serving the common good of the world.

Barbara Brown Taylor, the American episcopal priest, writer, and extraordinary preacher, writes in her book, *An Altar in the World: A Geography of Faith*: "Whoever you are, you are human. Wherever you are, you live in the world, which is just waiting for you to notice the holiness in it."[15] This has a fine resonance with the gospel. The treasure we seek is before us, just waiting for us to notice its holiness. It is the treasure of the poor; they constitute the true altar whose holy and sweet fragrance ascends to the Lord of heaven and earth. Chrysostom said the fragrance of the poor ascends not just to heaven but right to the top: "It passes beyond heaven itself, and the heaven of heaven, and arrives at the throne of the King."[16] Although your

13. Brown, *Through the Eye of a Needle*, 80.
14. Brown, *Through the Eye of a Needle*, 81.
15. Taylor, *An Altar in the World*, 17.
16. Chrysostom, "Homily 20."

work might indeed be undertaken silently and without fanfare, nonetheless your work speaks volumes.

On Taking the Crucified from the Cross

The church's vocation in the world is to preside at the third altar. This is a vocation to follow the Lord of the world to the altar at which the good and compassionate God presides. This ecclesial vocation has been powerfully and movingly articulated by Jon Sobrino in *The Principle of Mercy*.[17] The subtitle is telling: *Taking the Crucified People from the Cross*. Sobrino's context is one of poverty, suffering, and violence. And yet, he proposes an uncompromising theology of the church shaped by the principle of mercy. For Sobrino, such a church is pre-eminently "Samaritan" in character, or what Christopher Marshall calls the "compassionate justice of God."[18] Beyond mere sentiment or "works of mercy," something more radical is envisaged. "Mercy is a basic attitude toward the suffering of another, whereby one reacts to eradicate that suffering for the sole reason that it exists, and in the conviction that, in this reaction to the ought-not-be of another's suffering one's own being, without any possibility of subterfuge, hangs in the balance."[19]

The sense here that human life "hangs in the balance" is haunting, to say the least. Our very humanity is endangered to the extent that we refuse to live mercifully and with compassion toward the suffering of others. Taking the crucified people down from the cross is a costly and life-involving matter. The transactional accounts of mercy and compassion (Sobrino's "calculated mercy"), so much a feature of the Western philosophical tradition, are rendered null and void on this account.

What emerges into the full light of day is Sobrino's thoroughly christological interpretation of mercy. The primordial mercy of God—the structured form of love whereby the suffering on another is interiorized—"appears concretely historicized in Jesus' practice and message."[20] It is most powerfully narrated in the parable of the Good Samaritan—or might we say, "merciful Samaritan." Mercy is "fundamental to the structure of the life of Jesus."[21].

---

17. Sobrino, *Principle of Mercy*.
18. Marshall, *Compassionate Justice*, e.g., 217.
19. Sobrino, *Principle of Mercy*, 18.
20. Sobrino, *Principle of Mercy*, 17.
21. Sobrino, *Principle of Mercy*, 15.

What then of the people of the church? Their vocation is to "reiterate this mercy of God's, exercising it toward others and thus rendering themselves like unto God."[22] Sobrino's theology of the church, developed through the lens of the principle of mercy, offers a powerful kenotic ecclesiology patterned after Christ. At the heart of the mercy dynamic is a going out of oneself for the other. This mode of outreach is the very antithesis of a contemporary culture of narcissism driven by self-interest, twisted in on itself and its desires. The mercy dynamic identified above is not a one-way transactional type of relation. Rather, it involves genuine reciprocity, mutual accountability, and vulnerability. It is not simply the one to whom mercy is shown whose life "hangs in the balance," *but the one who offers mercy. It is the life of this one that hangs in the balance.*

Such is the nature of true mercy. It generates a reciprocal relation undergirded by a theology of kenosis. A kenotic ecclesiology is the natural theological home for the vocation of the church to be a body of compassion for the world. Such a radically shaped ecclesiology of compassion is inevitably an activity that generates scandal and lives in the shadow of the cross of Jesus and its attendant violence. Such is the shape and tenor of ministry and mission at the third altar. It has been a mark of Archbishop Philip's life and ministry.

---

22. Sobrino, *Principle of Mercy*, 17.

Bibliography

Brown, Peter. *Through the Eye of a Needle: Wealth, the Fall of Rome, and the Making of Christianity in the West, 350–550 AD*. Princeton and Oxford: Princeton University Press, 2012.

Florovsky, Archpriest Georges. "St. John Chrysostom: Prophet of Charity." *Catholic Culture* website. Accessed July 20, 2019. https://www.catholicculture.org/culture/library/view.cfm?recnum=5977.

Chrysostom. "Homily 20." In *The Homilies of St. John Chrysostom*, Volume 12 of the Library of the Nicene and Post-Nicene Fathers of the Christian Church, edited by Philip Schaff, 372–374. Edinburgh: T. & T. Clark, 1989.

Marshall, Christopher D. *Compassionate Justice: An Interdisciplinary Dialogue with Two Gospel Parables on Law, Crime, and Restorative Justice*. Eugene, Oregon: Cascade Books, 2012.

Taylor, Barbara Brown. *An Altar in the World: A Geography of Faith*. New York: HarperCollins, 2009.

Roth, Catherine P. Translation and Introduction. *St. John Chrysostom on Wealth and Poverty*. Crestwood, New York: St. Vladimir's Seminary Press, 1984.

Sobrino, Jon. *Principle of Mercy: Taking the Crucified People from the Cross*. Maryknoll, NJ: Orbis, 1994.

Stephens, W.R.W. *St. John Chrysostom, His Life and Times*. N.P.: Createspace, 2014.

Tillard, J. M. R. *Flesh of the Church, Flesh of Christ: At the Sources of the Ecclesiology of Communion*. Collegeville, MN: Liturgical, 2001.

14

When Theology Risks Life and Limb

The Role of the Church in Humanitarian Practice

Bob Mitchell[1]

THERE IS A PRESSING need to bring together the worlds of theology and contemporary humanitarian practice. There can be no better reason for doing so than this: it may save lives.

Theology is much more than a catalogue of dry beliefs. It extends to a consideration of how understandings about God inform human behavior. With this applied focus, the study of theology becomes socially relevant. It is also a more revealing process because what people actually think about God is often best disclosed by their actions or inactions.

The humanitarian sector is broad-based, consisting of government actors, well-known international NGOs, and civil defense organizations. It also includes local civil society organizations, like churches. As a permanent presence in communities, churches can have a vital role to play in disaster preparation and response. Churches are found in very remote places and are expected to be among the first responders when a disaster strikes.

---

1. The views expressed in this essay do not represent any organization and are the views of the author alone.

In his capacity as president of Anglican Overseas Aid, Archbishop Philip has always been a strong supporter of development and humanitarian programs. In particular, he has demonstrated a very keen interest in the challenges affecting our own region, including climate change. This is clearly reflected in the ongoing dialogue between Oceania primates, in which Archbishop Philip has played a central role. With this in mind, I have chosen to write about the way local theologies can affect Pacific communities in preparing for climate-related disasters.

Recent comprehensive qualitative research across four Pacific countries has revealed a clear communitarian outlook in their theological beliefs (consistent with traditional Indigenous culture), strong faith commitments that include a high regard for Scripture, and Christian values that firmly underpin community resilience and compassion. That said, some theological beliefs about natural disasters were reported that are inimical to humanitarian action. This research suggests that while there is much to both affirm and learn from in these Pacific settings, there are also some beliefs that should be respectfully revisited in the interests of better protecting Pacific communities.

The Social Legitimacy of the Church in the South Pacific

The South Pacific is vastly different from its rapidly secularizing neighbors, Australia and New Zealand. Countries such as PNG, Fiji, Vanuatu, and the Solomon Islands have a strong Christian identification, with a statistical affiliation of over 90 percent.[2] Fiji is a slightly different case, because there is a significant minority cohort of Indo-Fijians, many of whom identify as Hindu or Muslim. In general terms, however, the South Pacific remains devoutly Christian, with high rates of weekly church attendance and Sabbath observance.[3]

The role of churches in civil society in these countries should not be underestimated. Historically, many social services in these countries, like health and education, have been provided through the churches. This legacy dates back to the earliest colonial times and supports humanitarian engagement through churches. For example:

> Working with the churches in PNG is highly relevant for the PNG context. With strong legitimacy among the population, which is more than 95% Christian, churches can contribute to

2. Robbins, "*Pacific Islands Religious Communities*," 587–96.
3. Laking, *State Performance in the Pacific*, 16.

public policy in PNG, enhance government transparency and accountability, support social justice and peace building and develop social capital. In addition, the churches in PNG play a crucial role in service delivery—some 50% of health services and 40% of the schools in PNG are run by the churches. In the context of PNG, where the government is relatively fragile with very little capacity, the role of the churches is especially important.[4]

In Vanuatu, past governments have been criticized for completely abandoning their social responsibility to the churches. Professor Matthew Clarke notes that "there was an almost entire dereliction of duty by the dual-ruling French and English colonial powers within Vanuatu with direct involvement in the provision of health and education services not occurring until the mid-1960s."[5] In more recent times, there has also been a move to hand back schools for the churches to administer in both Vanuatu and the Solomon Islands.

It is significant, too, that church infrastructure is dotted throughout very remote island archipelagos and, in the case of PNG, across mountainous, heavily forested and isolated areas. The fact there are an estimated eight-hundred language groups in PNG is one indication of the isolating terrain.[6] It is a tribute to the intrepid efforts of early missionaries that the presence of the church has stretched far and wide and brought social services to many communities.[7] It is not surprising that the center of village life in the South Pacific is the church and that the church has retained a respected voice.

Localization in Humanitarian Work

The church has been involved in humanitarian efforts for two millennia. The New Testament records several instances of the earliest followers of Jesus organizing in a systematic way to achieve humanitarian purposes, both locally and internationally.[8] Almost all churches now have a social service or welfare arm, and these include many church-based organizations operating in the international space. In addition, several of the world's largest

---

4. Dart and Hall, *Church Partnership Program, PNG*, v.
5. Clarke, "Christianity and the Shaping of Vanuatu," 8.
6. Mitchell and Grills, *Humanitarian Collaboration in the Pacific*, 88.
7. Clarke, *Mission and Development*, 1–14.
8. Acts 6:1–4; 2 Cor 8; Acts 11:27–29

humanitarian organizations and networks have a distinctly Christian origin, for example, World Vision, the ACT Alliance, and the Red Cross.

Larger scale humanitarian intervention efforts now occur in a highly organized fashion. These involve complex questions of logistics, the prepositioning of supplies, coordination of multiple agencies, and liaison with government. Work is also required to analyze areas of greatest risk, to map local resources, and to identify potential evacuation centers. In recent decades, there has also been a better understanding that humanitarian engagement occurs in a cycle.

The United Nations General Assembly designated the 1990s as the International Decade for Natural Disaster Reduction. This recognized that a great deal can be done to mitigate the impact of naturally occurring disasters by risk identification, careful planning, and preparation. This is commonly referred to as DRR, or Disaster Risk Reduction. One aspect of DRR is to train up local community members and agencies in their role as first responders.

After this stage, coordinated interventions by government and/or international NGOs may be required to address issues such as the restoration of critical infrastructure, sanitation, and housing. A final phase is longer-term post-disaster recovery, which recognizes that it can often take years for a community to recover fully, economically and socially, and to deal with the legacy of trauma.

The church has a particular role to play in the first and last phases outlined. As a permanent community presence with established infrastructure, the church is well placed to prepare communities for anticipated disasters. There is also a strong community expectation that churches will provide immediate help in times of disaster. Again, as a permanent community presence, the churches have a distinctive role to play in focusing efforts on longer-term recovery and support.

An important emphasis since 2016 has been a renewed emphasis on *localization* in humanitarian response. A binding global commitment to greater localization was made at the World Humanitarian Summit in 2016.[9] The term "localization" recognizes that communities should have greater agency over decisions that affect them in humanitarian activity. This approach aims to achieve greater respect and dignity for communities while building up domestic and local capacities. This is in contrast to previous approaches, which were criticized as giving too much priority to international donor-driven agendas.

---

9. ICVA, *Localisation in Humanitarian Practice*, 1–7.

The localization emphasis has been widely applauded. It resonates with the valuable role that churches can play in preparing their communities for disasters. These roles include: acting as first responders; drawing on their local knowledge, especially of vulnerable persons and cohorts; and deploying local infrastructure—for example, church halls—which may be prepared as evacuation centers. The churches are also able to provide trusted leadership in rebuilding communities and in assisting with longer-term recovery and trauma.

Natural Disasters and Climate Change in the South Pacific

The Institute for Environment and Human Security of the United Nations University has prepared a country-by-country analysis based on annual data to determine those nations at greatest risk from natural disasters, including earthquakes, volcanic eruptions, floods, droughts, storms, and rising sea levels.[10] Countries in the South Pacific have the dubious distinction of having the highest risk. The analysis undertaken considered the likelihood of natural disasters occurring and the vulnerability of country populations given their overall susceptibilities, coping capacity, and ability to adapt. The results of this research were published in the World Risk Index report for 2018. The table below is reproduced from that report, and it lists the top ten countries (out of 172) in terms of their risk rating.[11]

Table 1. Countries with the highest risk from natural disasters worldwide as at 2018		
Country	Risk (%)	Ranking (out of 172 countries)
Vanuatu	50.28	1
Tonga	29.42	2
Philippines	25.14	3
Solomon Islands	23.29	4
Guyana	23.23	5

10. Heintze et al., *WorldRiskReport 2018*, 35–43.
11. Heintze et al., *WorldRiskReport 2018*, 48–51.

Table 1. Countries with the highest risk from natural disasters worldwide as at 2018		
Papua New Guinea (PNG)	20.88	6
Guatemala	20.60	7
Brunei Darussalam	18.82	8
Bangladesh	17.38	9
Fiji	16.58	10

The result of this analysis showed that the Oceania region has the highest global risk, a wretched combination of likelihood and vulnerability. Specifically, the countries of Vanuatu, Solomon Islands, PNG, and Fiji ranked first, fourth, sixth, and tenth respectively in the world. These are the four countries that are the subject of the theological research discussed later in this essay.

Feeding into that risk assessment is the impact of global warming, in particular the increasing frequency, intensity, and spatial range of climate-related disasters. The Fifth Intergovernmental Panel on Climate Change established clear links between rising sea temperatures and extreme weather events. This is not only manifest in cyclonic activity, but also in periods of prolonged drought.[12] Other consequences include tidal surges and rising sea levels and an existential concern for those communities situated in coastal areas or on low-lying coral atolls. These impacts have been identified as a major pastoral concern by church leaders across the Pacific.

Within the Anglican Communion, the impact of climate change has been a central focus of annual discussions between Primates in the Pacific region and a touchstone for advocacy efforts by the global Anglican Alliance.

Church Agencies Network—Disaster Operations

Australian churches have responded in a very constructive way to the challenge of recurring natural disasters in the Pacific. Apart from their own denominational efforts to influence public awareness about climate change, a programmatic consortium has been established between eight different church-related aid and development agencies. This consortium is called the Church Agencies Network Disaster Operations (CAN DO). At its heart,

---

12. Seneviratne et al., "Changes in Climate Extremes," 167–80.

CAN DO recognizes the dominant role of the churches within South Pacific society, the importance of DRR and localization in humanitarian practice, and the extreme risk to neighboring countries from natural disasters, including those influenced by climate change.

The eight Australian agencies involved in CAN DO are: Act for Peace (National Council of Churches), Adventist Development and Relief Agency, Anglican Board of Mission, Anglican Overseas Aid, Australian Lutheran World Service, Transform Aid (Baptist), Caritas (Roman Catholic, lead agency), and UnitingWorld (Uniting Church). The modus operandi of CAN DO is to work through the local church partners of each agency in the Pacific, and through national ecumenical councils.

CAN DO is a participant in a broader Australian government program, called Disaster Ready, which runs for an initial term of five years. As the name suggests, it has a strong emphasis on helping communities build up their skills in disaster preparation and response. CAN DO works primarily through churches, recognizing their central role in Pacific community life.

The intention is to achieve a broad coverage of Christian churches in the South Pacific through the various denominations involved. Key messages will reach into most areas and will be disseminated in a coordinated way through multiple denominations. This is important because messages will be reinforced not only among coreligionists but within the community more broadly where other denominations are represented.

Establishing CAN DO has been a major initiative in practical ecumenism both in Australia and among church partners in neighboring countries. A topic beyond the scope of this essay, but worthy of further and separate reflection, is how a practical unity can be achieved between churches by coming together to focus on a relevant area of social concern. The key to CAN DO seems to be its commitment to orthopraxy in the broader sense.[13] It is noted that CAN DO was commended as a significant and welcome demonstration of ecumenical collaboration at the seventeenth Annual General Synod of the Anglican Church of Australia in 2017. Other churches have recognized its significance in similar ways.

Research Purpose

The work plan for CAN DO involves working closely with church partners in the Pacific with the intention of training up church leaders and their communities in principles of disaster risk reduction. Working with

---

13. Mitchell and Grills, *Humanitarian Collaboration in the Pacific*, 92.

churches means engaging with a worldview informed by the teachings of Scripture and Christian theology, but which can also be heavily indebted to local customs and beliefs. It was recognized as part of the program design that it was important to understand the views of local churches and their communities about the natural disasters that affect them in a deeper and more comprehensive way.

A baseline qualitative survey was commissioned to gain a clearer picture about existing community beliefs concerning disasters. The work was carried out by local teams representing different CAN DO agencies in each country. These teams worked together with a doctoral candidate from Deakin University, Alice Banfield, who was engaged by UnitingWorld to lead this work on behalf of the consortium. The Australian Department of Foreign Affairs and Trade, who help fund CAN DO through its Australian Humanitarian Partnership scheme, saw the value in progressing this aspect of the program design.

The baseline survey is a first step towards developing a more comprehensive theology of Disaster Risk Management, a tool conceived to help Pacific churches in their management of natural disasters. This additional work will require the expertise of indigenous Pacific theologians adept in developing and tailoring culturally appropriate educational resources. The baseline survey is a prior step that "stems from the assumption that, in the Pacific context, Christian beliefs often strongly underpin people's responses to natural disasters and engagement in environmental stewardship, climate justice and disaster preparedness and that these beliefs can either hinder or motivate action."[14] The survey tested this critical assumption and mapped existing beliefs, highlighting potential barriers to program participation.

Methodology

The research undertaken was qualitative rather than quantitative and relied mainly on the administration of a survey across sites in PNG, Solomon Islands, Vanuatu, and Fiji. The bulk of the respondents in each case were church members from a spread of denominations.

The survey was administered by trained enumerators. Respecting the geographic context, "the research drew loosely on *Talanoa* research principles, an indigenous Pacific methodology which is collaborative and non-linear."[15] This meant that surveys were almost always administered face-to-face, often in group settings. The data gathering was usually discursive,

---

14. Banfield, *Baseline Study, PNG,* 4.
15. Banfield, *Baseline Study, PNG,* 8. All reports adopted a similar methodology.

going back and forth between different issues, and where necessary, surveys were translated into the local language. Most of the survey sites were in rural or regional settings, reflecting the dispersed nature of the general populations. A smaller number of more centralized workshops and interviews were held, especially with church leaders and humanitarian stakeholders.

Women were underrepresented in the community surveys, but much more significantly in the workshops held with church leaders. This reflects the dominance of men in senior roles in the Pacific churches.

The table below represents an overall summary of the survey data sources.

Table 2. Summary of data sources for baseline survey					
Country	Community surveys	Church leader workshop participants or interviews	Stakeholder workshop participants	Other	Total inputs
PNG	132	6	10		148
Fiji	37	10	46	1*	94
Vanuatu	201	7	8		216
Solomon Islands	190	11	10		211
Totals	560	34	74	1	669

*Interview with National Disaster Management Office

In summary, the research undertaken was comprehensive, strongly community-based, and sensitively administered.

Findings

This section reflects on some of the principle findings of the research. It does not attempt to discuss all relevant areas. Specifically, this essay does not cover community attitudes to inclusion, stewardship of creation, or traditional customs and beliefs. These areas were also considered by the research. The quotes selected from each baseline study are used with the permission of the author.

1. Disasters Are Seen as God's Retribution

A prominent finding of the research, across all the research sites, is that natural disasters are understood by communities as God's punishment or retribution for human sinfulness. Specifically, the research found that communities believe that moral failings, disobeying or neglecting God, or a lack of repentance can arouse the wrath of God and cause a disaster to be sent. While disasters are primarily about punishment, they are also understood as a vehicle to call the community back to greater faithfulness. The following quotes are a typical selection:

- "Disaster struck the community because of the disobedience of community members."—*Northern community, Vanuatu*
- "We believe that disaster can only happen if people over-enjoy the blessings of God and forget about the One that provides those blessings."—*Shefa community, Vanuatu*
- "Our own disobedience makes it happen. Don't blame others."—*Church leader, United Church, Solomon Islands*
- "Disaster is going to happen if we don't repent."—*Church members, Bougainville community, PNG*
- "People sin, disaster will happen. Disaster doesn't just happen for no reason. It is God who controls it and makes disaster strike."—*Church members, Highlands area, PNG*

Interestingly, in some locations there is a converse belief in protective piety. These communities see the avoidance of natural disaster as a reflection on their own righteousness compared with the assumed sinfulness of their disaster-struck neighbors.

- "People who were not affected by disaster are believed to be faithfully serving God. For those who were affected, it's a punishment from God."—*Community members, CMF, Fiji*

The belief in divine punishment as the cause of natural disasters may also be heavily influenced by more traditional community beliefs.

- "Looking at traditional beliefs, when people worshipped spirits, if they didn't do something they were supposed to do, then their god would be cross. Sometimes I think they have changed their god and they call him Jesus or Jehovah or whatever. But the way that they interact with that God is still the same. 'We haven't kept the gods happy, therefore we need to come back and pay our penance.'—*FBO representative, Solomon Islands*

Within many communities, disasters were traditionally ascribed to local gods or spirits. This causation had now been projected onto the Christian conception of God.

- "Disasters happen because spirits are not happy—that's the common traditional belief. When we translate that to Christianity, many people are saying God is not happy. So this traditional idea has in a way been translated to Christianity."—*Church leader, United Church, PNG*
- "My people [traditionally] believe disaster is made by a sorcerer, witchcraft, someone who makes spells. But since Christianity has come in, now people began to change their ways of thinking. Now people believe it was planned by God, created by God, and according to his purpose."—*Church leader, Salvation Army, PNG*

This series of beliefs poses significant challenges in designing a Disaster Risk Reduction program for a South Pacific community. Any program of this nature will depend for its success on strong community engagement. That engagement will be directly affected by these local theological convictions.

In short, communities may be reluctant to interfere with, or take steps to reduce, the impact of natural disasters because those disasters are seen as part of the inscrutable process of God's judgment. Communities may also see DRR activities as senseless because God's judgments cannot be frustrated or thwarted.

One way to overcome this problem is to reexamine theological beliefs. The CAN DO consortium is seeking to do this by working with indigenous theologians and church leaders. There does seem to be plenty of scope to reform these understandings.

Western theological reflection about natural disasters, and the problem of theodicy, has undergone significant revision over the last two centuries.[16] There is a greater tendency to accept that disasters are part of the natural order of things rather than punitive events. For example, it is understood that bushfires are necessary to germinate seeds and renew forests. Earthquakes and tsunamis may happen because of subterranean pressures or the movement of tectonic plates. These pressures must be periodically released to avoid even greater impacts and to regulate the earth's internal temperature. Cyclones occur due to a confluence of well-known atmospheric conditions including rising sea surface temperatures.

---

16. The 1755 Earthquake of Lisbon, which killed over 50,000 people, prompted a searing critique of Leibniz's *Theodicy* and sparked off this debate.

As one PNG church leader said: "Everything is not God. Sometimes it can be natural."[17] When disasters are understood as natural events, this is more conducive to communities taking steps to mitigate their impacts. This is because those communities are no longer positioning themselves against God's judgment but are taking rational human precautions.

It should be stated that belief in natural disasters as divine retribution is not confined to the South Pacific. Commentators and church leaders in the West have also occasionally attributed natural disasters to divine agendas. For example, American Evangelical leader Pat Robertson infamously attributed the 2010 Haiti earthquake to a pact made by former slave leaders with the devil; several commentators have attributed the 2011 Japanese tsunami to anti-Christian attitudes; and Pastor Danny Nalliah attributed the 2009 bushfires in Victoria to the liberalization of that state's abortion laws.

There is strong scriptural evidence that God does not seek to engage in any form of collective punishment, harming entire communities in order to judge a few. In Genesis 18, God makes it clear that he would not destroy Sodom and Gomorrah if any righteous people could be found there. In Matthew 5:45, Jesus explains that God causes his sun to rise on the evil and the good and sends rain on the righteous and the unrighteous alike. And in Luke 13, Jesus states that local incidents involving the slaughter of Galileans, and the collapse of the Tower of Siloam, did not impute greater sinfulness on the victims than other people. Jesus warns against *ex post facto* attributions of judgment, and instead counsels the living to attend carefully to their own relationship with God.

Despite this, there are statements in the Old Testament about God intending to inflict calamity by one means or another as part of the moral formation of his people or other nations. For example, the prophet Jeremiah relays God's message: "It may be that they will listen, all of them, and will turn from their evil way, that I may change my mind about the disaster that I intend to bring on them because of their evil doings" (Jer 26:3). Similarly, when Nineveh repents, the Book of Jonah records that "God changed his mind about the calamity that he had said he would bring upon them."[18] There are quite specific hermeneutical considerations applying to passages such as these. As a general comment, however, it would be a reductionist fallacy to regard every disaster—especially those occurring within a cycle or rhythm in the natural world—as the execution of God's judgment.

In more recent times, a very welcome theological development is the understanding that God suffers with his people in times of disaster.

---

17. Banfield, *Baseline Study, PNG*, 20.
18. Jonah 3:10.

Theologians like Jürgen Moltmann have stressed that all suffering and death are taken up by Jesus on the cross and are redeemed with him in his resurrection life.[19] The loving presence of God in disasters is made explicit through the actions of his people in living out real compassion and solidarity through times of crisis.

It is clear that a longer-term process of theological engagement is required to shift attitudes about natural disasters in the Pacific. Among better-educated church leaders, it is more common to hear that disasters are not God's judgment. This is encouraging and may also help shift the narrative over time. It is vitally important that this theological re-assessment is undertaken because ultimately it will save lives and will stop the insult being added to injury when the righteousness of communities is maligned in their most vulnerable hour.

2. Preparation for Disasters Occurs in Mainly Spiritual Ways

Currently, church-led preparation for impending disasters in South Pacific communities mainly takes the form of an interior, spiritual exercise. This is especially reflected in church preaching. There tends to be a strong emphasis on devotional piety with minimal accompanying practical steps or actions. This approach has a distinctly gnostic leaning, as communities are at times led by church leaders to preference spirit over matter.

The spiritualization of disasters can also be related to the idea discussed above that the catastrophes are God's punishment. For so long as the basic problem is diagnosed as sinfulness within a community, it is not surprising that the perceived antidote is a renewed commitment to piety. The data suggest that there is a kind of Platonic or dualistic thinking at play. While it is well-intentioned, this can be damaging to community welfare because it does not lead to practical action. The following quotes indicate the type of preparation involved:

- "Those who are mindful that cyclone season is near do prepare. The prayer warriors around here start to play their role in order to attack the changes about to hit."—*Community members, Fiji*
- "Prayer played a very important role. They prayed for God's protection on their family, so much so that they didn't put up shutters or take measures to protect themselves physically. They relied wholly on God for protection."—*Enumerator, Fiji*

---

19. Moltmann, *The Crucified God*, 276–78.

- "We don't prepare before or during times of disaster. We accept it as it comes. Before we know or get a warning from the disaster office in town, we just pray and hope for the best." —*Church members, Bougainville, PNG*

Faith should be accompanied by action. We live in a material world and must demonstrate our faith in practical ways. New Testament theologian Tom Wright reminds us that the canonical Gospels are about a very concrete existence of living for the kingdom of God on earth.[20] A robust Christianity will avoid the gnostic tendency to separate spirit from matter. We pray not to be removed from God's earth, even in times of great trial, but for God's kingdom to come within it. This means that we live lives of practical action, demonstrating the immanent reality of God's kingdom. For Wright, the corporeal resurrection of Jesus is supremely emblematic of the work that Christians have to do as they seek to live for God's kingdom in the present.[21] Some survey participants agreed with this position, complaining:

- "They spiritualise everything, referring to when the Bible says 'be ready.' But they don't translate those teachings to the practical. So, it becomes more like a theory . . . They need to translate the spiritual into the practical because we live in the world. We aren't in heaven yet." —*National church leader, inter-denominational, Vanuatu*

- "Some people don't understand that faith and works go hand in hand." —*Comment of enumerator reflecting discussion with church members, Fiji*

- "God is not a magic god. He looks after us through the actions we make." —*National church leader, inter-denominational, Vanuatu*

Christians are an active people who live both for God and for the world. Karl Barth puts it this way: "First and supremely it is God who exists for the world. And since the community of Jesus Christ exists first and supremely for God, it has no option but in its own manner and place to exist for the world. How else could it exist for God?"[22] Faith without works is dead; indeed, it is worse than dead, because it becomes a parody of what it truly means to have hope in Jesus Christ.

What practical action looks like will vary from context to context. It might mean rehearsing evacuation plans, ensuring that there are adequate

---

20. Wright, *Surprised by Hope*, 101–2.
21. Wright, *Surprised by Hope*, 160; chapter 13.
22. Barth, *Community for the World*, 499.

supplies of food and water, removing loose objects, securing windows and doors, and including vulnerable cohorts of people in disaster plans.

In terms of written resources offered to communities, it seems there is little on offer: "They only give the Bible. Everything we need is in the Bible. The church doesn't give out any other books."[23] Unfortunately, however, while there are relevant passages of Scripture that could be used to help communities to focus on practical action, they receive little attention:

- "The church leader admitted they don't preach directly about preparedness, though there is the same general preaching, like about the Second Coming."—*Enumerator feedback session, Apostolic Church, Vanuatu*

- "Maybe we need that talk to come out more in the pulpit. There are relevant passages we can use . . . But on the topic of preparedness for cyclones and things, there's not a lot at the moment."—*National church leader, Presbyterian, Vanuatu*

Some possible Old Testament stories that may resonate with South Pacific communities include the story of Noah and his family preparing for the anticipated flood (Genesis 6–8) and the story of Joseph (Genesis 41), who interpreted Pharaoh's dream and advised him to prepare for the years of famine that lay ahead. Proverbs also offers guidance about acting prudently to mitigate future risk.

In the New Testament, John reminds his readers to "love, not in words or speech, but in truth and action" (1 John 3:18) and the book of James urges followers of Christ to authenticate their discipleship in practical ways. The Parable of the Ten Virgins (Matt 25:1–13) and Luke 12:35–38 speak to the theme of readiness more generally. Helping communities to prepare for disasters in tangible ways is not merely an option for the church but, given its dominant voice, a moral obligation.

3. *The End Is Nigh*

Another theme to emerge from the data, and across all sites to a large degree, is the belief that their communities are living through the Last Days. By this, communities understand that they are in the midst of a pre-apocalyptic phase of existence that heralds the imminent return of Jesus Christ. While this theme tended to be associated more with Pentecostal and Evangelical churches, this was not exclusively so.

---

23. Banfield, *Baseline Study, Fiji*, 35.

The regular occurrence of natural disasters was seen as consistent with biblical Scriptures such as Matthew 24:7–8. These verses reference earthquakes and famines as signs that herald the consummation of the age. There is a strong possibility that the increase in climate-related disasters throughout the region is creating a self-reinforcing feedback loop. The increased number and intensity of these events may be strengthening existing perceptions about the Last Days.

The following quotes are an indicative selection:

- "Those things will happen in the Last Days. We are in the Last Days already. People need to prepare their lives."—*Church leader, Church of Christ, Vanuatu*

- "We are in the Last Days, and preparedness that is preached is more in relation to spiritual aspects."—*Community members, Seventh Day Adventist Church, Solomon Islands*

- "The Almighty's return is near. We preach in church that people must pray at all times."—*Church members, Highlands, PNG*

- "We believe [more] disaster is likely in future because the Bible tells us that a time comes when there will be turbulence, signs and wonders, and nation will rise against nation."—*Church members, Guadalcanal Province, Solomon Islands*

Strictly speaking, Christians having been living in the Last Days since the ascension of Jesus. Scripture indicates that no-one knows the exact time of Christ's second coming and warns against attempts to make predictions. In terms of DRR programs in the Pacific, the prevalence of a belief in the Last Days can operate either negatively or positively, depending on its broader theological framing.

On the negative side, there can be a sense of fatalism or resignation that militates against taking practical action on DRR. Why bother preparing for disasters if the world is about to end? For example:

- "A lot of people think Jesus' return is near. So, they don't prepare. It goes back to their pastor. People are looking forward to the second coming of the Lord. So, they are reluctant to evacuate."—*Humanitarian stakeholder, civil society, Vanuatu*

A related problem is to give priority to spiritual forms of preparation for the Last Days rather than taking practical actions, which may seem to be of lesser eternal significance. Thus, there is a very direct relationship between perceptions about the Last Days and the highly spiritualized nature of disaster preparation discussed in the last section.

A more helpful theological lens through which to approach this topic is a reminder that at no time is Christian responsibility to one another suspended. On the contrary, a genuine belief in the escalation of disasters should be met with a corresponding escalation in social care and responsibility. Followers of Jesus are to continue to care for one another right throughout the Last Days because this is a way to confidently and publicly demonstrate the hope they have in the resurrected Lord. It is for this reason that disciples are counseled to refrain from idle speculation about the return date of Jesus; Christians should vigilantly demonstrate their faithful discipleship at all times.

4. Community Resilience Through Faith

A very positive theme to emerge from the data was the role of Christian faith in rebuilding and strengthening communities after a natural disaster. This seems to be a unique role for the church in the South Pacific. There is no other type of organization that can so effectively focus goodwill and compassion and rebuild social capital following a natural disaster. Nor is there any other type of organization that can deploy volunteers in a localized and highly targeted way, especially in remote locations.

The qualitative evidence indicated a number of distinct contributions that fed into the theme of community resilience. Some of the main motifs were thankfulness for survival through adversity; a heightened empathy and encouragement for others; a renewed sense of community spirit; and finding personal meaning by looking for the good that can come from a bad situation. Each of these elements was framed in terms of the participant's understanding of Christian faith.

THANKFULNESS

Living through a disaster, even when it is understood through the lens of divine punishment or retribution, can imbue a sense of relief, thankfulness, and personal blessing. These types of sentiments spur people on to make a positive contribution to serve others. This is not survivor guilt but a much more purposeful sense of gratitude:

- "The first thing that happens is we realize we need to give praise and thanks back to God for his protection . . ."—*Church leader, Vanuatu*

- "When a disaster or bad time happens, it doesn't get us down. We are full of peace . . . [There might be a] shortage of food and water, but God's blessing remains, and we are inside his gates."—*Church members, Highlands, PNG*

Empathy/Encouragement

Another post-disaster motif is the role of church members in providing encouragement and empathy for others. This involves pastoral care, listening, and being present for others:

- "[After a disaster], continuous encouragement is given to people about how to each have confidence in their lives in the love of God, who is the foundation of their life."—*Church leader, Catholic, Vanuatu*
- "The first thing the church must do is to comfort those affected [to remind them that] even though hard times are upon them, God is still with them. As a church leader, I must feel the same pain that that person is in."—*Church leader, Presbyterian, Vanuatu*
- "After a disaster, much emphasis is placed upon our resilience as Christians and teachings are based in accordance with that, but at the same time allowing people to understand that God is very present during those times."—*Church leader, Salvation Army, Fiji*

Communitarian Spirit

A natural disaster can bring out the best in people as they seek to pull together to help one another out. For people living in Pacific communities, this is often framed as an outworking of their Christian faith. It is also a traditional community attitude. This motif was strongly reflected in the data:

- "We believe that we are here to help our people and our neighbor, carrying one another's burdens."—*Northern community, Vanuatu*
- "Historically, that's how we lived in Vanuatu. Melanesian societies have been called collective societies. Before anything else came, we helped one another. When the Bible came, it dovetailed with what we already had in the fabric of our society. So, there aren't too many problems in this area."—*Church leader, Anglican, Vanuatu*
- "Sometimes when disasters happen, it affects Anglicans, Catholics, SSEC, etc. We are talking about human persons that are affected.

Problems will unite people together, regardless of whether you are Catholic or Anglican. Inclusiveness is based on the fact that 'we are all people who suffer.'"—*Church leader, Anglican Church of Melanesia, Solomon Islands*

- "In the eyes of the Lord, we are all one. During disaster, we should help each other out."—*Church members, Methodist, Fiji*
- "It is our Christian duty to help our neighbors."—*Church members, Bougainville, PNG*

Refracting Good from Bad

Unsurprisingly, the experience of a natural disaster is often a time for personal reflection. In making sense of a bad situation, people may seek more positive meanings from their experience. A common occurrence reported throughout the data is people re-embracing their faith and the church, although sometimes that enthusiasm was short-lived. In other cases, however, the experience of disaster was a lasting turning point and became an opportunity for personal growth:

- "[The spiritual outcomes from disaster] depend on the level of the community. For a community which is Christian, where they have teaching which builds them up, the result is growth from that situation."—*National church leader, Vanuatu*

For others, the good to be found came from stronger relationships or more utilitarian considerations:

- "We faced disaster in order to help bring families together."—*Community members, Shefa province, Vanuatu*
- "Sometimes disaster becomes a blessing. For example, now they have much better buildings from aid after Cyclone Pam."—*Enumerator, Vanuatu*

Overview

It is acknowledged that the data for the baseline survey was drawn predominantly from Christian sources and may reflect the biases of Christian enthusiasts. That said, the qualitative evidence indicated that Christian faith was seen as a powerful coping mechanism in times of trial and beyond. This finding is consistent with other research, including my own.[24]

More than this, however, is the power of the Christian gospel itself. It provides an existential meaning and purpose that is highly relevant in times of stress and disaster. At bottom, the gospel is the story of God's limitless love demonstrated in the triumph of life over death. This provides a firm and hopeful foundation reflected powerfully in the image of the resurrected Christ. The gospel narrative, which speaks of new life rising from seeming impossibility, is a wonderful analogue for post-disaster recovery work:

- "We talk about the power of the resurrection. It is power which gives hope to everyone, victory over death, victory over the evil in this world. Despite everything, God is love. He is alive with us. He is always with us. He will be with us forever. That should give hope to us Christian people."—*Church leader, Catholic, Vanuatu*

Conclusion

The Australian Government is to be commended for funding this important baseline study. It is absolutely clear that humanitarian programs in the Pacific must take into account existing theological convictions if their effectiveness is to be assured. Put the other way, without engaging these beliefs, DRR work is likely to be seriously compromised, and a great deal of money could be wasted. Churches have a unique role and responsibility and are very well placed to encourage understandings that will lead to the better protection of communities in the most disaster-prone countries on earth.

To undertake such a role with integrity, Pacific churches must wrestle with difficult questions of theodicy. This will inevitably involve a reconsideration of the character of God in relation to natural disasters. There are helpful approaches that could be further developed within local contexts, and these may move the church away from the harsh implausibility of collective punishment or self-congratulatory notions of preventative piety.

It is equally important to embrace a biblical holism that firmly locates this world as the locus of God's saving action and renewal. Faith and works, prayer and action, preaching and preparation must be conjoined. Only then will an adequate account be given of the biblical witness.

There is ample evidence of many churches meeting the finest ideals of humanitarianism in their response to disasters. This contribution is applauded, especially the frequent role of churches as first responders and its

24. Mitchell, *Faith-Based Development*.

ongoing challenge in dealing with longer term recovery and trauma. There are no organizations better placed to rebuild and refocus community life. On the preparation front, however, enthusiasm for the Last Days may have in some cases imbued a kind of fatalism that is corrosive of true Christian social responsibility.

The key to progressing many of these issues is longer-term indigenous theological engagement and careful attention to ministerial formation and in-service training. The production of carefully considered, theologically informed, and contextually appropriate DRR resources remains a high priority.

Bibliography

Banfield, Alice. *Theology of Disaster Risk Management: Baseline Study, Fiji.* Sydney: CAN DO Consortium, 2018.

———. *Theology of Disaster Risk Management: Baseline Study, Papua New Guinea.* Sydney: CAN DO Consortium, 2019.

———. *Theology of Disaster Risk Management: Baseline Study, Solomon Islands.* Sydney: CAN DO Consortium, 2018.

———. *Theology of Disaster Risk Management: Baseline Study, Vanuatu.* Sydney: CAN DO Consortium, 2018.

Barth, Karl. "The Community for the World." In *Theological Foundations for Ministry*, edited by R. S. Anderson, 499–533. Edinburgh: T. & T. Clark, 1979.

Clarke, Matthew. "Christianity and the Shaping of Vanuatu's Social and Political Developments." *Journal for the Academic Study of Religion* 28 (2015) 24–41.

———. *Mission and Development: God's Work or Good Works?* New York: Continuum International, 2012.

Dart, Jess, and James Hall. *Church Partnership Program, Papua New Guinea: Case Study Report.* Canberra: AusAID, 2011.

Heintze, Hans-Joachim, et al. *WorldRiskReport 2018.* Aachen, Germany: Bündnis Entwicklung Hilft, 2018. https://reliefweb.int/sites/reliefweb.int/files/resources/WorldRiskReport-2018.pdf.

International Council of Voluntary Agencies (ICVA). "Localisation in Humanitarian Practice." Accessed March 19, 2019. https://www.icvanetwork.org/resources/localisation-humanitarian-practice.

Laking, Rob. *State Performance and Capacity in the Pacific.* Manila: Asian Development Bank, 2010.

Mitchell, Robert, and Nathan Grills, "A Historic Humanitarian Collaboration in the Pacific." *Christian Journal for Global Health* 4 no. 2 (2017) 87–94.

Mitchell, Robert, *Faith-Based Development: How Christian Organizations Can Make a Difference.* Maryknoll, NY: Orbis, 2017.

Moltmann, Jürgen. *The Crucified God: The Cross of Christ as the Foundation and Criticism of Christian Theology.* London: SCM Press, 1974.

Robbins, Joel. "Pacific Islands Religious Communities." In *The Oxford Handbook of Global Religions*, edited by Mark Juergensmeyer, 587–98. Oxford: Oxford University Press, 2006.

Seveviratne, Sonia, et al. "Changes in Climate Extremes and their Impacts on the Natural Physical Environment." In *A Special Report of Working Groups I and II of the Intergovernmental Panel on Climate Change*, edited by Christopher B. Field et al., 109–230. New York: Cambridge University Press, 2015.

Wright, Tom. *Surprised by Hope.* London: SPCK, 2007.

15

Te Rongopai, Te Tiriti, Te Pouhere; Gospel, Treaty, Constitution

Church, Culture, and Justice in Aotearoa New Zealand

Philip Richardson

PHILIP FREIER AND I were ordained as bishops as one millennium gave way to the next. Ordained on opposite sides of the Tasman Sea within a few months of each other, we first met when Bishop Philip attended a meeting of the New Zealand House of Bishops as the Australian guest. As brand-new bishops, we struck up a friendship, and two years later I spent time with Philip and Joy in the Northern Territory before he and I traveled to Perth for a meeting of the Australian House of Bishops, at which I was the New Zealand guest.

I regard this friendship as one of the most providential of my ministry. We are Primates of our respective provinces at a time when communication, understanding, and mutual support between Aotearoa, New Zealand, and Polynesia and the Anglican Church of Australia is important for the proclamation of the gospel in Oceania. Our friendship has assisted that relationship.

My visit to the Northern Territory introduced me to Philip's deep commitment to building his personal understanding of Aboriginal cosmology, culture, language, and art. I have come to realize how much this has contributed to his instinctive empathy for the way the Anglican Church in Aotearoa New Zealand has developed. Philip "gets us" in a way that many parts of the Anglican world do not.

One simple example was an occasion when there had been a series of significant interventions in the polity of the Church of Australia by a New Zealand Anglican leader, and this had created tension. By then Archbishop and Primate, Philip knew that letter writing or appeals to the Archbishop of Canterbury were not the preferable way of engaging with us in all our cultural diversity. It needed to be *kanohi ki te kanohi* (face to face). He came, we talked, we acted.

This commitment to listen and engage across cultural difference with respect and with an open heart and mind is welcomed and respected by the Church in Aotearoa New Zealand and Polynesia, and we regard Archbishop Philip as a very good friend and colleague.

I count it a personal honor to contribute to this collection of essays recognizing, on the occasion of his sixty-fifth birthday, his significant contribution to the Anglican Church in Australia and beyond.

The Gospel in Aotearoa New Zealand

Indeed, friendship was a hallmark of the story of the establishment of the first Christian mission in these islands, and therefore of the Anglican Church in Aotearoa New Zealand. Australia played a significant part in that friendship.

On Christmas Day in 1814, the Christian gospel was proclaimed for the first time on the soil of Aotearoa at the beautiful beach at Oihi in the Bay of Islands. It is important to remember that this historic moment was many years in the making and to acknowledge that its potential is still to be fully realized. It was only possible at all because of grace-filled hospitality.

It is true that the Ngā Puhi Chief, Ruatara, offered that hospitality. It was Ruatara who invited Marsden to bring a small party of missionaries to settle in that quiet bay just below the protection of his fortified village, Rangihoua.

It is also true that the friendship forged between Ruatara and Marsden began with Marsden's kindness to Ruatara, whom he had met in a sad state of health. Ruatara, during a period as a sailor, had been maltreated on the long journey to England from Australia. Upon reaching London, sailors had simply transferred him onto a returning ship with little care for his physical state. It was on this ship that Marsden met Ruatara and helped him back to health. This friendship was strengthened when Marsden invited Ruatara to stay with him on his farm at Parramatta.

But it is also true that Ruatara's invitation to Marsden was in spite of actions that could have derailed the welcome completely. Te Pahi, Ruatara's uncle, who had formed a friendship with Marsden some years before, was accused of having been involved in the massacre of the crew and the sinking of the sailing ship *Boyd*. Te Pahi's home was attacked in retribution, and Te Pahi was mortally wounded. Marsden, after investigation, was convinced that his old friend was falsely accused.

In many cultures and societies, there would have simply been an escalation of mistrust and hostility. Instead, Ruatara extended to Marsden and his companions a grace of welcome and patronage, which secured the small mission settlement and inaugurated a vision of partnership that undergirds our potential as a nation to this day.

In essence, therefore, we are a church born out of a grace-filled act of sacrificial generosity. What Ruatara offered was more fundamental than the English word hospitality can possibly convey. Ruatara lived out the values of manaakitanga: costly, self-giving generosity, a deep respect for the other, putting the holistic wellbeing of the other first.

These are the values on which the hand of friendship was offered at Oihi. These are the values that undergirded the first real partnership between *tangata whenua*[1] and Christian settlers.

At the center of this first Christian service on the soil of Aotearoa, Samuel Marsden preached on the text from the Gospel of Luke: "Behold I bring you glad tidings of great joy"! These "glad tidings," this good news, is the same today as it was in 1814 and is just the same as it was 2000 years ago.

I want to explore three intertwined strands that bind the life and practice of the Anglican Church in Aotearoa, New Zealand, and Polynesia. They reflect the constant, daily challenge at the center of what it means to be Anglican in these islands. These three strands are *Te Rongopai*, *Te Tiriti*, and *Te Pouhere*; Gospel, Treaty, and the Constitution of our three tikanga[2] church.

It is these three things that bind us to each other.

- They bind us in a way that means we cannot let each other go.
- They bind us in a way that means that we must seek each other's good.

1. The "people of the land"; the first peoples to settle in Aotearoa.
2. Three "cultural streams."

- They bind us in a way that means that when one part of this body is suffering or unable to live out their potential then we are all weakened and diminished.
- We are bound in such a way that we recognize that all of the resources we have at our disposal come from God and are for the whole body in the service of the gospel.

Te Rongopai (Gospel)

Central to the gospel is the proclamation that God loves all that God has made and that God reaches out to each of us in Jesus Christ.

We are disciples of Christ because we know that we are beloved of God, that this love has been offered anew and made known in Jesus Christ, and that we find ourselves drawn to follow his way. At the heart of the gospel message is God's unceasing offer of relationship.

There are no bounds to the extent to which God will go to draw us back. This is Good News. Our identity, individually and collectively, rests first in this reality: we are each made in the image of God, and we are each redeemed by God in Christ. That compels me into a certain relationship with others and with this earth. I can do no other than to seek the best for my brothers and sisters and for this fragile and vulnerable earth.

We have a responsibility for one another and particularly for the most vulnerable members of our community, and we must work unceasingly for justice, for peace, and for righteousness. It begins with the simple things like treating each person we meet with the same value, with the same respect, with the same genuine interest, and living out the simple truth that every person we meet is beloved of God and must be treated as such.

The kind of community we are called by the gospel of Christ to work for is a community based on this mutual respect and interdependence. It is a vision of a community in which each person's worth is measured not by their economic value but by their intrinsic value as a human person made in the image of God.

This simple gospel message would have resonated in that quiet bay with a people who already understood very well the principles of *manaakitanga* and *whanaungatanga*[3] and the radical inclusion that these principles or values represent.

---

3. Relationship, kinship, sense of family; a relationship through shared experiences and working together, which provides people with a sense of belonging. It develops as a result of kinship rights and obligations, which also serve to strengthen each member of a kin group. Importantly, it extends to others with whom one develops close familial,

Of course, the tragedy—scandal, even—is that so many people do not experience lives of dignity, safety, or simple happiness and joy.

Aotearoa New Zealand is a nation with abundant natural beauty and resources. We are a people known for innovation, creativity, and a "can do" attitude. We are a small nation. We each feel as if we are a part of a diverse, dynamic, extended family. We have taken on the world in many fields and have excelled.

We value a society in which all can achieve and where all can reach their potential. But we have seen developments in our society where this is increasingly difficult:[4]

- From the mid-1980s to the mid-2000s, the gap between the rich and the poor has widened faster in New Zealand than in most other developed countries. This gap continues to widen.
- The average household in the top 10 percent of New Zealand has nine times the income of one in the bottom 10 percent.
- The top 1 percent of adults own 16 percent of the country's total wealth, while the *bottom half* put together have just over 5 percent.
- Housing is becoming increasingly inaccessible not only for the poorest but for middle New Zealand.
- Our church social services are reporting dramatic increases in homelessness and increased demands on food banks and other services. Notably, there are increases in the proportion of people on wages who are needing to access this support.
- Our incarceration rates and reoffending rates are unconscionably high.

Māori are disproportionately represented in all these figures.

We have also seen a growing cynicism in our public life and discourse. There has been a shift to engagement in some aspects of this public life where individuals are attacked and demeaned as a way of furthering ideological goals and ambitions. While the incomprehensible events at two mosques in Christchurch on March 15, 2019, were at one level unique, we do well to remember a history of atrocity perpetrated against Māori as land was alienated by force and by illegal confiscation. The Waitangi Tribunal settlement processes have, at very least, detailed this history in an incontrovertible way. Reconciling that history and our broken relationships remains the greatest challenge we face as a society and as a church.

---

friendship, or reciprocal relationship.

4. Much of the following information is derived from Rashbrooke, "Why Inequality Matters."

Social, economic, and political frameworks exist to serve the people and to provide the environment for human flourishing. The health of a community is measured by the experience of the most vulnerable, the most marginal. What we are seeing is that these things are creating a deep chasm in our society.

Christian mission is not a form of palliative care. We are called to radical intervention to build societies and communities for human flourishing, because this is God's intention for human beings. This is rooted in the simple gospel proclamation that all are loved of God, all have ultimate worth before God, and all are created to flourish.

Te Tiriti (Treaty)

The gospel as the first imperative of my identity quickly leads to a second: The Treaty of Waitangi.

I am located at a particular point in a history of relationships. I was born to Barbara and Bill. I am the grandson of Vera and Frank, Winnie and William, great grandson of . . . and so on. This is my whakapapa, which is much more than simply my lineage or descent. It defines me; it speaks of the diversity woven into me: North Country English, Irish, German, Jewish.

But I am also located in a particular land and nation with a very particular history. I was born in this place, in this land. But I have joined its history recently. My parents were migrant people. They sailed here and met on the long sea journey. They made their life here. I was given the gift of life here.

Part of my identity is that, as the child of immigrant parents, I have a place to stand in this land because of a covenant established with the first people of this land: *Te Tiriti o Waitangi* (The Treaty of Waitangi).

My identity, then, is also as a child and a beneficiary of te Tiriti. And I have to understand this covenant and my rights and obligations under it.

We know all too well the cost of the failure to do so. It is a cost borne disproportionately by Māori. I want to quote at length from Archbishop Brown Turei's[5] reflection on the occasion of the 175th anniversary of the signing of the Treaty in 2015:

> In 1940, during the 100th Anniversary of the signing of the Treaty, leaders and chiefs gathered once more at the sacred ground of Waitangi. Sir Apirana Ngata stood and said:

---

5. The Most Reverend Brown Turei served as a priest for over sixty-five years, a bishop for twenty-five years and Archbishop for eleven years. He died, still in office, at the age of ninety-two in 2017.

"I do not know of any year the Māori people have approached with so much misgiving as this Centennial Year ... In retrospect what does the Māori see? Lands gone, the power of chiefs humbled in the dust, Māori culture scattered and broken. What remained of all the fine things said 100 years ago? Before proceeding further with the new century, it is the clear duty of the Government to try to wipe out the mistakes of the past 100 years."

By 1990, and the 150th Anniversary of the signing of the Treaty, the relationship between Māori and Pākehā had improved, and Treaty grievances were being acknowledged and settled. But, as the then bishop of Aotearoa Te Whakahuihui Vercoe noted in his speech at Waitangi that day, there was much more to be done:

"Some of us have come here to celebrate, some to commemorate, some to commiserate, but some to remember what happened on this sacred ground. But since the signing of that Treaty 150 years ago I want to remind our partners that you have marginalized us. You have not honored the Treaty. We have not honored each other in the promises we made on this sacred ground. May God give us the courage to be honest with one another, to be sincere with one another, and above all to love one another in the strength of God."

Now we find ourselves here in 2015, the 175th year since the signing of the Treaty of Waitangi. What can we say has changed since the signing of the Treaty? What has changed since the 100th Anniversary of its signing? What has changed since the 150th Anniversary?

Some may say that much has been done to right historic wrongs, but I feel that the offer of a few cents as reparation for every dollar stolen falls far short of the promise and potential of the Treaty of Waitangi.[6]

If we can renew within ourselves the faith and the courage of our forebears who first signed the Treaty, we may well rise to fulfil our true potential as one people.

If our sense of servanthood can overpower our sense of entitlement, if our hunger for justice can overpower our selfish greed, if our hope can be more relentless than our grievance, and if our love can be more powerful than our litigation, we will fulfill the greater promise of the Treaty of Waitangi: One people, united.

---

6. Archbishop Brown Turei, "Reflecting on the Treaty's Moral Promise," *Taranaki Daily News*, February 10, 2015.

> Until then, we need to pray for peace, and to strive to deal with injustice and oppression.
>
> Nā tōu rourou, nā tāku rourou, ka mākona te iwi.
>
> We are all in this together.

As Anglicans we have a particular responsibility in relation to the Treaty. We are inheritors of the work of our missionary forebears, who toiled hard to secure the signing of the Treaty, and our Māori forebears, who trusted that friendship and believed that they were laying the foundations for a genuine partnership without surrendering any of their traditional lands, resources, or sovereignty. We carry that kaupapa[7] and responsibility for it.

Te Pouhere (Constitution)

A powerful set of opportunities and obligations rest with the Anglican Church in Aotearoa New Zealand. This church, which for the first decades of its history was undeniably Māori in shape, worship, and ethos, all too quickly marginalized Māori. In this predominantly Māori church, there were no Māori signatories to the 1857 Constitution.

For more than one hundred years, the church could not accept the idea of autonomous but interdependent Māori oversight of Māori ministry. There was hospitality of a kind, offered by the Diocese of Waiapu, which established the bishop of Aotearoa as a suffragan bishop of Waiapu with oversight of Māori ministry within that diocese.

Finally, in 1978, General Synod established the bishop of Aotearoa "to share in partnership with the Diocesan Bishops." This happened by way of an amendment on the floor of the General Synod.

There was hope that real progress had been made. Chief Judge Eddie Durie expressed that hope in this way: "I am a Māori Anglican. The Bishopric of Aotearoa serves to assure me that I need not cease to be a Māori in order to have a place in God's home, and a home within the Anglican Communion."[8]

But by 1982, concerns were being expressed that while the bishop had the status of a diocesan bishop, there was no clear jurisdiction. As a result, the General Synod established the Bi-Cultural Commission, which in 1986 presented its report, *Te Kaupapa Tikanga Rua: Bi-Cultural Development*. Most of the report's recommendations were adopted by the General Synod in that year.

---

7. Purpose, issue, theme, plan, agenda, matter for discussion, initiative, subject.
8. "What Binds This Church?" *Taonga News*, May 6, 2016.

In 1992, the church adopted a new constitution, providing for three partners who were enabled "to order their affairs within their own cultural context: Tikanga[9] Māori; Tikanga Pākehā; Tikanga Pasefika."

I was growing up at the time of the Bi-cultural Commission and lived through the consultation and controversy of that process. I understand that this three tikanga church was birthed out of what was fundamentally a wrestling with the consequences of the Treaty of Waitangi for the life of the church in Aotearoa New Zealand.

Pasefika moved from being a missionary diocese to a full and equal partner in our three tikanga church. As Archbishop Jabez Bryce acknowledged: "Formerly our people felt as though we were an appendix to the Church, we did not qualify for resources. Now we are a full, integral and equal partner in the life of this Church, and we are so grateful not just for the sharing of resources, but for being able to participate fully in the life of the Church."[10]

The fact that things moved so quickly for Pasefika was a source of some pain for Māori, who had struggled for so long in a context where ministry by and for Māori was marginalized, but they gracefully accepted that such a step had to be accommodated at that point in time.

In the Anglican Church of Aotearoa New Zealand and Polynesia, our constitutional framework seeks to honor the gospel and Treaty imperatives that have shaped our history. The framework establishes a basis for mission that recognizes that effectiveness in mission needs to allow for differences in language, culture, and worldviews.

The framework provided for in Te Pouhere demands a constant commitment to relationship, which does not allow us to live in silos but requires us to strive for each other's good, even to sacrifice ourselves and our own aspirations for the good of our partner.

John Paterson, former Primate and retired bishop of Auckland, put it this way:

> The absolute key for me lies in the concept of mana. It is the mana of the Treaty of Waitangi that has caused the Church to set its own house in order so that in a decade of evangelism we can invite others into that house who also respect it in the manner we respect it. Pākehā can only be Pākehā in this place because in the Treaty Māori guaranteed the right to Pākehā to come and live here, as Pākehā.

---

9. Cultural strand or stream.
10. Bluck, *Wai Karekare, Turbulent Waters*, 72.

> Until the mana of the Treaty of Waitangi is recognized equally by both Māori and Pākehā, it will not be possible for Pākehā to be truly and authentically Christian Pākehā in this place . . . Whether we like it or not, our identity in relation to our partner has to take the matter of mana into serious consideration. What we do simply has to be mana enhancing for our partner. We cannot enhance our own mana in isolation. We cannot build more self-esteem for ourselves by ourselves. We can endeavor to enhance the mana of our partner and thereby enhance our own."[11]

Partnering into the Future

Anglicans in Aotearoa New Zealand have grappled with the obligations and possibilities of partnership, with limited success, for more than 200 years.

We have wrestled with what it means to live with people whom God made differently to us—people who don't see things as we do or share our understandings, experiences, and values. Sadly, a lack of compassion by the settler church led it to being complicit in the marginalizing of Māori in, and from, their own land. Only in the latter portion of that 200 years, after decades of struggle, have we arrived at a constitution that enshrines respectful ways of being church together.

We are a church made up of colonized and colonizer. We have a difficult history. But it is a shared history. We know the language, the face, and the consequences of colonization. For Māori, disenfranchisement, alienation from whenua (land), racism, and poverty are consequences of this shared history.

Our nation is founded on Te Tiriti o Waitangi, which our church helped to broker. The Treaty offered, and still offers, a framework for nationhood that allows for the flourishing of all in these islands. Our church's constitution, Te Pouhere, provides for the potential of a genuine and just partnership.

The gospel of Jesus Christ is woven into both Treaty and Constitution. These two are not simply founding documents. They are lived realities. They are enlivened by 200 years of shared history and relationships in the gospel. And, they are deeply rooted in the historic faith first shared by the CMS missionaries and welcomed and spread by Māori.

As a church, we continue to be challenged by enormous internal and external inequities: we are a reflection of our society. To be Anglican in this

---

11. Bluck, *Wai Karekare, Turbulent Waters*, 19.

land requires that we face this shared history so that we can help shape a common future for all people based on peace, justice, and righteousness.

We are committed to meeting the challenges of the gospel imperatives, to working out the consequences of our shared history and to honoring our relationships. Māori are a people of whakapapa, whenua, and Treaty, and will stay true to those roots—they cannot be replicated elsewhere. A church is not recognizable as Anglican in these islands if it does not encapsulate these 200 years of relationship and history.

I look around our church and I see people who are my family, some of whom have been in my life for most of my life. I look around, and I am left wondering why we find it so hard to have this conversation with each other, a conversation about seeking each other's good. So much of the potential that lies in this partnership between Māori and Pākehā remains unrealized. But partnership is in our DNA now, as a church and as a nation.

Glenn Colquhoun sets this out in his poem, *The Trick of Standing Upright Here*:[12]

> The trick of standing upright here
> Is the art of using both feet.
> One is for holding on.
> One is for letting go.

The poem is a list of bicultural images of ordinary events and activities. We can recognize ourselves, Māori and Pākehā.

> Bread is walking back from a dairy with milk.
> It is the smell inside of tea-towels . . .
> Seafood is a fish on the plate with lemon.
> It is the rattle of cockles in a pot . . .
> Remembering is a statue in the park.
> It is the face carved in wood.

However inadequate our conversations might be, we simply have to talk with each other—and we have to keep the dialogue going. We need to be clear about practical and achievable outcomes.

---

12. Reprinted with the author's permission. Glenn Colquhoun is a doctor, poet and children's writer. His first poetry collection, *The Art of Walking Upright*, won Best First Book of Poetry at the 2000 Montana New Zealand Book Awards. In 2003 he won the Poetry Category and also became the first poet to be awarded the coveted Montana Readers' Choice Award.

We have an obligation rooted in Gospel and Treaty and mandated in our Constitution to work to fulfil the potential our forebears set the foundations for.

I am deeply hopeful about the future for the Anglican Church Te Hāhi Mihinare, in these islands, if we wholeheartedly commit to this. We do need to be clear that it is an ongoing task, but we have an opportunity to begin a process, at every level in this church, that will lead to a quality of engagement together in mission that will transform us and our ministry—as tikanga and as a church.

Bibliography

Bluck, John. *Wai Karekare, Turbulent Waters: The Anglican Bi-cultural Journey 1814-2014*. New Zealand: Anglican Church of Aotearoa, New Zealand and Polynesia, 2012.

Rashbrooke, Max. "Why Inequality Matters." In *Inequality: A New Zealand Crisis*, edited by Max Rashbrooke, 3–23. Wellington: Bridget Williams, 2013.

Theology and Personhood

16

Identity Angst

Narrative Identity and Anglican Liturgy

BRIAN ROSNER

THIS ESSAY EXPLORES AN aspect of contemporary Western culture that is relatively novel in human history and of critical importance to a host of issues, namely, the way in which we form our personal identities. In keeping with the title of this volume, included in my reflections on this aspect of our culture will be a consideration of its relevance to the church and its mission. It is a pleasure to dedicate this essay to Archbishop Philip on the occasion of his sixty-fifth birthday in gratitude for his irenic and faithful leadership.

In traditionally structured societies, people tend to look outwards at their roles and places in the community to find their identity. Increasingly, however, in our post-modern pluralistic world we take for granted the obligation to find and define, or even invent, ourselves for ourselves. The frequently heard advice in many contexts is: "be true to yourself," "follow your heart," "be yourself," and the most recent and hippest version, "you do you." Self-definition is the self-evident route to identity formation in our day. It is often labeled expressive individualism. Ours is a do-it-yourself self.

The regular advice today, as *New York Times* columnist David Brooks notes, is for people to "follow their passion, to trust their feelings, to reflect and find their purpose in life. The assumption behind these clichés is that when you are figuring out how to lead your life, the most important answers are found deep inside yourself."[1]

Charles Taylor states it well: "Modern freedom and autonomy centres us on ourselves, and the ideal of authenticity requires that we discover and articulate our own identity."[2]

Interest in personal identity is on the rise in our society, with expressive individualism fast becoming the unquestioned and exclusive approach to identity formation. And personal autonomy is the trump card in almost every ethical debate. In such issues as gender, sexuality, abortion, assisted dying and so on, to speak against deciding for individual choice is a modern-day heresy.

A key dimension of personal identity is the story we inhabit that narrates our lives over time. Jonathan Gottschall's *The Storytelling Animal: How Stories Make Us Human* puts it well: "Our life stories are who we are. They are our identity."[3] We each have what Timothy Keller calls a narrative identity: "Everyone lives and operates out of some narrative identity, whether it is thought out and reflected upon or not."[4] Such narratives give meaning to our lives, sketch our character in outline, and tell us what is important in life. As Alister McGrath puts it: "The story we believe we are in determines what we think about ourselves and consequently how we live."[5]

According to Gottschall, the power of stories to shape us is far-reaching:

> "Story teaches us facts about the world; influences our moral logic; and marks us with fears, hopes, and anxieties that alter our behavior . . . Research shows that story is constantly nibbling and kneading us, shaping our mind without our knowledge or consent. The more deeply we are cast under story's spell, the more potent its influence."[6]

Stories have "sculpting power."[7] And this is no truer than in the stories we tell about ourselves.

1. Brooks, *Road to Character*, 21.
2. Taylor, *Ethics of Authenticity*, 81.
3. Gottschall, *Storytelling Animal*, 161.
4. Keller, *Reason for God*, 15.
5. McGrath, *Deep Magic, Dragons and Talking Mice*, 947.
6. Gottschall, *Storytelling Animal*, 148.
7. Gottschall, *Storytelling Animal*, 152.

The expressive individualism approach to narrative identity is predictable. Each of us chooses the stories that define us (or at least we think we do). And in such stories, we take the starring role, as well as act as director, producer, script writer, and narrator.

Personal identity is a huge topic of growing importance and bewildering complexity. It can be addressed from a variety of angles and from a range of disciplines.[8] This modest essay considers four questions related to narrative identity formation:

1. How successful is expressive individualism as an approach to narrative identity formation?
2. How realistic is expressive individualism as an approach to narrative identity formation?
3. What does the Christian faith offer in terms of our narrative identity?
4. What, if anything, has Anglican liturgy got to do with narrative identity formation?

Let's consider each of these in turn.

1. Expressive Individualism Produces Unintended Negative Outcomes

There are many obvious benefits to inventing yourself as a way of doing personal identity. Psychologists generally regard authenticity, being true to yourself, as a basic requirement of mental health. As Karen Wright observes:

> "Authenticity is correlated with many aspects of psychological well-being, including vitality, self-esteem, and coping skills. Acting in accordance with one's core self—a trait called self-determination—is ranked by some experts as one of the three basic psychological needs."[9]

Or as Charles Taylor puts it: "Authenticity points towards a more self-responsible form of life . . . at its best it allows for a richer mode of existence."[10] Expressive individualism acknowledges that people are re-

---

8. For a biblical-theological treatment see Rosner, *Known by God*, 245–62. This essay builds on the final chapter, in which I discuss how we can know ourselves as we are known by God.
9. Wright, "Dare to Be Yourself," 72.
10. Taylor, *Ethics of Authenticity*, 74.

sponsible individuals with particular talents and passions and treats them as such.

However, there are also some major problems with "you do you." What kind of self does self-definition produce? For all its potential and strengths, expressive individualism is prone to five unintended outcomes.

First, *ironically, the self-made self produces a self that is fragile and unstable*. Whereas once identity formation almost took care of itself, nowadays everything about who you are is up for grabs. And the pressure to live your best life now can be oppressive. The dreaded midlife crisis notwithstanding, in the recent past the identity of most people was set during their adolescence when they accepted, rejected, or adapted the identity handed to them by their parents in their childhood. These days, life-cycle dilemma experts believe that for many people identity transitions occur earlier than midlife and much more often. The "age of discontent" can happen at any and every age, the obligation to define or design yourself being always at hand. You don't have to wait for midlife to have doubts about how your life is tracking. The dreaded "thrisis" awaits those turning thirty, who having climbed the ladder of success are disillusioned to discover it's leaning against the wrong wall.[11] And those of us turning forty, fifty, or sixty years of age might experience "cuspiety," the anxiety associated with reaching the precipice of so-called cusp ages.

In our day, a myriad of factors weighs against having a stable and satisfying sense of self. Living our lives in the separate compartments of home, work, and leisure can produce superficial relationships and problems for genuine self-knowledge. Multiple careers and marital breakdown can lead to confusion about some of the most basic of answers to the question of who you are, namely, your occupation and marital status.

The digital age has added a new dimension to the question of personal identity. The web is now the platform on which many of us live our lives. With social media, the internet is the way you tell the world not just what you are up to and what you are thinking but *who you are*. Regular profile and status updates on sites like Facebook, Instagram, and Snapchat have taken defining yourself to a new level. Many believe that the web has affected our very identity.[12] And even if social media has made self-definition appealing, as Peter Leithart notes, if humans have always worn masks, "with the arrival of postmodern communication technologies the masks have become thicker and more concealing."[13]

---

11. See Edwards, *30 Something*.
12. E.g., Harkin, *Cyburbia*.
13. Leithart, *Solomon Among the Postmoderns*, 123.

Secondly, *the self-made self can cultivate unrealistic expectations for life and is ill-equipped to cope with serious setbacks and disappointments.* Social researcher Hugh Mackay has identified what he calls the "utopia complex, a world we dream of and think we are entitled to with outcomes that are always positive."[14] The difficulty is that in embracing such high expectations, we are setting ourselves up for a fall. Along with the rise in high expectations for life, some economists today see the rise of the "precariat," (playing off the word, "proletariat"), a growing social class formed by people suffering from precarity, existence without predictability or security.[15] Lack of job security and the stubborn trend of underemployment in our economy makes it unlikely that "living the dream" will become a reality. As much as we might like to think that we are the author of our lives, life's unscripted moments—redundancy, illness, bereavement, relationship breakdown and the like—means that all of us belong to the precariat.

Thirdly, *the self-made self is prone to pride and envy.* Here we may note the widely reported rise in narcissism across our society. Studies show that narcissistic traits are on the rise: psychologist Ross King suggests that the number of those possessing such traits has jumped from 3 to 10 percent in three decades.[16] "In 1950 a personality test asked teenagers if they considered themselves an important person. Twelve percent said yes. By the late 1980s, 80 percent said yes."[17] Simon Smart writes:

> A generation brought up on an endless diet of their own specialness appears to be struggling with the hard truth that most of us are just ordinary . . . According to a [recent] survey by the National Youth Mental Health Foundation, university and TAFE campuses are reporting epidemic levels of mental health issues, with 70 per cent of students reporting high to very high levels of psychological distress.[18]

---

14. Simon Smart, "The Generation Brought up on Self Esteem is Struggling," *Sydney Morning Herald* online. Last modified April 13, 2017. http://www.smh.com.au/comment/the-generation-brought-up-on-selfesteem-is-struggling-20170413-gvk4ng.html

15. Veronica Sheen, "The Precariat Is Recruiting: Youth, Please Apply," *The Conversation*, January 10, 2013. Accessed July 17, 2019. http://theconversation.com/the-precariat-is-recruiting-youth-please-apply-10550

16. Chloe Booker, "Narcissism Is on the Rise, but Are You a Narcissist? Take Our Quiz," *Sydney Morning Herald* online. Last modified July 1, 2017. http://www.smh.com.au/national/health/narcissism-is-on-the-rise-but-are-you-a-narcissist-take-our-quiz-20170701-gx2qze.html

17. Brooks, *Social Animal*, 191.

18. Smart, "Generation Brought Up."

It seems likely that the focus on the self, that is intrinsic to the self-made self, has contributed to this rise in pathological self-centeredness. Many psychologists claim that overuse of social media, that great tool of self-definition and expression, is strongly linked to narcissistic behavior and low self-esteem.[19]

Fourthly, *the self-made self is easily given to self-centeredness.* What room is there for the weak and lowly, for example, in a narrative of following your heart and achieving greatness? Will such people simply be regarded as obstacles on the path to self-actualization? As Charles Taylor asserts, "our ties to others, as well as external moral demands, can easily be in conflict with our personal development."[20]

Fifthly and finally, *the self-made self, focused on itself and its own image, can lack empathy for others.* In the past, an indiscretion might lead to being shunned at a party; nowadays a single poorly worded tweet can lead to worldwide censure and opprobrium. As one author has said in the context of the online world, "hatred is everywhere; empathy and its cousin, civility, are nowhere. [We live in a] culture of reflexive outrage."[21] The phenomena of internet pile-ons and rabid "twitch hunts" would suggest that the self-made self is easily angered.

People point in many directions for an explanation of these unfortunate societal trends: not enough mindfulness, technology addling our brains, the failure of major institutions (e.g., politicians, churches, media, banks), loss of shared values, absence of community cohesion, etc. However, some of these are symptoms rather than causes. I suggest that a shift in the way we do identity formation in our day is a big part of the problem. While the fragile self, the utopia complex, the rise in narcissism, our culture of reflexive outrage, and the absence of compassion in our society cannot all be blamed on the self-made self, it is hardly surprising that such an approach to identity seems to produce a personal identity that is self-centered and self-absorbed.

---

19. Joanne Black, "It's All About Me: The Rise of Narcissism," *Noted* social media website. May 19, 2012. Accessed July 17, 2019. http://www.noted.co.nz/archive/listener-nz-2012/it-s-all-about-me-the-rise-of-narcissism/

20. Taylor, *Ethics of Authenticity*, 74.

21. Michael Shammas, "Outrage Culture Kills Important Conversation," *Huffpost*. January 27, 2016. Last modified January 27, 2017. http://www.huffingtonpost.com/mike-shammas/from-liberal-college-camp_b_9070894.html

2. Expressive Individualism Neglects the Fact That Our Stories Are Part of Some Bigger Story

But not only is expressive individualism as an approach to identity formation causing a number of unintended outcomes, it is also seriously flawed as a strategy for identity formation. Humans are social beings, and we come to know ourselves by being known by those closest to us. (I explore this angle on personal identity in full in my book, *Known by God: A Biblical Theology of Personal Identity*.) It is also a mistake to think that our life stories are simply our own making and played out in isolation from others. The big story, or metanarrative, in which each of us lives, is often a shared story, a combination of defining moments and goals and expectations of life related to stories handed to us by our families and related to the stories of our nations, ethnicities, social classes, and religious faiths.

Concerning which shared stories we inhabit, Alister McGrath suggests that:

> "Some of us live under the assumptions of the Western story of societal progress, that civilisation—technologically, socially, or morally—is continually improving. Others live under the story of individual progress of the sort peddled on daytime talk shows, that the self is the most important thing there is and that more or better information will organically produce better selves. Still others subscribe to the victim metanarrative, that their personal choices have little impact on the world they live in."[22]

As it turns out, in inventing themselves by looking inwards, many people elevate and absolutize one aspect of their identity (e.g., their race, gender, social class, occupation, age, and so on), which connects them to a group that shares these features and brings with it the template of a life story. Such narratives are often driven by a legitimate desire to seek justice for the group. However, they can also lead to a distorted view of the world in which every situation is judged in simplistic ideological terms, and an ugly tribalism emerges. At worst, such groups can be united not by common objects of love but by their mutual hatred for other groups. In *Known by God*, chapter 3, "The Foundations of Personal Identity," I argue that the Bible regards such markers of personal identity to be important, but not all-important, and that defining ourselves by such means can lead to idolatry.

---

22. McGrath, *Deep Magic*, 58.

3. The Christian Faith Commends the Life Story of Jesus Christ for Our Narrative Identity

The Christian faith believes that while each of us has a unique story, all of our stories are part of some bigger story.[23] And this is most certainly true of the people of God. In both the Old and New Testaments of the Bible, God's people are defined by the story of their redemption, shared memories, and a common defining destiny. In the case of Israel, it was release from slavery in Egypt and the prospect of entering the promised land;[24] for followers of Jesus Christ it is release from the reign of sin by the death of Christ and the hope of eternal life.

In a passage like Colossians 3, the life story of Christ is the Christian's narrative identity. Christ not only died in our place; there is a sense in which we also died with him. We share his death, and we will share his resurrection:

> You died [our shared memory], and your identity is now hidden with Christ in God. When Christ, who is your life story, appears, then you also will appear with him in glory [our defining destiny] (Col 3:3-4; my own translation).

This is why Paul can say in Galatians 2:20: "I have been crucified with Christ and I no longer live, but Christ lives in me. The life I now live in the body, I live by faith in the Son of God, who loved me and gave himself for me." Indeed, Paul's language of "putting on" Christ (or the new self) in several of his letters is a call to embrace this very story as one's own and live according to it.

When it comes to life stories, Christian faith asks—to take a line of Pink Floyd's song, "Wish You Were Here," out of context—"Would you exchange a walk-on part in the war for a lead role in a cage?" The choice for all of us is between striving for a starring role in our own short story, the genre

---

23. For example, DeSilva, *Sacramental Life*, 168: "Story gives shape to our identity, direction and purpose."

24. Horton, *The Christian Faith*, 86-87, explains the significance of such shared memories for personal identity with reference to the Old Testament people of God: "The present generation makes history their story . . . History is not only rendered contemporary; it is internalized. One's people's history becomes one's personal history. One looks out from the self to find out who one is meant to be. One does not discover one's identity, and one certainly does not forge it oneself . . . Instead, it is the consequence of what are presented as the acts of God . . . Israel began to infer and to affirm her identity by telling a story." See also DeSilva, *Sacramental Life*, 168: "The greatest danger for the Israelites on entering the Promised Land was forgetting the story of God's redemption and salvation and that they would then start living out another, distorted story."

of which could be a farce or a tragedy, or a bit part in the grand story of God and the redemption of the world.

According to Alister McGrath, "Christianity doesn't just make sense of things. It changes our stories. It invites us to enter into, and be part of, a new story."[25] McGrath contends that C. S. Lewis illustrates well in *The Chronicles of Narnia*, through the character of Lucy and the story of Aslan, how our life stories can be given new direction and purpose by the story of Jesus Christ:

> Lucy—who is in many ways the central human character of the series—became shaped by the story of Aslan. Lucy's love for Aslan is expressed in her commitment to him. She wants to do what he wants; she wants her story to reflect who he is. As a result, Lewis speaks of Lucy feeling "lion-strength" flowing within her. She has become part of the story of Aslan. But—and this is a hugely important "but"—she has not lost her own identity. Her story remains her own. However, her story now makes more sense because Lucy has gained a sense of value and meaning. By embracing the story of Aslan as central to her story, she has gained a new sense of identity and purpose.[26]

As Christians, how well we inhabit the story of Jesus Christ and are sculpted by it makes all the difference.

The church needs to give people a story they can live by; not one that leads to a naïve optimism about life, but one that can cope with and give meaning to hardship, serious setbacks, and grief, that is not given to hubris, that can respond to enemies and injustice with proportion, and that looks on the less fortunate as equals. That story is the story of Jesus Christ, which we are invited to mirror in our lives.

How does this Christian metanarrative measure against the five unintended outcomes of the self-made self I listed above? In brief, it supplies the resources and gives the direction to those living it to do much better. It offers a stable and satisfying sense of self as a child of God united to Christ. The shared memory of dying with Christ gives meaning to our suffering and instils in us a measure of comfort and hope. We have good grounds to be humble and consider others to be more important than ourselves, in imitation of Christ, who humbled himself to the point of death on a cross. Similarly, the weak and lowly we come across are to be respected and assisted, given that in the cross God chose human weakness as the means of saving the world; in identifying with Christ in his death, we die to pure self-interest and are raised to live lives of sacrificial love. And in contrast to

25. McGrath, *Deep Magic*, 947.
26. McGrath, *Deep Magic*, 889.

the outrage culture, the story of Jesus Christ calls on his disciples to turn the other cheek in imitation of his own extreme example.

The cross is the answer to the postmodern objection that all metanarratives, including the Christian one, are by definition self-serving and oppressive. Rightly understood, the Christian story into which we are invited is one that champions the oppressed and calls for self-sacrifice. While Christians, and especially Christian leaders, do regrettably often behave out of self-interest, it is not the story's fault that they've lost the plot and gone off script.

Stories have the power to inspire imagination and imitation. On this score, Gottschall points to the disturbing and extreme case of the influence of the nineteenth-century German composer Richard Wagner on Adolf Hitler. I hesitate to cite it, given that my own father and his parents suffered under Nazi terror. But it does offer a sharp example of the power of story to form character and behavior. Gottschall writes:

> Wagner was not just a brilliant composer. He was also an extreme German nationalist, a prolific author of inflammatory political tracts, and a virulent anti-Semite who wrote of a "grand solution" to the Jewish menace long before the Nazis put one in place. Hitler worshipped Wagner like a god and called Wagner's music his religion . . . He considered the composer to be his mentor, his model, his one true ancestor . . . Hitler lived Wagner's work, he believed himself to be a Wagnerian hero.[27]

Hitler himself said that "whoever wants to understand National Socialist Germany must understand the works of Wagner."[28] The aim of churches is to be able to say: Whoever wants to understand Christian people must understand the story of Jesus Christ.

4. The Place of Anglican Liturgy in Narrative Identity Formation

Alister McGrath contends that a central task of the mission of Christianity is "to show that it can tell a more compelling and engaging story that will capture the imagination of its culture."[29] Whole books could be written on how the church can and must tackle this challenge. Central to any discussion should be the gospel of our Lord Jesus Christ and its power to change people

---

27. Gottschall, *The Storytelling Animal*, 143–4.
28. Gottschall, *The Storytelling Animal*, 144.
29. McGrath, *Deep Magic*, 728.

now and forever. My aim in this closing section is to attempt something more modest, asking the question: What, if anything, has Anglican liturgy got to do with narrative identity formation? While I am by no means a liturgist (or the son of a liturgist),[30] my hope is that this neglected function of the church's liturgy might be more widely recognized and taken further by better qualified people in service of the church's mission.

My thesis is that many elements of Anglican liturgy contribute to the task of telling the story of Jesus Christ as the life story of every believer. On the broadest canvas, the liturgical calendar itself is a means of enabling believers to inhabit the Christ story. As John E. Colwell argues:

> The seasons of the Christian Year are a liturgical unfolding of the Christian story, and, as such are a means of indwelling that story . . . The Church journeys through the Christian Year with Christ whose story is here narrated; the Church joins him in his journey and reaffirms his journey as its own journey, the journey by which it is defined and in which it participates.[31]

On this score, it is significant that the seasons in the first half of the year trace the story of Christ, and the second can be seen as narrating our story in the light of the story of Christ. This gives the framework and setting for the weekly service. Thus, the seasons of Advent, Epiphany, Lent, and Easter recount the birth, death, resurrection, and ascension of Christ. The reading of Acts each year in the season of Easter reminds us that we are in continuity with the early church in spreading the gospel throughout the world. In the gospel readings through the season of Ordinary time, we join with the disciples in their journey with Jesus, learning from his story (and the stories he told), the big story of the Bible, and through them our story. In this season, through the Old Testament readings we are reminded over many weeks that the history of God's people is our history, and in the New Testament readings we hear from Paul and the apostles what it means for us to be the church. Where commemorated, saints' days and minor feasts don't just celebrate individual "heroes" of the faith but help connect us with our history as the church (see Heb 12:1–2).

With regard to the function of liturgy and storytelling, James K. A. Smith, in *Desiring the Kingdom: Worship, Worldview, and Cultural*

---

30. I wish to record my thanks to George Hemmings for research assistance and help in preparing this section.

31. Colwell, *The Rhythm of Doctrine*, 6–7. See also Smith, *Desiring the Kingdom*, 156: "Just the space of worship would tell a story that actually organizes time—an indication that here dwells a people with a unique sense of *temporality* [emphasis original], who inhabit a time that is out of joint with the regular, mundane ticking of commercial time or the standard shape of the academic year."

Formation, claims that we are defined and driven by what we desire or love, which is bound up with our view of human flourishing. Liturgy, then—and Smith argues that the world is full of competing liturgies—helps to shape and cultivate our desires, so it is worth paying attention to what they are and what they are doing. Being human takes practice, and liturgy is where we learn. Smith contends, for example, that in the Eucharist, itself a "microcosm" of the whole liturgy of worship, we are placed in the midst of the story of God's work: "It's as if the story we've been hearing and rehearsing now comes live with illustrations."[32] For Smith, sharing in the Lord's Supper is supremely affective and transformative: "Just as a song makes words stick in our memory, so the sights, smells, and rhythms of the Eucharist seem to make the story both come alive and wriggle into our imaginations in a way that it wouldn't otherwise."[33]

We may briefly consider some of the common elements of an Anglican service, showing how they encourage us to inhabit and live the story of Jesus Christ.

In the opening prayer we mark ourselves out as different from the world; far from being self-made, we confess our brokenness and need for God to fashion us anew. He knows us better than we know ourselves:

> Almighty God,
> To whom all hearts are open,
> All desires known,
> And from whom no secrets are hidden;
> Cleanse the thoughts of our hearts
> By the inspiration of your Holy Spirit,
> That we may perfectly love you
> And worthily magnify your holy name,
> Through Jesus Christ our Lord.

Confessing our sins reinforces the same ideas and makes explicit that we are not able to write our own life stories. Or as Smith puts it, "we confess our failure 'to *be human*.'"[34]

Baptism signifies our past joining to Christ in his death and resurrection, our present journeying with Christ in a new life of obedience, and

---

32. Smith, *Desiring the Kingdom*, 198.

33. Smith, *Desiring the Kingdom*, 199. See also Colwell, *The Rhythm of Doctrine*, 10: "To celebrate this story is to participate in this story is to be shaped and transformed by this story. No re-telling of this story, therefore should occur other than worshipfully, with the prayerful expectation that such transformation will occur."

34. Smith, *Desiring the Kingdom*, 178.

our future resurrection with Christ in his glorious kingdom. In baptism, we affirm that we are, "not closed, self-sufficient autonomous units."[35] Whenever we witness a baptism, it summons us to recall our own baptism and to cherish the shared memory and defining destiny that form our identity in Christ. Note the connection between being baptized, being children of God, and the story of Christ in the 1662 *Book of Common Prayer*:

> And as for you, who have now by Baptism put on Christ, it is your part and duty also, *being made the children of God* and of the light by faith in Jesus Christ, to walk answerably to your Christian calling, and as becometh the children of light; remembering always that Baptism representeth unto us our profession; which is, to follow the example of our Saviour Christ, and *to be made like unto him; that as he died, and rose again for us; so should we, who are baptized, die from sin, and rise again unto righteousness*; continually mortifying all our evil and corrupt affections, and daily proceeding in all virtue and godliness of living.[36]

There are many reasons to say the creed: to teach doctrine; to underscore our links with Christians of all ages and across denominations; to worship God; to combat heresy. A further, oft-neglected purpose is to affirm our identity as the people of God. As Michael F. Bird puts it, "The creeds remind us who we are as Christians and that we are part of God's plan to gather his people around himself and to bring all of his children into his new creation."[37] In affirming that we are part of the story of God, Christians at the same time deny that they are part of another story. As N. T. Wright notes, when we recite the creed we affirm that "we are renewed as *this people*, the people who live within *this* great story, the people who are identified precisely as people-of-this-story, rather than as people of one of the many other stories that clamor for attention all around."[38]

Matt Chandler makes the same point specifically with reference to the Apostles' Creed:

> When the early church recited the Apostles' Creed, it was simultaneously their greatest act of rebellion and their greatest act of allegiance. When the church gathered [in this way] . . . they rejected the popular narratives of their day. So in Rome they rejected that Caesar was lord. They rejected the narrative of

---

35. Smith, *Desiring the Kingdom*, 186.
36. Closing charge for service of adult baptism, "The Ministration of Publick Baptism to Such as are of Riper Years, and Able to Answer for Themselves." Italics added.
37. Bird, *What Christians Ought to Believe*, 40.
38. Wright, "Reading Paul, Thinking Scripture," 64. Italics original.

the first century and said, "No, no, no. I reject that. I believe that Jesus is Lord." They said, "We don't believe the story our culture is telling." That story has some similarities, but it has changed throughout human history.

In our day, by reciting the Apostles' Creed we're saying, "We reject the narrative of materialism. We reject that stuff will satisfy our souls." We're saying, "We reject the notion that what I need to be physically satisfied is more and more and more partners. I reject that there's not *a* way but everybody has their own." We just fundamentally reject that narrative. Our narrative is that we believe in the God of the Bible.

> When the church recites this creed, distilled, pulled from, wrung out of the Word of God, we're saying, "We reject the modern narrative. We believe the historic narrative, the narrative that God has come into the world to save sinners, that Jesus Christ has died for our sins, and we believe and trust that he has made known to us the path of life."[39]

When we say the Apostles' Creed, we repudiate the creeds of alternative visions of what it means to be a human being in our day. Or as Smith puts it: "In reciting it [the Creed] each week, we rehearse the skeletal structure of the story in which we find our identity."[40]

Praying the Lord's Prayer together demonstrates the role prayer plays in recalling and rehearsing key narratival aspects of our identity. We do not simply pray to receive good gifts from God. The act of prayer itself reminds us who we are in relation to God. Praying the Lord's Prayer marks out the main lines of the journey believers are on; it reminds us of to whom we belong, what we are a part of, what we need, and where we are headed. Likewise, intercessory prayer brings into focus that we are to live for others and not for ourselves and that we are part of God's mission to the world.

In reading the Bible and hearing it preached, we not only learn about God but also about ourselves. For the Bible knows the human condition and tells the human story. From our creation as God's offspring in the garden, through our ruinous rebellion, to God's determination to set things right, the human story, "warts and all," is the main plot of the Bible's larger narrative. And the history of Israel as God's chosen people, from the covenant promises through Abraham, the conquest, kingship, to the exile and

---

39. Matt Chandler, "The Apostles Creed: I Believe In," sermon transcript, August 22, 2015. Accessed July 17, 2019. https://www.tvcresources.net/resource-library/sermons/i-believe-in

40. Smith, *Desiring the Kingdom*, 192.

return, is the backstory of every believer's narrative identity.[41] And with the coming of Christ, the second Adam, the human story takes a decisive turn. Again, as Smith notes, "the Scriptures function as the script of the worshiping community, the story that narrates the identity of the people of God."[42]

The communion service is an identity forming and confirming emblem of the gospel. In taking communion, believers are prompted: (1) to *look back* to a shared memory; (2) to *look around* at their brothers and sisters in the family of God; and (3) to *look forward* to their defining destiny. Michael F. Bird puts it well:

> The meaning of the Eucharist is ultimately anchored in a story, in fact, *the story*. It is a snapshot of the grand narrative about God, creation, the fall, Israel, the exile, the Messiah, the church, and the consummation. The bread and the wine tell a story about God, redemption, Jesus, and salvation.[43]

The *Kenyan Anglican Communion Liturgy* closes with words that point to our shared memory of dying with Christ and our defining destiny of rising with him: "Christ has died, Christ is risen, Christ will come again. We are brothers and sisters through his blood. We have died together, we will rise together, and we will live together."

If baptism dramatizes our initiation into Christ's body and our identification with him, communion is the second act in the drama of salvation, or more accurately a rehearsal for the final act. Its performance reminds us that we are no mere spectators when it comes to the death, resurrection, and final destiny of God's Son. In eating his flesh and drinking his blood, we declare that, "Christ is our life" (Col 3:11). And we reserve our seats for the banquet to end all banquets!

Finally, "the sending out" reminds us that as we participate in the story of God through worship; we are trained to play our part in his mission. Smith argues that having had our identity reinforced and affirmed in worship, we're sent out to be witnesses, to invite others to find their identity in worship.[44]

---

41. Paul writes to the Christians in Corinth concerning "*our* ancestors" (1 Cor. 10:1), referring to the history of the nation Israel. Matthew opens the New Testament with a genealogy that demonstrates the continuity of "Jesus Christ, the son of David, the son of Abraham" (1:1) with the story of Israel.

42. Smith, *Desiring the Kingdom*, 195.

43. Bird, *Evangelical Theology*, 777–78. Italics original.

44. Smith, *Desiring the Kingdom*, 206.

Jonathan Gottschall observes that "the more absorbed readers are in a story, the more the story changes them."[45] A major task of the church today is to plant God's grand story deep in the psyche of believers in Christ so that it reverberates throughout their lives.

If done well, combined with faithful proclamation of the gospel from the Scriptures, Anglican liturgy can be an effective means of doing this very thing.

---

45. Gottschall, *The Storytelling Animal*, 151.

Bibliography

Bird, Michael F. *Evangelical Theology: A Biblical and Systematic Introduction*. Grand Rapids, MI: Zondervan, 2013.

———. *What Christians Ought to Believe: An Introduction to Christian Doctrine Through the Apostles' Creed*. Grand Rapids, MI: Zondervan, 2016.

Brooks, David. *The Road to Character*. New York: Random House, 2015.

———. *The Social Animal: A Story of How Success Happens*. New York: Random House, 2011.

Colwell, John E. *The Rhythm of Doctrine: A Liturgical Sketch of Christian Faith and Faithfulness*. Milton Keynes: Paternoster, 2007.

DeSilva, David A. *Sacramental Life: Spiritual Formation Through the Book of Common Prayer*. Downers Grove, IL: IVP, 2008.

Edwards, Kasey. *30 Something and Over It*. Sydney: Random House, 2009.

Gottschall, Jonathan. *The Storytelling Animal: How Stories Make Us Human*. Boston: Mariner Books, 2012.

Harkin, James. *Cyburbia: The Dangerous Idea That's Changing How We Live and Who We Are*. London: Little Brown, 2009.

Horton, Michael. *The Christian Faith: A Systematic Theology for Pilgrims on the Way*. Grand Rapids, MI: Zondervan, 2011.

Keller, Timothy. *The Reason for God: Belief in an Age of Scepticism*. London: Hodder & Stoughton, 2009.

Leithart, Peter J. *Solomon Among the Postmoderns*. Grand Rapids MI: Brazos, 2008.

McGrath, Alister. *Deep Magic, Dragons and Talking Mice: How Reading C. S. Lewis Can Change Your Life*. London: Hodder & Stoughton, 2014.

Rosner, Brian S. *Known by God. Biblical Theology for Life*. Grand Rapids MI: Zondervan, 2017.

Smith, James K. A. *Desiring the Kingdom: Worship, Worldview, and Cultural Formation*. Cultural Liturgies Volume 1. Grand Rapids MI: Baker Academic, 2009.

Taylor, Charles. *The Ethics of Authenticity*. London: Harvard University Press, 1991.

Wright, Karen. "Dare to Be Yourself." *Psychology Today* (May 2008): 72.

Wright, N. T. "Reading Paul, Thinking Scripture." In *Scripture's Doctrine and Theology's Bible: How the New Testament Shapes Christian Dogmatics*, edited by Markus Bockmuehl and Alan J. Torrance, 59–74. Grand Rapids, MI: Baker, 2008.

17

"Walking with a Limp"

Some Personal and Pastoral Reflections on Trauma

John Harrower[1]

ARCHBISHOP PHILIP FREIER COMMENCED his term as Primate of the Anglican Church of Australia one year into the work of the Royal Commission into Institutional Responses to Child Sexual Abuse (2013–2017). On the first day of the final hearing into the Anglican Church by the Royal Commission, the Primate made a strong statement committing himself and the church to action: "We eagerly await the Royal Commission's recommendations. We believe that the rigorous and independent scrutiny the commission has provided is greatly to our benefit. There is a pronounced appetite for change inside the Anglican Church. We are determined to apply best practice so that the Church is truly a safe place for children."[2]

Much work has been done, and there is more work yet to be done.[3]

---

1. I am grateful to OSL Healing Ministries for the invitation to deliver the Pearce Memorial Lecture 2017 in which I had the opportunity to explore this theme at the Triennial Conference, "Walking in Faith into the Future." Melbourne, 2017.
2. Freier, "We Are Ashamed."
3. Gladwin, "Remembering our Future."

During his episcopal ministry as bishop of the Northern Territory (1999–2006) and currently, serving as Archbishop of Melbourne from 2006 and Primate from 2014, Archbishop Freier has been immersed in the leadership task of creating safety for children and responding appropriately to perpetrators and survivors.[4] This has exacted a heavy toll, as expressed in his unequivocal statement of our church's failure:

> Anglicans have been truly shocked and dismayed at the unfolding in the Royal Commission of the scope of our failure to tackle child sexual abuse within the Church and the depth of survivors' pain and suffering. We are deeply ashamed of the many ways in which we have let down survivors, both in the way we have acted and the way we have failed to act.[5]

The Primate clearly acknowledged the depth of survivors' pain and suffering as a devastating effect of abuse and an area in which the church failed to understand the evil, tragedy, and traumatic nature of child sexual abuse. Trauma is a devastating consequence of such abuse, and dealing with trauma is serious business: it results from profound suffering, it is debilitating, and its consequences are long lived.[6]

This article is an exploration of ways by which people of Christian faith live with trauma, even when the consequences of traumatic events cause them to "walk with a limp." This is not a dispassionate academic exercise, and it may prompt emotional responses. Some readers may have experienced traumatic events or know people who have experienced or are experiencing trauma. We never know when the outworking of deep traumas can erupt and express themselves. Therefore, while reading this article, be free to hit the pause button.

Introduction

When discussing a person who is suffering from trauma, how many of you have you heard someone comment along these lines:

"Get over it!"
"Deal with it!"
"Pray believing!"

4. See, for example, Freier, "Presidential Address."
5. Freier, "We Are Ashamed."
6. See Barker, *Tackling Trauma: Global, Biblical and Pastoral Perspectives,* for a volume of thought-provoking essays by Christian professionals of diverse cultures and expertise and their practical engagement with people and communities around the world who have suffered from traumatic events.

"Toughen up!"

"Go for a walk, get some fresh air, smell the roses. You'll be fine."

But, no! Not so! A flippant dismissal of trauma is a gross misunderstanding of trauma. These reactions show ignorance or perhaps deep fears held by the speakers themselves.

Tragedy strikes and trauma follows. Although the effects of the violence (emotional, physical, intellectual, and spiritual) may lag behind the tragic event by years, trauma does come.[7] When a person is suffering from trauma, they feel down, down, down. Crying, weeping, hopeless and alone, despairing, a failure, embarrassed, humiliated. But neither is wallowing in trauma with the tears, sadness, brokenness, and hopelessness an option. Is it possible to deal with trauma at all? And if so, how?

Let me say at the outset that I make no claims to professional expertise in the area of trauma or dealing with its consequences. My aim is to learn from the experience of some people who have suffered traumatic events in order that we might better walk with people who are suffering from trauma. This essay is a personal and pastoral exploration of a complex and pain-laden issue.

My Own Experience

Bessel van der Kolk's significant book, *The Body Keeps the Score: Brain, Mind, and Body in the Healing of Trauma*,[8] presents case study after case study of the ways in which tragic events and their traumatic aftermath are stored in our bodies. There is, if you like, a cumulative effect emotionally, intellectually, and physically/medically from traumatic events. As the years go by, we are less able to contain them: the body keeps score.

Two years ago, I viewed the biographical war drama movie *Hacksaw Ridge*.[9] It tells of the courage of a conscientious objector in the US Army who was bullied during military training and yet who rescued, under enemy fire, seventy-five of his wounded comrades. Crawling among the dead and wounded while dodging Japanese soldiers, he lowered these seventy-five wounded comrades by rope, one-by-one, down the steep cliff of Hacksaw Ridge to safety.

It was a movie with plenty of body parts, and yet I found watching it was okay until the end of the movie when the courageous soldier, now

---

7. A taxonomy of horrors in outlined in Harrower, *God of All Comfort*, 26–38.

8. See Van der Kolk, *The Body Keeps the Score*.

9. Mel Gibson (director) and Andrew Knight and Robert Schenkkan (writers). *Hacksaw Ridge*. Australia: Icon Film Distribution, 2016.

an elderly man, was interviewed. The interview was a surprise, and he was diffident about the attention being given him. I found his gracious manner and the warm acknowledgement he received overwhelming. My body began to shake. I struggled to stay upright in my seat. My beautiful bride of forty-seven years stayed and comforted me as the movie ended and people filed out of the theatre.

My reaction was unexpected, embarrassing, upsetting. I realized once again that I can no longer guarantee that I have control over myself. It all seemed so wrong. The film had a "happy ending": The man's courage in persisting as a conscientious objector and his bravery and sacrifice as a medic under enemy fire were being celebrated. Yet for me, it was too much. I unraveled emotionally and physically. I suffer from vicarious or secondary trauma, arising from events that have occurred over some decades. I may be seeking to deal with trauma, but it is also true that trauma continues to deal with me!

Events of the past continue to weaken my walk. I no longer stride; I walk with a limp.

I first broke down publicly in front of a hundred clergy and lay workers. It was 2013, and I was saying how delighted I was that Prime Minister Julia Gillard had established a Royal Commission into Institutional Responses to Child Sexual Abuse. As bishop of Tasmania, I had been calling for such a royal commission for eleven years. And now it had happened. What a wonderful moment! But then my body began to shake. I gripped the lectern to stay upright. I could not speak. Fighting back tears, my chest heaving, "No, Lord, not here!" was my inner cry. My colleagues were kind, generous. They comforted me. With the encouragement of my leadership team, I commenced counseling.

When I commenced counseling, I well recall the psychologist saying, "It's all right to cry."

"But I don't want to cry. I don't want to cry in public." (Me)

"What's the problem with crying?"

"It's embarrassing."

"Okay, tell me about that."

And so, we talked. I am profoundly grateful for these sessions with a psychologist in Hobart, Tasmania.

My trauma had been cumulative: a troubled childhood, years living in Argentina with my wife and sons during a military dictatorship and war with Great Britain in the Falkland Islands, the recent deaths of two close friends, and my role leading a response to survivors of child sexual abuse by Tasmanian Anglican Church workers. In this role, I had met, cried, apologized, prayed, and sought to walk with survivors of child sexual abuse. Their suffering affected me deeply: I struggle with vicarious traumatization. These traumatic events have taken their toll on me.[10]

With the psychologist's assistance, my wife's love and forbearance, the understanding and sacrifice of work colleagues, and the deep confidence that I was God's son, I was able to continue my ministry. But I was not as emotionally robust as I had been. I was less stable. I was walking with a limp.

My "limp," the accumulated trauma from tragedy and threatening events, had weakened my emotional resilience. My health was not what it had been. I learnt to avoid some things. Now, I rarely watch the evening news. This was a loss, as it had been a staple part of my life. In my time as bishop of Tasmania, I had been regularly called upon by the media and church community to respond to current issues.

I shared my struggles with a friend, who recalled his farewell gift from missionary service in Tanzania: a walking stick! In reply to my obvious puzzlement (for he did not use a walking stick in daily life) he explained the symbolism of the walking stick. In the tribe where he was working, a walking stick is a symbol of respect, of honor and status. It acknowledges leadership and its cost. The tribe recognizes that a life of service is marked by suffering, and suffering takes its toll on a person's health, hence the walking stick.

I mentioned this to another friend, who exclaimed, "I was given a walking stick in Tanzania!" We live in a small world. My friend had been coaching Tanzanians in a school project to assist abandoned children. The project was led by a converted Maasai pastor, whose farewell gift to him was a walking stick. Moreover, upon my friend's return to his hotel, he became conscious that the African room staff took notice of the walking stick and were treating him with great deference. The walking stick is a badge of honor. Walking with a limp is not to be disparaged. It recognizes challenge, struggle, and pain.

Trauma from tragic events accumulates through life and can grow to become a toll too heavy to bear; we need to recognize our need for help, that we are walking with a limp.

Some Strategies for Dealing with Trauma

There are strategies in seeking to deal with trauma. Note that I have used "in seeking"—the present continuous tense. Dealing with trauma is an

---

10. For further resources for church leaders see the Resources section at the end of this essay shaped by Dr. Barry Rogers MAPS.

ongoing thing, a continuing walk, a walk that is in some way hampered, hence "walking with a limp."

Professional Help

The following areas are vital when seeking to deal with trauma: First, accept that trauma is real. It is serious business and it needs to be addressed. Second, acknowledge the importance of supportive friends and family, the wisdom of avoiding of places of vulnerability, and the value of safe places of grace and peace—"safety valves" for when pressure builds.[11] Third, there is the need for counseling.

How do we know when a person is just down and perhaps need a good "kick in the pants" or when a person is suffering from trauma and needs professional help? This question is not easy to answer. But one thing that I have learnt along the way is that when in doubt, see a GP and a professional counselor. Make an appointment!

Regarding counseling, it is helpful to clarify options:[12]

1. Psychological counseling, with a psychologist who has had some trauma training, is one pathway. This pathway, under a GP mental health care plan, allows for a Medicare rebate, which will assist some people who otherwise might not seek counseling support.

2. Others may be able to access psychological counseling under their health fund benefits if they have private health cover.

3. Some people in church contexts would prefer a person of Christian background. Support can be found via a counselor who is registered with the CCAA/Christian Counsellors Association of Australia. This

---

11. In my professional life as a chemical engineer, I learnt that it is imperative to have a safety valve on a vessel. Should the pressure of the fluid inside a vessel become too high for the integrity of the vessel, the vessel's safety valve will open, and the dangerous pressure will be reduced as the fluid is released in a safe manner to a safe place. This will save the vessel from rupture and the factory from possible major damage. I recall an occasion when a safety valve did not open, and the pressure of the fluid grew until it ruptured the top of a tank showering liquid product on nearby houses. This was not appreciated! I understood that if we don't have safety valves, or if we don't maintain them, then when pressures build, vessels can be damaged and or even destroyed. People also need "safety valves" to protect themselves for those times when the pressures of trauma build and need release in a safe manner. These safety valves could be going out with friends or taking time to smell the roses or whatever relaxes us and brings release, peace, and, hopefully, joy; these things help us survive. We wisely build "safety valves" into our lives.

12. I am grateful to Dr. Barry Rogers MAPS for setting out these options.

is likely not Medicare rebated unless the counselor is a psychologist or mental health professional.

Beliefs That Sustain

Something else that I and others have learnt concerns the beliefs that we hold.

What are the beliefs that sustain us? Or put another way, what songs do we sing when the going gets tough?

Imagine you are in a plane when it plunges, lifts, plunges, steadies, and then begins to gently "wobble." Imagine yourself hearing the concerned, calming voice of the captain over the gasps and cries of passengers.

I recall such a frightening event. My distressed fellow passenger grasped the arm rests and gasped repeatedly, "No! Ah! Oh, no!" This contrasted sharply with the man a few rows back vainly trying to calm his mate who had burst into hysterical laughter. We humans are a mixed bunch.

Prior to "the plunge," I had been revising my sermon for the installation of the incoming Dean of Hobart. My text? A hymn of the early church: the "Song of Christ" in Paul's Letter to the Colossians (1:15–20):

> He (Christ) is the image of the invisible God, the firstborn of all creation; for in him all things in heaven and on earth were created, things visible and invisible, whether thrones or dominions or rulers or powers—all things have been created through him and for him. He himself is before all things, and in him all things hold together. He is the head of the body, the church; he is the beginning, the firstborn from the dead, so that he might come to have first place in everything. For in him all the fullness of God was pleased to dwell, and through him God was pleased to reconcile to himself all things, whether on earth or in heaven, by making peace through the blood of his cross.

My sermon challenge was to be: "Will you, the Dean and Cathedral congregation, sing this Song of Christ?" However, God has this habit of turning a preacher's words back on himself, and at that moment in the plane I heard, "John, will you—yes, you yourself—sing this Song of Christ, even as the plane plunges?"

When the plane plunges, when my world comes crashing down, when loss and grief are unbearable, where are the strong beliefs that sustain my walking in faith? What songs am I singing? The following "songs" or truths are fundamental to my walking in faith as I continue dealing with tragedy and trauma:

- Christ's promise of his presence: "And remember, I am with you always, to the end of the age" (Matt 28:20).
- In Jesus Christ, I see the character and purposes of God (John 14:9)
- The "love one another" of the brothers and sisters is both supportive and a living reminder of the love that suffers—of the Lover who knows of suffering and human anguish, who died that we might live (John 13:34).
- The resurrection of Christ is my trust and hope (John 20:28).
- The promise of my eternal dwelling with Christ, where there will be no more tears and sorrow, give me hope, comfort, and resilience to continue walking in faith (Rev 21:4).

A question: What are the songs that I, you, we, sing?

I'll let you in on a secret. For over fifteen years, Elvis Presley was my traveling companion in Tasmania. Yes, Elvis Presley! His Gospel songs filled my car and my heart and mind (and passengers) with gospel truth. And "Elvis" even made a surprise appearance at the conclusion of my farewell service as bishop of Tasmania at St. David's Cathedral, Hobart, in 2015, leading us all in singing *Amazing Grace*.

Well, that's some of my singing. These might not be the songs for you. What, then, are songs that nurture your life?

Christian songs nurture our walking in faith. They speak of God's character, life's meaning, and hope, which are founded in the biblical record. An Australian theologian wrote recently:

> Matthew's Gospel . . . (offers) the possibility of meaningful living, hope, and reversal despite the presence of horror in the world. . . . Matthew's Gospel makes the reader aware of the means by which this hope may be sustained in the midst of, and after, horror and trauma. These include a life of prayer, imitating the character of God, belonging to the community of faith, and the ritual of the Lord's Supper. . . . This hope and the life recommended by Matthew's Gospel may enable those who appropriate its message by faith to [be on] the journey of partial recovery from horror's traumas.[13]

---

13. Scott Harrower, "Coping with the Horror and Trauma of Life Today," *The Melbourne Anglican*, August 26, 2016.

18. This theological and pastoral approach, which examines both a horror reading and blessed reading of the Gospel of Matthew, is developed in his *God of All Comfort*. Also of relevance is Nils Von Kalm, "When Grief is Overwhelming, How Do We Cope?" *The Melbourne Anglican*, September 18, 2017.

Hope

Hope plays a vital role in the survival of a woman who suffered terrible burns in the 1983 Victorian bushfires. Hit by a massive fireball, Ann Fogarty was literally on fire and only saved by being lifted into a pool, where her skin peeled off her. Serious burns to 85 percent of her body required surgical treatment that extended over years. She showed extraordinary courage in living with the traumatic physical, emotional, social, and spiritual consequences of such horrendous injuries.

And what of the unanswered, "Where are you, God? Where were you, God, when my body, mind, and soul were being destroyed, ripped apart?" In her autobiography, *Forged with Flames,* Ann Fogarty recounts her struggle to live, her wrestling with God, family life, physical health, and her post-traumatic stress.[14] It is what gained her autobiography the award of Australian Christian Book of the Year in 2013. The award judges described *Forged with Flames* as a "distinctively Australian saga."

> Ann brings to her writing the same humour, honesty and courage with which she suffered the pain, doubt and despair . . . The hope forged by this extreme experience is shared with simplicity and an open heart. It is profoundly comforting to follow her growing assurance of God's presence and loving care. Ann's story is compelling, unforgettable and inspiring.[15]

Prayer and the Bible

In *Child, Arise!*, a handbook for survivors of sexual abuse and those who support them, Jane Dowling, a survivor of child sexual abuse, shares in vulnerability and hope the spiritual resources she discovered in her own journey through suffering.[16]

At twenty-one years of age, Jane Dowling entered an international Catholic missionary community of prayer and ministry of the Bible. In her mid-twenties, the trauma of her abuse erupted in pain and anguish. Then followed a two-decade-long quest for healing.

There are no words to describe the betrayal and trauma of child sexual abuse, and Jane Dowling does not detail her sexual abuse except to say that

---

14. Fogarty and Crawford, *Forged with Flames.*

15. Emma Halgren, "Compelling, Unforgettable, Inspiring' Story Wins Australian Christian Book of the Year." *The Melbourne Anglican,* August 9, 2013.

16. Dowling, *Child, Arise!* is an outstanding and multifaceted book. Little wonder it was awarded the Australian Christian Book of the Year 2016.

it occurred from early childhood to her mid-teens by a family relation, then during her teenage years by a Catholic priest. This brief statement sets a record of her abuse. But her actual abuse is not the focus of her book.

Child, Arise! tells the story of the destructive consequences of the author's abuse, her suffering, and her survival from God's perspective. In her trauma, the author sought God and God's resources to raise her life from its deathbed of betrayal by years of child sexual abuse. Significantly, the words Jane Dowling chose as the title for her book are the words spoken by Jesus when he restored Jairus's dead daughter to life (Luke 8:54). God's words are powerful and bring life from death.

The author's vulnerability in the telling of her story, her prayerful listening to God's voice, and her decision to trust God in the living of what is heard, usher the reader into spaces that inspire and challenge our faith.

The first part of the handbook is a compilation of truths about God and about humankind's identity, dignity, purposes, and strengthening. Jane Dowling recaptures the power of the word of God to change lives. This is meaning-making of the highest order. Listening to our personal story from the perspective of a loving God brings comfort and healing.

In the second part of the handbook, Jane Dowling shares her personal engagement with aspects of trauma such as hopelessness, lack of self-esteem, and being harsh with herself, and ways of gaining strength to stand to face them, such as channeling anger for good and being set free from paralysis and panic attacks.

Here is one illustration from the handbook. Jane's struggle and pain on the day of her private hearing with the Royal Commission into Institutional Responses to Child Sexual Abuse were immense.[17] The fear the abusing priest had instilled in her was overpowering. The anticipated re-traumatization from retelling her childhood abuse was overwhelming.

Struggling to prepare herself to attend, Jane turned to her Scripture reading, Isaiah 43:1–3, and spent time praying the verse that entered into her head and heart: "You will not be burned; the flames will not consume you." Jane saw her story from God's perspective. She was strengthened to attend her private hearing, and she testifies to the power of God's transforming grace through the prayerful reading of the Bible while in deep pain and suffering.

Importantly, the author affirms the role of counselors, family, friends, and community in her struggle for survival. All of these resources are to be marshaled for the survivor to stand again, scarred but not broken.

17. See Peter McClellan (chair), "Royal Commission into Institutional Responses to Child Sexual Abuse," Final Report, 2017. https://www.childabuseroyalcommission.gov.au/.

A further reflection from this personal experience of trauma relates to the resources that we have in responding to trauma. Jane Dowling had deep disciplines in prayer and the Bible due to her life in the Catholic missionary community. It was this investment in her personal life, in her relationship with God, that was such a rich resource when the trauma of abuse burst within her. Jane Dowling alerts us to deepen our walking in faith, our discipleship, with the prayerful reading and living out of God's word, the Bible. What we invest in today is our resource for tomorrow.

The Role of Community

Jason Russell's story is the tragic story of a decorated firefighter whose life disintegrates under a combination of factors, including vicarious trauma suffered throughout years of firefighting and counseling his fellow firefighters. Struggling, he started to self-medicate with illicit drugs, his career fell apart, his family was devastated, and he suffered drug addiction and homelessness.

Jason Russell shared his poignant story in conversation with Philip Freier, the Anglican Archbishop of Melbourne.[18] When commenting on his process of recovery, he highlighted the importance of affordable housing and community. He found community at St. Mark's Fitzroy and the Lazarus Centre at St. Peter's Eastern Hill: "I went to St. Mark's Community Centre. I went and washed the dishes. This gave me respect, dignity. They asked if I would help at the reception. I had something to do, somewhere to be."

The Power of Story and Symbol

Four Australian stories—Ann Fogarty, Jane Dowling, Jason Russell, and my own story—have shown some ways of addressing trauma. They have spoken of the importance of personal disciplines, prayer, Bible reading, family, friends, Christian community, counselors, courage, meaning, hope and belief in God's character.

I have learnt about living with trauma from two superb novels: *Les Miserables* by Victor Hugo[19] and *Cry, the Beloved Country* by Alan Paton.[20]

---

18. Jason Russell, "Conversations with the Archbishop: The Homelessness Crisis," *AnglicanMediaMelbourne*, September 20, 2017, see https://www.youtube.com/watch?v=1byS5uctsuI.

19. Hugo, *Les Miserables*.

20. Paton, *Cry, The Beloved Country: a story of comfort in desolation*.

Les Miserables: Silver Candlesticks as Symbols of Redemption

Do you recall, in Victor Hugo's masterpiece, the silver candlesticks given to the convict Jean Valjean by the forgiving bishop? For the forgiven Valjean, the candlesticks become an enduring symbol of rescue and meaning.

Can you even begin to imagine being imprisoned for stealing a loaf of bread to feed your sister and her children and being brutalized over nineteen years of incarceration? Upon his release from prison, the former convict Valjean is harshly excluded from food and accommodation at inns, until he is directed at last to the local bishop's home. There, he is welcomed with a meal at which he is honored as a guest: the table especially set with the bishop's inherited six pieces of silver cutlery. Following the meal, Valjean is offered a bed, and the household retires for the night. During the night Valjean wakes, steals the silver cutlery, and flees, but is soon apprehended by gendarmes and brought to the bishop on the accusation of theft of the bishop's cutlery.

To Valjean's astonishment, the bishop pretends that the silver cutlery was a gift; to emphasize that all is well between the former convict and himself, the bishop also gives him the set of silver candlesticks. The bishop farewells him, "Jean Valjean, my brother, you no longer belong to what is evil but to what is good. I have bought your soul to save it from black thoughts and the spirit of perdition, and I give it to God."[21]

Through seasons of prosperity and hardship, the silver candlesticks remain Jean Valjean's companion. They are not sold to finance his new life. They are kept to finance his memory: memory of grace received. The candlesticks were a reminder of personal and societal darkness, of rescue, of grace, of release, of light, of a new day dawned in his spirit, of his life bought for God.[22] The candlesticks were with him when he died: "He lay back with his head turned to the sky, and the light from the two candlesticks fell upon his face."[23]

What symbols do we have? Do you have? Do I have? I have a copy of this novel, *Les Miserables*. I read it for the first time in my teens and I continue to browse, indeed "graze," in its pages. I have written of its significance in my life.[24] The book is a symbol, a reminder of God's grace and presence. It is a place of nurture, of safety. What symbols do you treasure? What are the safe pages and places that nurture you?

21. Hugo, *Les Miserables*, 111.
22. Hugo, *Les Miserables*, 117–18.
23. Hugo, *Les Miserables*, 1200.
24. John Harrower, "A Book That Changed Me," *The Melbourne Anglican*, September 2017.

Cry, The Beloved Country: The Lord's Supper Strengthens Us

Jesus Christ gave his disciples a meal by which to remember his great love for us and in which the Holy Spirit nurtures and strengthens us.

At times I find a certain heaviness descends upon me, maybe because of continuing events: the persecuted church around the world, the pain of women and children suffering domestic violence, my own country's indifference to asylum seekers—it is all so sad. Yet, I look to God who raised Christ from the dead for our deliverance, for freedom from the suffering of this earthly life. I look forward to the ultimate dawn of the second coming of the Son of God, of the new heaven and the new earth, where "death will be no more; mourning and crying and pain will be no more, for the first things have passed away".[25]

This resurrection hope amidst grief is poignantly captured in the closing scene of Alan Paton's majestic South African novel, *Cry, the Beloved Country*. We see the tragic figure of the stricken father awaiting the dawn that would herald the execution of his delinquent son in faraway Johannesburg. The father's heartbreaking lament over his son and country is yet fused with the comfort of the coming of another dawn; for he is a Christian, the impoverished Zulu Anglican priest of a rural African village.

The "comfort in desolation" depicted in the closing paragraphs of the book is stark. "He (the father) looked out of his clouded eyes at the faint steady lightening in the east. He calmed himself and took out the heavy maize cakes and the tea, and put them upon a stone. And he gave thanks, broke the cakes and ate them, and drank of the tea."[26] Here, the priest is partaking of Holy Communion, the Lord's Supper, the sacred ritual, this sacrament which feeds and strengthens us. In the words of the Anglican Prayer Book for Australia, "Come let us take this holy sacrament of the body and blood of Christ in remembrance that he died for us, and feed on him in our hearts by faith with thanksgiving."[27]

Returning to Cry, the Beloved Country:

> Then he [the father whose son is to be executed at dawn, this father and priest] gave himself over to deep and earnest prayer, and after each petition he raised his eyes and looked to the east. And the east lightened, till he knew that the time was not far off. And when he expected it, he rose to his feet and took off his hat

---

25. Rev. 21:1-4.
26. Paton, *Cry, the Beloved Country*, 236.
27. Anglican Church of Australia Trust Corporation, *A Prayer Book for Australia*, 142.

and laid it down on the earth, and clasped his hands before him. And while he stood there the sun rose in the east.

Yes, it is the dawn that has come. The titihoya [bird] wakes from sleep, and goes about its work of forlorn crying. The sun tips with lights the mountains of Angeli and East Griqualand. The great valley of the Umzimkulu is still in darkness, but the light will come there. Ndotsheni [the village] is still in darkness, but the light will come there also. For it is the dawn that has come, as it has come for a thousand centuries, never failing. But when the dawn will come, of our emancipation, from the fear of bondage and the bondage of fear, why, that is a secret.[28]

The Anglican priest awaiting his son's execution took meaning and hope from the character of God revealed in Jesus Christ, in the sacrament of the breaking of the maize cakes and drinking of the tea—"Do this is remembrance of me" (Luke 22:19)—as he awaits the coming of the Son, the new dawn.

The father's lament led me to write my own lament as we await the dawn of Christ, the Son of God. A brief excerpt:

> *Oh, we await, with yearning*
> *while working*
> *with deep assurance,*
> *for the dawn does come,*
> *the Sun does rise*
> *the Son did rise*
> *the Son is risen*
> *the Son will come again!* [29]

Our final emancipation, our deliverance from trauma, is founded in Jesus Christ, the resurrected Christ, who promises that those who believe in him will live, even though they die. Recall Jesus' words to Martha at Lazarus's tomb:

> Jesus said to her, "Your brother will rise again." Martha said to him, "I know that he will rise again in the resurrection on the last day." Jesus said to her, "I am the resurrection and the life. Those who believe in me, even though they die, will live, and everyone who lives and believes in me will never die. Do you

---

28. Paton, *Cry, the Beloved Country*, 236.
29. John Harrower, "The Dawn Will Come," *Tasmanian Anglican*, August 2015.

believe this?" She said to him, "Yes, Lord, I believe that you are the Messiah, the Son of God, the one coming into the world."[30]

Martha knew the character of God was revealed in Jesus Christ, the Messiah, the Son of God, and this enabled her to make meaning of life and gave her hope in the face of trauma.

May God almighty, the Father, the Son, and the Holy Spirit, strengthen us in our own "walking with a limp." Amen.

---

30. John 11:23–27.

Resources

The following books relate to information on trauma pathways and support church leaders in dealing with trauma. These have been recommended by Dr. Barry Rogers MAPS, who has given his permission for this resource information to be shared with other people who may benefit from it.

- Professor Stephen Joseph. *What Doesn't Kill Us: The New Psychology of Posttraumatic Growth*. London: Piatkus, 2011.

The foreword is by Terry Waite; you'll recall he was Archbishop Robert Runcie's Assistant for Anglican Communion Affairs and was kidnapped in the late 1980s in Lebanon. Chapter 3 of this very readable book is on the biology of trauma; those who have experienced trauma directly or vicariously could really be helped by its clear explanation of the brain processes associated with trauma impacts.

The book is particularly helpful for those who have had some time distance between their initial trauma and dealing with life's stressors now. It is also a very insightful, practical resource for church leaders who are providing pastoral support to other leaders.

- Dr. Bessel van der Kolk. *The Body Keeps the Score: Brain, Mind, and Body in the Healing of Trauma*. New York: Penguin, 2015.

This book, written by one of the world's foremost experts on trauma, explores the ways in which tragic events and their traumatic aftermath are stored in our bodies, literally reshaping the brain. It also offers hope for recovery. A helpful aspect of this book is its personal stories, which present deep insight into how trauma impacts people relationally, cognitively, and physically/medically. Group reading of such case histories can begin to generate opportunities to address personal trauma for in church-based senior leadership groups—as long as such groups are safe, supportive, and confidential.

One website review of the book, linked here, provides the de-identified client story of "Marilyn." This is worth reading in relation to the multifaceted aspects of trauma and its developmental impacts: https://www.psychotherapy.net/article/body-keeps-score-van-der-kolk.

The New Scientist book review included here is also helpful to pass on to other leaders who may benefit from reading the book: https://www.newscientist.com/article/mg22429941-200-the-lifelong-cost-of-burying-our-traumatic-experiences/.

Bibliography

Anglican Church of Australia Trust Corporation. *A Prayer Book for Australia*. Sydney: Broughton Books, 1995.

Barker, Paul A., ed. *Tackling Trauma: Global, Biblical and Pastoral Perspectives*. Carlisle: Langham Global Library, 2019.

Dowling, Jane. *Child, Arise! The Courage to Stand: A Spiritual Handbook for Survivors of Sexual Abuse*. Melbourne: David Lovell, 2015.

Fogarty, Ann, and Anne Crawford. *Forged with Flames*. Melbourne: Wild Dingo, 2013.

Freier, Philip L., "Presidential Address." Delivered to the 17th General Synod of the Anglican Church of Australia, September 4, 2017. http://www.anglicanprimate.org.au/2017/09/04/primate-renews-apology-at-general-synod/.

———. "We Are Ashamed." Media release from the Office of the Primate, March 17, 2017. http://www.anglicanprimate.org.au/press/we-are-ashamed-primate/.

Gladwin, Michael, ed. "Remembering our Future: The Response of Australian Churches to the Recommendations of the Royal Commission into Institutional Responses to Child Sexual Abuse." *St. Mark's Review* 245 (2018) 3.

Harrower, Scott. *God of All Comfort: A Trinitarian Response to the Horrors of This World*. Studies in Historical and Systematic Theology. Bellingham, WA: Lexham, 2019.

Hugo, Victor. *Les Miserables*. Sydney: Penguin Classics, 1982.

Joseph, Stephen. *What Doesn't Kill Us. The New Psychology of Posttraumatic Growth*. London: Piatkus, 2011.

Paton, Alan. *Cry, The Beloved Country: A Story of Comfort in Desolation*. Ringwood: Penguin, 1958.

Van der Kolk, Bessel. *The Body keeps the Score. Brain, Mind and Body in the healing of trauma*. New York: Penguin, reprint 2015.